THE GONG
AND
THE FLUTE

THE GONG
AND
THE FLUTE

African Literary Development
and Celebration

Edited by
KALU OGBAA

Contributions in Afro-American and African Studies, Number 173

GREENWOOD PRESS
Westport, Connecticut • London

Library of Congress Cataloging-in-Publication Data

The gong and the flute : African literary development and celebration /
    edited by Kalu Ogbaa.
        p. cm.—(Contributions in Afro-American and African
  studies, ISSN 0069–9624 ; no. 173)
    Includes bibliographical references and index.
    ISBN 0–313–29281–7 (alk. paper)
    1. African literature—History and criticism. I. Ogbaa, Kalu.
  II. Series.
  PL8010.G66   1994
  896.09—dc20   94–16121

British Library Cataloguing in Publication Data is available.

Library of Congress Catalog Card Number: 94–16121
ISBN: 0–313–29281–7
ISSN: 0069–9624

First published in 1994

Greenwood Press, 88 Post Road West, Westport, CT 06881
An imprint of Greenwood Publishing Group, Inc.

Printed in the United States of America

The paper used in this book complies with the
Permanent Paper Standard issued by the National
Information Standards Organization (Z39.48–1984).

10 9 8 7 6 5 4 3 2 1

To

Michael J. C. Echeruo

Teacher, Critic, Poet, and William Safire Professor of Modern Letters

Syracuse University, New York

Contents

Preface

Modern African literature was developed out of orature, a body of African oral texts, which has gone through several periods of retardation and triumph. As a literary tradition, orature is as old as Africa, the origin of humankind and civilization, and continues to inform African literature. Yet, to date, a literalist tendency inWestern thought—that literature can exist only in written and not in oral form—continues to deny or obscure the existence of "literary" activities in Africa before slavery and colonialism. Such denial or obcurity was, however, popularized by early European explorers and colonial writers, who used the misrepresentation of Africans and their cultures as a means to acquire either personal economic power or literary fame, and to influence their home countries' political perspectives on Africa. They claim that, since most of Africa was illiterate and lacked culture and civilization before the coming of Europeans into Africa, it was a misnomer to characterize African oral texts as a viable literature worthy of internatinal attention and recognition.

That European position on traditional African literary culture was expressed in high places as part of the white man's overall sociopolitical grand plan to dehumanize Africans and other nonwhites the world over, so as to justify and legitimize both colonialism and slavery. That is the picture painted in "the novels of Africa" by such colonial writers as Joseph Conrad and Joyce Cary, whose compulsory texts were taugh to African students by British University Colleges in Africa, including Ibadan in Nigeria, Achimota in Ghana, Fourah Bay in Sierra Leone, and Makerere in Uganda.

Those students, of course, knew that what they were being taught was not true of the Africa they lived in, and it disturbed them. Also, they knew that slavery and colonialism were a rape of their cherished continent. So, it had to be challenged, if not stopped, by informed African writers, critics, and teachers, who had to develop their own literature out of the existing oral tradition comprised of folktales, proverbs, folksongs, rituals, and folk dances,so as to set the records straight, as it were. While the students prepared to do battle with their colonial teachers, African political leaders struggled to win independence from their European colonial masters. Thus we find that African literary development has been closely connected with the renewal of African cultural and political consciousness after the demoralizing periods of slave trade and colonialism.

Their colonial university education over, the erstwhile students began writing and teaching their own independent literature. Ironically, African literary development began as a protest effort by those Karin Barber calls "a tiny and precarious intelligentsia who were removed by education from the culture and experience of the majority of the population, and assigned to a ruling elite which was both unstable and rapacious. They were politically disaffected from the elite, often at great personal risk, and alienated from metropolitan powers that kept it in place." Still they persevered until African literature was developed to a point of celebration, to a point where readers and critics can agree with Barber, who comments in Richard Priebe's *Myth, Realism and the West African Writer* (1988), that: "If you see an elephant, don't say 'I saw something flash by;' you'd better acknowledge that what you saw was the mightiest of beasts." Critics have certainly acknowledged modern African literature for the formidable animal it is. Indeed, they have erected such a towering apparatus of literary history, commentary and analysis around it that "we are likely to forget that less than thirty years ago it did seem, precisely, to flash onto the scene, arriving suddenly with a turbulent dazzle."(ix)

Another foreign commentator on African literature, Robert M. Wren, was so fascinated by the courage and accomplishments of the"tiny and precarious intelligentsia" that he wrote a book, *Those Magical Years: The Making of Nigerian Literature: 1948-1966*, to lionize them. Among those mentioned in the book is Professor Michael J.C.Echeruo, whose creative, critical, and professional achievements inspired the production of this collection of essays on African literary development and celebration.

As a student, Michael Echeruo was fortunate to have been taught by professor Molly Mahood of Britain who was a great influence on not only him but also such other literary figures as Chinua Achebe, Wole Soyinka, Christopher Okigbo, Flora Nwapa, John Pepper Clark, Ben Obumselu, and John Munonye—a crop of students that Mahood encouraged to develop their own literature, while they studied European literature. With that encouragement, they began publishing articles and poems in such magazines as *The Horn, Ibadan, Nigeria Magazine,* and *Black Orpheus.*

The books that most of these people published, after graduation, became the bedrock of Modern African Literature. What is unique about Echeruo, however, is that, apart from publishing books of poetry and criticism, he has remained a devoted university professor and scholar. That role continues to make it possible for him to develop African literature as both curriculum and content, and to train students who have developed themselves professionally to the point of becoming university professors and administrators. They, like their mentor Echeruo, have joined in the business of training other persons as well as developing and celebrating African culture and civilization through its literature.

In recognition of Echeruo's role in the development and promotion of Nigerian (and Igbo) literary and cultural tradition, Isidore Okpewho in "The Dignity of Intellectual Labor..." gives a synopsis of the writings of Echeruo the critic and poet, and sees them as "criticism of culture" as well as "intellectual history" of Africa. Okpewho's critical evaluation of the writings and his personal recognition of the rigorous intellectual labor that produced them enable him to assert that "of this few [literary scholars today in Nigeria], Echeruo is the undisputed guru."

In Chapter 1, "Some Sources of Joyce Cary's *Mister Johnson*," Ben Obumselu opines that *Mister Johnson* is the effect of the imposition of an alien [European] code of morals and manners upon a native [African] culture. For that reason African writers have been infuriated by the very idea of Johnson so that they have made the decision to become the interpreters of the culture and experience of their own people. Hence he quotes Echeruo who, in *Joyce Cary and the Novels of Africa*, argues that European novels of Africa are in the nature of things bound to focus interest on the domestic concerns of European culture. However, while agreeing with the "infuriation" of the African writers and critics, Obumselu recognizes the fact that from imperial stereotypes of prelogical consciousness, Cary derived a comic plot heavily laced with racial smugness and bigotry; but Cary humanized that plot when looking into the mirror of his own mind and recognized, perhaps unconsciously, that he was also primitive, and with that dim awareness a deep current of fellow feeling and compassion entered the stream. Obumselu's overall reading of *Mister Johnson* not only complements the research findings of Echeruo but also proves that, considering the colonial encounter between Europe and Africa, both the Europeans and the Africans are, after all, primitive, a knowledge that should reduce the racial smugness of the former and the fury of the latter.

That effort to interpret his people's culture and experiences is made in Chukwuma Azuonye's essay which discusses the development of Okigbo as a poet, as it highlights the literary, cultural, and political import and implication of such a development. From the essay, one learns that just before his demise, Okigbo had begun to abandon the obscure symbolism of his earlier poems for "more direct statements of faith and ideology"—a change which was not to be as a result of the 1967-70 Nigeria-Biafra War that claimed the life of the poet. Overall, the chapter reminds readers of the importance of Okogbo's poetry to Nigerian, indeed Igbo, literary and cultural studies which have continued to attract Echeruo's literary evaluation and commentary.

While he applauds the Nobel Citation which praises Soyinka as a writer who "in a wide cultural perspective and with poetic overtones fashions the drama of existence," Edward Okwu reminds readers in Chapter 3 that

Soyinka is no less a poet than he is a playwright. Okwu attempts to persuade readers to accept that Soyinka's central artistic concern is a continuing attempt to show the significance in human terms of the Ogun archetype, and to acknowledge the central position which the poem "Idanre" occupies in Soyinka's scheme: Idanre, the Yoruba god of iron, war, creativity, and harvest is Soyinka's prototype of modern creative man burdened by his own complex personality in an even more complex existential reality and striving to achieve a unified consciousness. Okwu's reading of "Idanre" raises the ancient question of the roles of the gods in human affairs—an issue that is touched upon in Echeruo's own poetic corpus.

Chinyere Nwahunanya's chapter on "Nigerian Drama and the Theater of the Absurd" demonstrates how the dramatic trend referred to as "the absurd" is the modern men's literary responses to contemporary experiences that have cut across international boundaries. Tracing the roots of the trend to Eugene Ionesco through Beckett and Camus, Nwahunanya sees a link in the plays of the artists which derives from a common way of looking at man's predicament in the contemporary world. He evaluates the success of such established Nigerian playwrights as Soyinka, Clark, and Rotimi experimenting on the new dramatic trend, and makes the conclusion that the most significant relevance of the "absurd" plays to contemporary Nigerian reality is that the playwrights' anguish (portrayed in the anguish of absurd characters) stems from their need to change the world; hence their plays serve as a progressive call for a rejection of the fatalistic attitude, which both the artists and their audience have developed from the mistaken belief that their condition is not only hopeless but also unchangeable.

In Chapter 5, Afam Ebeogu recognizes the tendency for teachers and students to split literature into genres (prose, poetry, and drama), and drama into its various components for purposes of formal analysis as a "compartmentalization syndrome, necessary, no doubt, but often exasperating." Therefore, he attempts a synoptic and comparative analysis of what he calls "the burden of dramatic experience" which is a holistic approach to the study and appreciation of drama, the African drama specifically. His own reading of select African plays reveals that in pre-literate society, literature was "one"; but oral literature was more serious and more embracing of life values. Ebeogu emphasizes that "it is less pretentious, and therefore, less amenable to prostitution and cant." Also, he claims that more recent researches in the area reveal that "the entertainment quotient in traditional African performances is quite higher than surface observation is prepared to acknowledge. And the evidence is really all around us, even in the Igbo society where it is generally agreed that people take life rather too seriously." By way of conclusion, Ebeogu affirms that the dramatic experience is the living of life itself, recommending that ritual action and myth should be woven into dramatic action, a point which Echeruo apparently makes elsewhere in his essay on the development of Igbo drama.

Ernest Emenyonu, in Chapter 6, makes a case for literature in indigenous languages, because he claims, "literature in indigenous languages is the most neglected in Africa, especially in Nigeria" where "anything popular to one language group is assumed to be a means of sanctioning ethnicity and, therefore, forestalling national unity." He cites *Devil on the Cross* originally written in Gikuyu by Ngugi and translated into English. The novel not only conveys in original African language the powerful theme of the obligation of the Kenyan people to overthrow the neo-colonialist powers that dominate their lives, but also portrays effusively such abstract concepts as imperialism, capitalism, neo-colonialism, and marxism to the level of the Kenyan masses. Emenyonu lionizes J.F. Schon, a German missionary, D.O. Fagunwa, Bishop Ajayi Crowther, and Pita Nwana all who wrote what could be regarded as the foundation literature in indigenous Nigerian languages. After giving the genesis of the development of Igbo literature, Emenyonu calls on schools, universities, and government agencies to encourage and support the good output of Igbo literary works which must be complemented by expert mastery of the Igbo language.

Donatus Nwoga, in Chapter 7, continues the argument for Igbo studies, an aspect of which Emenyonu makes in Chapter 6. Nwoga's point is that Igbo scholars should give Igbo studies definition and direction. Nwoga reviews the progress so far made in the development of Igbo language and literature, and demonstrates how scholars can forge "for our people a language which can bear the burden of giving expression to their experiences and communication to their ideas." In other words, such a language "must be adaptable and expansive, a language which does not retrain their efforts to accommodate their experience, a language receptive to new ideas and technology." Concluding his essay, Nwoga tells the Igbo how not to waste their emotional and creative energies in internal conflict over whose dialect is to be selected, so they can give Igbo language the status of competing for national use and interest.

Chinua Achebe, Africa's foremost novelist, was the first to decide to become "the interpreter of the culture and experience of his own people," we are reminded in Obumselu's essay. So in this book, we have included two essays that give readings of two of Achebe's novels, *No Longer at Ease* and *Anthills of the Savannah*. Nnadozie Inyama, in Chapter 8, interprets Igbo social behavior as it concerns the Igbo family history, as fictionalized by Achebe in *Things Fall Apart* and *No Longer at Ease*. In his view, one of the most striking things about the two novels is that, in spite of their small sizes, Achebe has been able to cram into them the histories of four generations of a family. Furthermore, Inyama asserts, "Perhaps one of the most remarkable aspects of Igbo social behavior is the people's concern with family histories. It is a concern which can prove decisive or disastrous in interpersonal relationships of any depth, whether in business ventures or marriage alliance." Inyama's critical analysis of the interpersonal relationships in *Things Fall Apart* and *No Longer at Ease* helps to explain the tragic dimensions of Okonkwo's and Nwoye's characters, which stem from the effeminacy of the head of the Okonkwo family, Unoka.

In Chapter 9, Kalu Ogbaa demonstrates that although Achebe's artistic techniques and style have changed somewhat in his latest novel, *Anthills of the Savannah*, yet the novelist has maintained consistent commitment to his art: the thematic concerns of the novel prove that he still plays the role of keeper of the conscience of his people and defender of the values of individual freedom and human rights. Even in this novel which appears more *urban* than his earlier novels, Achebe still adopts the historical approach in dealing with modern problems, making use of the same people and names as characters; the same West African geographical areas as setting; the same gods, goddesses, oracles; and the same rituals and ceremonies, etc, which form the bases of his thematic materials. Ogbaa discusses Achebe's views on bad governance, revolutions, and victims, as well as the novelist's literary activism. He is of the opinion that "playing his usual self-imposed role of the novelist as teacher, Achebe has used *Anthills of the Savannah* as a forum to discuss the issues of bad governance and misrule in most West African countries... In the end, Achebe does not prescribe revolution as the only solution to the hydra-headed problems of the nations." Instead, he has told West Africans where the rain started to beat them. Now they know; they ought to get to their destination quicker.

Chapter 10 is Emmanuel Obiechina's critical exploration of the theme of victimization as expounded in select African plays and novels. He traces the history of victimization to the slave era, and opines: "Starting with the slave trade, the african peoples have probably produced more human victims than any other races of mankind in recent times. Imperialism and white racism on the continent have also brought their own dimensions of human wastage. More recently still, the emergence of post-independence black dictatorships and bad governments has brought new styles and degrees of human destruction that provide additional material for writers whose role it is to constantly explore and evaluate the state of social and psychological health."

Obiechina finds that African writings, from the very beginning, has been the literature of victims. In that literature he notices that writers have distinguished between two classes of victims—namely, individual victims and group victims; and the writers have also suggested in fictional modes how to deal with victimization on the two levels of group and individual consciousness. His study of victimization as handled in the chosen texts leads him to remark that the authors' handling of the theme of victimization varies considerably, but they share one dominant attitude in common: ambivalence. "They see the sacrifice of victims as logical to the communal system and to certain types of human situations, but their sympathy is always with the victims and the victims' struggle to defend the flicker which they carry within them, which is indeed their own lives."

The Gong and the Flute is intended as a tribute to those who sounded the gong for African literary development, and as a path-finder for those celebrating Modern African Literature with the flute. I am greatly indebted to my friends and professional colleagues who have contributed the essays that follow. Indeed, the contributors have raised issues that touch on the research interests and professional output of their literary mentors, so, the essays do complement their work and those of other researchers in the field of Nigerian and Igbo Studies. It is my hope, therefore, that reading the book will challenge other Nigerian and Igbo scholars to make further substantial contributions to language and literary studies, especially in the area of Igbo Studies, which require urgent attention.

—Kalu Ogbaa

Acknowledgments

We are indebted to Professor Emmanuel N. Obiechina, whose essay, "The Theme of Victimization in Select African Plays and Novels," is reprinted by permission of the author. Its revised version, "Victimization as Theme," appears in a Howard University Press book, *Language and Theme: Essays on African Literature*, by Emmanuel N. Obiechina. Copyright © 1990 by Emmanuel N. Obiechina. We are also indebted to Professor James D. Newman and Jessie L. Jones of Southern Connecticut State University, for typesetting the book; and to all other contributors who have waited patiently for the eventual appearance of *The Gong and the Flute*.

1

Some Sources of Joyce Cary's
Mister Johnson

Ben Obumselu

It is usual to read *Mister Johnson* (1939) as a representation and a criticism of the African character. Early reviewers noted the hero's emotional instability, his comic illusions of grandeur combining so ill with a dismal record of dissipation and crime, and the guilelessness which makes him a variation on the theme of the noble savage. "*Mister Johnson* is a brilliantly accurate miniature of Africa as it is today," the *Times Literary Supplement* concluded. Forest Reid in the *Spectator* pointed out Cary's unexpected association of innocence with crime: "At least it seems odd," he said, "until we remember that animals never are corrupt—a rather disquieting thought for moralists." The reviewer for the *Guardian* saw Johnson as a child and felt "a protective and remonstrant love for this absurd, dishonest, irrational creature. It is impossible to be angry with him as it is to punish a foolish, blundering puppy for eating the slipper."

Scholars and critics also interpret the novel in the same way. The first full-length study, Andrew Wright's *Joyce Cary: A Preface to His Novels* written in close consultation with the novelist, does indeed point out that *Mister Johnson* and Cary's other stories set in Africa have universal themes. "Their interest is not in explaining Africa to England, nor in making a plea for this or that course of action vis-à-vis Nigeria; the interest is in the drama played against a backdrop which by its very brilliance lays bare human motivation."[1] Later critics do not, however, follow this cue. Arnold Kettle, noting the clash of contrasted cultural styles and mores in the novel, asserts that "the theme of *Mister Johnson* is the effect of the imposition of an alien code of morals and manners upon a native culture."[2] According to Frederick Karl, "This basically humorous novel has as its main theme the changes taking place in Africa that put natives like Johnson in a no-man's land between two cultures."[3] Golden Larsen similarly argues that Johnson is ruined by the consequences of his sentimental dream of civilization "not through malice on the part of any particular individual or system but through the very nature of the institutionalizing and abstracting process and his unavoidable ignorance."[4] Harold Collins and Henry Barba comment in a similar vein on the hereditary disabilities of black peoples and their power to stultify Europe's civilizing mission in Africa.[5]

Understandably, African writers and critics have been infuriated by the very idea of Johnson. Africa's foremost novelist, Chinua Achebe, has said that the kind of distortion which Johnson represents was partly responsible for his decision to become the interpreter of the culture and experience of his own people.[6] In *Joyce Cary and the Novel of Africa*, Michael Echeruo argues that European novels set in Africa are in the nature of things bound to focus interest on the domestic concerns of European culture; "only indirectly, as it were by accident, are these novels about Africa in any important sense." If *Mister Johnson* appears to give a positive image of its African hero, this, Echeruo argues, is because that novel anticipates the impending change in Cary's art in which he turns his attention to the wider humanities of English life. In any case, *Mister Johnson* is far more "the story of Rudbeck's education than that of Johnson's magnificent existence."[7] To Abdul JanMohamed, all Cary's African stories merely dramatize the usual polarities of an imperial system: "It is the allegory, of the elect and the damned, of superiority and inferiority, of the self and the other."[8]

A review of the major antecedents which showed Cary the way he might go in *Mister Johnson* must begin by carefully distinguishing between the hero of the novel and the supporting African characters. If the hero is a fool child, the minor characters are shrewd. If he is primitive in the grand literary and romantic meaning of the word, they are primitive only in the sense of being unenlightened, frustrated, predatory, and cruel. And, if he is resistant to interpretation, they need no interpretation.

All Cary's African stories use the same backdrop more or less; and there can be no doubt that the nightmare world depicted in that backdrop is a genuine attempt to recreate the real Africa that Cary knew. Starting from incidental sketches in the letters he wrote to his wife (1916/19), the abandoned drafts of *Daventry* and *Cock Jarvis* which date back to 1918/19, *Aissa Saved* (1932), *An American Visitor* (1933), *The African Witch* (1936), *Castle Corner* (1938), and *Mister Johnson* (1939),[9] there is remarkable unity of tone and impression. The letter of February 13, 1919, in which Cary presents a snapshot from Kenu, has been cited again and again: "Kenu 13th: This den of thieves is very peaceful. A large deputation of brigands met me on the road and escorted me in. The old chief is blind—and came to me led by a small boy. He looked like Lear." Langa in the *Daventry* manuscript is another village chief. "His head was quite bald, and his face withered like old hide. The gristle of his nose had fallen away, and he seemed to have no teeth, one hand was bright pink with leprosy, and the dirty rags hanging from his vulturelike shoulders could not conceal the extreme emaciation of his miserable old carcass."[10] Zegi in *Aissa Saved* is a walking skeleton. "His face had tumbled in so that it appeared like that of a dried head up on some battle-field, and his little red eyes blinked at the bottom of deep round holes" (p. 101). Henry in *An American Visitor* is "not more than the dirty framework of a negro hung with the rags of an old khaki shirt" (p. 14). From *The Case for African Freedom* comes a real person, Tasuki, who also appears in his own name as the bridge builder in *Mister Johnson*. "He was ragged and dirty, usually in pain from a complication of diseases including syphilis, and always laughing." "He had been flogged by at least one court."[11] Cary's use of Tasuki and the clerk Montague as fictional characters in *Mister Johnson* should tell us that in the backdrop of this novel he kept close to actual experience.

Right to the end of his life Cary believed that contemporary Africa was, generally speaking, paleolithic. "Nine tenths of the people belong in mind to at least five thousand years back," he says in *The Case for African Freedom*;[12] and in *Mister Johnson* he shifts the time scale back in describing Fada village, whose people "would not know the change if time jumped back fifty thousand years" (p. 99). He thought that tribal life featured a deadly diarchy: "a combination of totalitarian government and authoritarian church in their most oppressive forms, a system that has succeeded with the help of the climate in preventing almost all progress."[13] Africa as he saw it was not the inexhaustible reservoir of physically superb humanity but "a rubbish heap of castaways," "a museum of disease and frustration."[14] Only sentimentalists, he thought, imagined that Africans lived intensely and deeply. "From my own experience, the reverse is true . . . , a complex civilization shows higher standards of imagination and a deeper power of feeling."[15]

Cary's Africans do not read the eternal deep; nor do the great forms of nature nourish their hearts. They are not like Lawrence's grooms, gypsies, and Mexicans, whose spontaneous creative fullness of being rebukes Europe's sterile braininess. The high passion of Forster's Italian peasants which is, for good and ill, a glorification of life is entirely alien to their nature. In particular, they are not romantic children. Cary states this quite firmly: "In spite of common talk, Africans are not children, they are shrewd and hardworking peasantry with the natural feelings and limitations of illiterate peasantry everywhere you find it."[16]

But in a writing life spanning a quarter of a century, the novelist had plenty of time to contradict himself. In his occasional prose and sometimes in the depiction of tribal life—even in *Mister Johnson*—he often gave way to the orthodox view that African experience must be as dizzy as a drink party. But this idea contradicted his experience and accorded ill with his deepest beliefs. For he was absolutely sure that there is only one life which subsists and moves through all things, one character of being actualizing itself in the multitudinous variety of historical cultures and individual persons. In writing about Africa, he could not possibly have asked himself what African life was like; to do so would have led to an acknowledgment of ignorance. "My interest is not so much in the black man's mind as in everybody's mind," he affirmed in a letter to H.S.W. Edwardes.[17] Like Melville, Conrad, Synge, and Malraux, he was not deeply interested in the relativities of morals and manners. Exoticism features peripherally to his themes, serving only to highlight the abiding forms of experience. Africa as he imagined it differed from Europe only because "basic obsessions which in Europe hide themselves under all sorts of decorous scientific or theological or political uniforms, are there seen naked in bold and dramatic action."[18] Whether a novel was set in Borgu, Shanghai, a Pacific whaling ship, the Malay peninsula, or the home counties, the aim would always be to strike a responsive chord of feeling in the reader and make life recognize itself as an experience of value. For the Borguwa, the American and the English share a common substance:

The Mohammedan judge, subtle and learned, the great chief with his political shrewdness, the hospital assistant, the village headman, the lorry driver, the sergeant-major; put any of them into a white skin and they would take their place, in the same rank of European society, on equal terms. They would appear like the rest, the lawyer among lawyers, the chief among statesmen, the government clerk among officials; the sergeant-major among that natural aristocracy of the soldier's career—the non-commissioned officers.[19]

Cary prefixed a note to *The African Witch* to tell readers that the novel is "a work of imagination, and not . . . a picture of contemporary conditions in West Africa" (p. 7). But the novel was still read ethnologically. Ultimately it was the failure of English reviewers and readers to see the general human interest behind and beyond the ethnological material which made the novelist turn to the English setting. "Tho' I have several other African books in various stages, my next will probably deal with English tribes, pagans and witch doctors."[20]

Molly Mahood has shown how extensively *Mister Johnson* uses material from Cary's experiences in Nafada, Borgu, and Kaiama.[21] Despite this fidelity to life, we must recognize also that the African background of the novel is part of an imaginative construction. Although Fada is a primitive village no better than a rabbit's warren or a badger's burrow, and its people hold themselves "with crooked languor as if just out of hospital" (p. 25), the British colonial administration in the novel is a part of the same wasteland waiting for the rain. Fada government station has been on a temporary site for twenty years. It is like the imperial system, itself a makeshift structure going to rot where the first empire builders left it without creative impetus or historical purpose. "It is as if some giant had tossed down a few scraps of old rotten hay on a mangy lion skin, tufted with moth-eaten fragments of the hair and scarred with long white seams" (p. 14). Characteristically the officials lack a meaningful vision and their quarters are no better kept than Fada village. "Blore's bed is a ruin. Its net poles are tied up with string; its net has even more plugs of wool than Johnson's" (p. 47). When there is enterprise, it is of the housekeeping variety like Tring's punctuality to the office, his scrutiny of accounts, his inspection of the treasury, and his prison reforms. Tring's interest in prisons needs to be compared with the central symbol of the novel, the building of the great north road with which Johnson is associated. While Tring, without knowing it, acts to confine the scope of human freedom, Johnson spontaneously enlarges it. Similarly, Blore's gait, "like a man pushing his feet through deep slush" (p. 20), speaks of the fear of progress; and it may be compared with the symbolic ballet dancer's gusto of Johnson's walk, always "between a trot and a lope" (p. 19). At this level *Mister Johnson* does not invoke any real life contrasts between Europe and Africa. What it involves is a symbolic antithesis realized in the novel itself between decaying systems and a dynamic process of growth. Cary returns to this theme in *To Be a Pilgrim* (1942), where Victorian England is portrayed as a decayed old house into whose once graceful rooms a thresher must be driven to bring it back into the stream of life.

In *Mister Johnson* the hero is the primitive energy and joy of life standing in opposition to the representatives of the social order grouped round him. To Bamu, Aliu, Ajali, Blore, and Tring, Johnson is a fool child, a madman, a wild Dionysiac "who defies the laws of being and still goes unpunished" (p. 196). He is maladjusted, alien, and turbulent, while they have learned to accept the daily routine. He breaks out in unexpected ways as lover, burglar, entertainer, work leader, and murderer, while they criticize and marvel. He is light and winged and insanely happy, while they bear their lot grudgingly. He is a fiery child and they are prematurely old. Clearly Johnson is not cast in the same mold as the supporting characters, who come straight out of Cary's memory of his African experiences. It may be, as Michael Echeruo argues, that in portraying his hero, the novelist remembered two of his last African subordinates, Graves, who copied documents inaccurately, and Musa, the political agent who took bribes.[22] But these details are inessentials. The essential thing is that in the romantic infantilism which distinguishes Johnson from the other characters, Cary represents the anarchic creativity of the unconscious.

The initial notes for Johnson emphasize the clerk's infantile and anarchic nature: "The book then is the study of a human soul giving way to crime— showing how it happens, from uncertainty, from ignorance of self. Johnson does not know till the end whether he is very wicked or very clever. General idea, that he ought to be taught what is true and right and the nature of himself and the world. What is good that gives liberty and procures happiness; what is bad that restricts it."[23] The hero's tragedy is prefigured in the first sketches. In the final text, Johnson sleepwalks from one misadventure into another until the moment he finds himself before the hangman; but his enchantment is so deep that he does not wake up to the cruelty of real life. Where does this conception come from if it is not a part of Cary's Africa?

The stereotype of the primitive as a child was widespread in the late nineteenth century; by the early twentieth century it had become a part of the theology of empire. As we have seen, Cary often spoke against it. It was nevertheless a theory on which there was agreement among such venerable authorities as Sir Harry Johnston (*British Central Africa* [1897]), Lucien Levy-Bruhl (*Les Fonctions mentales dans les sociétés inférieures* [1910] and *La Mentality primitive* [1923]), Lebon (*Lois psychologiques d'évolution des peuples* [1914]), Sir Charles Eliot (*East African Protectorate* [1905]), Sir Frederick Lugard (*The Dual Mandate in British Tropical Africa* [1926]), and General Jan Smuts (*Africa and Some World Problems* [1930]). It would be useful to indicate briefly how much Johnson's character and the plot of the novel in which he features owe to this body of ideas about the primitive.

Levy-Bruhl was the great early twentieth-century authority on pre-logical consciousness. Surveying and synthesizing a vast literature of travel, missionary effort, and imperial settlements, he argues that the primitive is childish and mystical. Like a mystic, he takes no account of logical contradictions in his experience and does not distinguish objective things from their emotional and spiritual correlatives. He confounds time present with time past and time future, living, as it were, in a timeless continuum which he shares with ancestors and the unborn. Like a child he is impermeable to experience and enjoys sensations richer and more complex than those of the European.[24] It is to this quality of consciousness that Cary refers when, describing Johnson's inflammable emotions, he says that "to him Africa is simply perpetual experience, exciting, amusing, alarming, or delightful; which he soaks into himself through all his five senses at once . . ." (p. 92).

Smuts too speaks about the infantile and mystical blessings of the primitive African mind: "A childlike human being cannot be a bad human, for are we not in spiritual matters bidden to be like unto little children? Perhaps as a direct result of his temperament the African is the only happy human being that I have come across."[25] On the same theme, Lugard, writing specifically about the West African, says that "the virtues and defects of this race-type are those of attractive children," that he is "a happy, thriftless, excitable person lacking in self-control, discipline and foresight"; and "his thoughts and feelings are concentrated on events and feelings of the moment, and he suffers little apprehension for the future or grief for the past."[26] Sir Charles Elliot descends one step in the order of creation. His African is "far nearer the animal placidity and want of desire to rise beyond the state he has reached."[27]

Despite the rich flavor of his life, the primitive African is presented in this theory as being singularly exposed to the slings and arrows of chance. Drawn magnetically to a life of pleasure, to wine, women, and song, he sidesteps the serious business of life, which he dimly glimpses only as obstacles to his dissipations. In Harry Johnston's opinion, it is early sexual indulgence which stunts African minds and holds the continent back.[28] Even black musical talents of which writers of the Harlem renaissance and the negritude movement boast, are, in this theory, derivative from a self-indulgent temperament. For the black professional, it is said, will quiver involuntarily at the sound of a drum. Lugard instances the specially portentous case of Marcus Garvey, "Provisional president of Africa, arrayed in a flowing robe of crimson slashed with green . . . parading the streets of New York with six hands."[29] The hero of *Mister Johnson* does not merely quiver and parade the streets, "He sings alone, falsetto, dancing with peculiar looseness as if all his joints are turned to macaroni" (p. 36). He crouches down, "wriggles and skips in that position; then jerks himself three feet into the air, bent backwards at almost a right angle, with a scream even louder than the old women" (p. 133).

Just as theorists of primitive consciousness predict, Johnson drifts by slow degrees into dissipation, debt, burglary, and murder. But he is unapprehensive even while awaiting execution. Lugard tells the story of a Makonde who breaks into a fortified stockade to steal a cow as thoughtlessly as Johnson breaks into Rudbeck's and Collup's bedrooms though he knows that these men have loaded pistols ready. Lugard adds that "criminals condemned to death show the same lack of apprehension until the moment of execution arrives."[30] Johnson is not only unapprehensive, he dies "triumphing in the greatness, the goodness and the daring inventiveness" of the man who shoots him (p. 225). One of Cary's colleagues in Nigeria, A. C. Hastings, claims that "scallywag employees of my own, or native officials whom I have dismissed or sent to prison, have greeted me, months later, with beaming faces of recognition as though I were their greatest benefactor, as perhaps I was."[31]

Johnson abundantly illustrates the absurdities of the African character as European theorists perceived it at the turn of the century. But the novel does not merely recreate, it also transfigures, the stereotype. It recalls the mental profile, the stock comic episodes, and the expected justice of fate. But if that were all, the novel would have been a Sarah Gertrude Millin or a Rider Haggard melodrama. Cary's originality lies in his reinterpretation of the character in terms of a Blakean psychology of creativity, in the new heroic dimension which he gives the comic material, and in the metamorphosis of Johnson from a wog to a maker of civilization. For the clown of whom Levy-Bruhl and Lugard speak cannot have overcome the institutional inertia of the British empire and the Moslem emirate to build the symbolic road which opens a new way for the human spirit.

Cary first mentions Johnson in the notes he made for a projected book of short stories to be called "Fame and Other Stories." In the outline for "The Favourite," Cary describes a clerk whose embezzlement of funds is condoned by his English boss because of the clerk's imaginative powers. "He gave them life, stirs their imagination. This frightens the D.O. who is done for, but excites the wife, the Chesters and Grosby."[32] A later jotting adds: "The man has idea of trade roads, zungos, bridges, swindles to get it, and is let down." These notes emphasize initiative and imagination; and in the last remark it is apparent that Cary himself excuses the theft, not on the grounds of Johnson's childishness, but on the grounds of the social usefulness of the initiative he takes.

Cary's decision to make Johnson responsible for the building of a trade road took the novelist back in imagination to his own work in Borgu in the last quarter of 1919. A detailed account of that period in his life has been rendered again and again, by Cary himself in *The Case for African Freedom*, by Professor Molly Mahood in *Joyce Cary's Africa*, and by Malcolm Foster in *Joyce Cary: A Biography*. For our purpose, there are two main points. In deciding to finance local road improvements without budgetary authority, Cary showed an individual spirit of enterprise in a bureaucratic situation which normally discouraged it; and, legally speaking, he misappropriated (that is, stole) the divisional votes for police uniforms, stationery, and secret services to see the work through. Moreover, it was in the context of these personal interventions in the making of history that Cary told his wife, who was urging him to come home, how proud he was to be an official of the empire: "Now even if I never write a book worth reading, I know that I have done something in the world—work which can be respected, which is good, and has been good for others. My children need not be ashamed of me, if I am never more than an officer in this service."[33] In a subsequent letter, Cary placed his work on the Borgu roads in a blinding historical light by comparing himself to a Roman engineer in ancient Britain:

This is as some Roman engineer felt when he strolled down the long reaches of Watling Street, and wondered how long he would be permitted to foretell the future of Britain—with one eye on the disturbances in Rome. Shall we all be recalled by the breaking of the Empire. And shall some Blackman in the year 4000 trace my road for a paper in the Kaiama Archeological Society, and debate learnedly the ancient greatness of Britain. It is certain.[34]

Cary was very proud of his road. For him to ascribe that specific initiative to Johnson meant giving the African fool child a supreme historical value which inevitably changed the very conception of the character. It meant, moreover, that while writing, the novelist could look into his own memory of the Dionysian stream of vitality which made him flout regulations and risk his career in a thankless course of action. Johnson would still be immature and even comical. Cary had every reason in 1939 to be amused at his own callow youth. But selfderision, being in this instance one of the guises of self-justification, would be so conducted as to account for "the protective and remonstrant love" which many readers feel in reading Johnson's story. Johnson so conceived cannot represent the primitive anarchy of Africa; he represents the seething pressure of creative excitement which ambitious youth cannot control.

To suggest that Cary is Johnson would be too simple a formula. But just as Cary himself argues that Dostoievsky created Stavrogin and Aloysha out of his own impulses, so we may hypothesize a submerged level of personality out of which he created Johnson. The records show that even as late as 1919 Cary was still struggling against the kind of romantic boyishness which Johnson supremely represents. Looking back many years later, he explained his troubles as the result of "the rootlessness of a boy uprooted from the long romantic tradition of a family domain."[35] He had been unable to settle down to the study of painting in Paris and Edinburgh (1906-09); to the study of law at Oxford (1909-11); to the writing of fiction in Stores Street, London, in 1912; and had come to Africa to prove to himself and his fiancée's family that he could take the yoke of steady work. But even after six years in Nigeria, he was still impulsive, unsteady of purpose, flight "The Raft" and "Bush River," and the uncompleted novel *Daventry* show Cary wrestling anxiously with his own quixotic nature.

We expect as we read the first pages of "The Raft" that this is a story about the eternal youthfulness of Africa. For the black askaris, maneuvering near German outposts during the Cameroonian campaign of the First World War which is the background of the story, shout with laughter as they cut down the trees which their English officer indicated. The officer's protests do not restore order and he walks away telling himself that Africans will never grow up. But with the falling of the tree minutes later, it is the officer who flees in childish terror. This, however, is not the point of the story, which brilliantly recreates the anxieties and forest scenery of that war. The climax of the action comes when the completed raft is launched. It sinks immediately. The Africans have been laughing at the ignorance of the young foreigner who dared to instruct them on local timber. "Bush River" ends on a similar note when the British officer who ignores the advice of his African subordinates faces "the spectacle of his own enormous folly," "the monster of his own stupidity." In *Daventry* the crisis of immaturity is even more devastating. The English hero is a romantic imperialist attracted to Africa by the mystery of the dark continent and the opportunities it offers for storybook adventures. So blinded is he by his temperament that the barking of hyenas is like water bubbling from a bottle. Warned that he would be marching through a hostile area, he insists on taking only a ceremonial retinue made up of pipers, drummers, carriers, a political agent in a new turban and a tasseled sword, and six mounted spearmen in red turbans: "This was a proud beginning. Such a beginning as could not end in failure, or worse than failure, triviality. Nothing would ever be accomplished if youth believed in death, if pride really took a fall into consideration. It was not making an unusual revelation to admit that D would have liked some of his people at home to see him ride along." The moment of truth comes when his cook, transfixed by a poisoned arrow, rejects his offer of first aid. "What for you come here? You no fit do nuffin." Daventry's swagger, his love of pageantry, his indifference to realities may remind us of Johnson; but there are several autobiographical touches in the story (based on the destruction of Malthy's party when they rode unarmed into Tel country in 1916) which suggest that Cary was thinking about the temptations of his own romantic immaturity.[36]

Worried, lonely, often ill, and deprived of all comfort as Cary was in 1919, his usual riot of excitements made him happy. He was writing steadily, sometimes working on three different stories simultaneously, and much enjoyed the characters he created as he told his wife in a letter of October 6, 1919: "I trot about all day when I'm not doing official work, chuckling over the situations I invent. I get much more fun out of my books than any reader ever will."[37] We may see an implicit parallel between the novelist and Johnson as mythomaniacs; and Cary himself recalls that even as a schoolboy at Clifton he used to keep his friends awake at night by making up stories for their amusement. Apart from these joys of the imagination, Cary also enjoyed his work on the Borgu roads in 1919. "I cannot explain the pleasure of seeing a road which one has planned and surveyed in actual being, but it is a very unusually keen pleasure."[38] When he went for a ride on the road, "I found myself performing little jumps— shooting down declivities and flying out of river beds."[39] Elsewhere, he recalls how travelling with his pony "we danced along together all the way."[40] Right to the end of his Borgu days, Cary enjoyed these Johnsonian intoxications of emotion though at the very end his excitements were chastened by a steadying sense of social purpose.

In 1919 Cary did not have an anarchic African clerk to fiddle accounts for him and inspire his road gangs. Whatever had to be done, he did himself. Johnson should, therefore, be seen as the creative second self who gave him the power of historical initiative during those last years in Nigeria. How delightful the experience revived in memory was may be seen from the extraordinary zest and fluency with which Cary renders the character of his double; and he surrounds Johnson's tragedy with poetic sentiment and compassion of a kind that he does not evince for any other of his heroes.

Apart from imperial stereotypes of the primitive and the novelist's memories of his own romantic youth, there is a third factor which has contributed to the conception of the hero of *Mister Johnson*: Cary's imagination was formed by theories of creativity which have their origin in romanticism, the aesthetic and symbolist movements, and the beliefs of the artistic avant garde at the turn of the century. This is not a topic that can be presented briefly. But some indication can be given by considering two contemporary sources of these ideas, Blake and Baudelaire, both of whom exercised tremendous influence on Cary's mind and art.

Cary says in "My Religious History" that he studied Blake in 1910 and was deeply stirred by the poet's vision of the world.[41] His copies of Edwin Ellis's edition of *The Poetical Works of William Blake* bought in 1910 and the Everyman edition of *Poems and Prophecies* are both heavily scored with annotations and endnotes. From the allusions made by Gulley Jimson in *The Horse's Mouth*, it is clear that Cary knew "Milton," "Lament of the Daughters of Albion," "Jerusalem," "America," and "The Mental Traveller" remarkably well. "The Mental Traveller" is definitely one of his favorite poems; and it may be inferred from *The Horse's Mouth* that he interpreted the poem as a parable of the artist's relationship with his society. At birth the artist is faced by the authority of a dominant style of life and art: "Who nails him down upon a rock, catches his shrieks in cups of gold. She binds iron thorns around his head, she pierces both his hands and feet, and she cuts his heart out at his side to make him feel both cold and heat." Johnson's first relationships with the world round him are painful. Bamu's family strips him. His creditors make common cause against him. Blore suspends him from his work. Waziri holds him in a blackmailer's grip. Johnson is no better able to deal with these problems than an art student can handle aesthetic form or a primitive manage his world. In a sense the relationship with Bamu is central; it sums up Johnson's failure to achieve control. But the moment arrives when he breaks his fetters. He burgles the office. He becomes a father. He is Rudbeck's righthand man and Waziri's friend: "Then he rends his Manacles and binds her down for his delight. He plants himself in all her Nerves, just as a Husbandman his mould; and she becomes his dwelling place and Garden fruitful seventy fold . . . He feeds the Beggar and the Poor and the Wayfaring Traveller: for ever open is his door." Bending or disregarding all the rules, Johnson creates new forms of experience to enrich the life around him. At the height of his career, he literally houses the wayfarer and feeds the poor. But Blake's scheme envisages a reversal of the gyres of history in which the relationship between institutional forms and the creative individual favors social authority. In this antithetical phase, the social order now represented by Tring, Collup, and Rudbeck as lawgivers re-assumes the initiative and the story rapidly moves to its tragic close.

Cary's knowledge of Baudelaire goes back to his art student days in
Montmartre in 1906. Some of the poems included in the slim volume of
verse which he published in 1908 reflect his reading of the French poet.
That the interest continued may be seen from *The Drunken Sailor,* which
Cary wrote in 1947 on the model of Baudelaire's "Le Voyage," and Cary's
poem takes its title from "ce matelot ivrogne" of Baudelaire's poem. The
hero of "Le Voyage" who dreams of paradise while wallowing in the mud
may remind us of Johnson, just as Baudelaire's idea of the "animally
ecstatic gaze of the child confronted by what is new"[42] sums up a conception which links Johnson with the cultivated primitivism of the artistic
vision. In speaking of the utter selflessness of this vision Baudelaire
apparently explains why Cary gives Johnson a character in which imaginative powers are one and the same as promiscuity of affection. "What men
call love is a very small, restricted and weak thing compared with this
ineffable orgy, this holy prostitution of a soul that gives itself utterly, with
all its poetry and charity, to the utterly emergent, to the passing unknown."[43]

Baudelaire's account of the fate of the artist in "Benediction"[44] is similar
to, though less schematic than, Blake's:

> Lorsque, par un décret des puissances suprêmes,
> Le Poéte apparaît en ce monde ennuyé
> Sa mére épouvantée et pleine de blasphèmes
> Grispe ses poings vers Dieu, qui le prend en pitié. (ll.1-
> 4)

These hostilities follow the artist into adulthood. His friends spit into his
food. His wife threatens to cut his heart out and feed it to her dog. Rejected
by mother, peers, and spouse, the artist ought to be miserable. But he is
insanely happy as he converses with the wind and is drunk with the sun:

> Pourtant, sous la tutelle invisible d'un Ange,
> L'Enfant désherité s' enivre de soleil,
> Et dans tout ce qu'il boit dans ce qu'il mange
> Retrouve l'ambroisie et le nectar vermeil. (ll.21-24)

The cruelty which the creative individual has to endure is explained in the
myth of the artist. He is an alienated person who will not accept the shared
graces of the common routine. Instead of lying down with the rest of the
herd, he is uncontrollable, self-willed, and disruptive. For according to

Cary's undergraduate friend, John Middleton Murry, "art is movement, ferocity, tearing of what lies before. . . . It comes to birth in irreligion and is nurtured in immorality."[45] Cary himself adds that "the artist in creating new experience is a source of life in the strictest sense—upsets a balance."[46] Rising out of the unconscious, the artist's idea is perceived as a visitation entirely outside normality and destructive of the normal, having nothing to do with reason, practical judgment, or common sense. "The conscious ego is swept along on subterranean current, being nothing more than a helpless observer of events," according to Carl Jung.[47]

At least ten times explicitly and twice as many times implicitly, Johnson is presented to the reader as an artist. "'Look at that, Sozy,' he says with the pride of an artist showing his masterpiece; 'the finest cloth in Fada'" (p. 106). "In that exciting atmosphere of gin and poetic sympathy which belongs only to artists and drink parties, Gullup and Johnson often pursue their own creations simultaneously" (p. 128). "The situation has been given into his hand, like wood to be carved or a theme to be sung" (p. 34). Whenever Cary had occasion to speak about the novel, he invariably referred to Johnson as "the artist in life, creating his life," "the artist of his own joyful tale."[48]

Blake, Baudelaire, and avant garde romanticism account for that distinctive quality of Cary's mind and art, his insistence on the spirituality of common experience. Enid Starkie, one of his closest Oxford associates, reports how amusing it is in daily life to see Cary "turning some humble and unattractive barnyard fowl into a noble bird, and it seemed to me often that his view of people was quite unrealistic."[49] Cary's readers and critics have simply been unable to conceive how he could make dazzling swans of such ducklings as Johnson, Bonser, Jimson, and Nimmo; and his reputation has suffered because of this incomprehensible Blakean legacy. From Blake, Baudelaire, and the artistic avant garde he also derived a view of the world in which the primitive and the child are types of the artist. For the primitive and the child enjoy the artist's mystical intensity of vision in which fact and value are fused, both have the virgin spirit which experience does not defile, both contemplate the world with an ecstatic gaze, both live in a storm of feeling that would not let them rest, and both rush into creation to make a new world that would accord with heart's desire. Although they are bruised in their collisions with the permanent forms of things, they often effect a change in the existing order. "History is chiefly made by those who are ignorant of its lessons," Cary says in his Borgu Notebook.[50]

Under the influence of Blake and Baudelaire, *Mister Johnson* became a meditation on the relative powers of reason and emotion, calculation and spontaneity, culture and nature, in the processes of human renewal. It is because the novel raises questions of this order that it can stand beside the works of Cary's great contemporaries, D. H. Lawrence and E. M. Forster.

Finally, we may consider Cary's debt to *Billy Budd* (1891). Melville's novelette may not have modified the overall conception of Johnson's character as the other sources so far discussed have, but it certainly contributed something vital to Cary's final episode and in that way influenced the mythical resonance of the story. It may also have shown the novelist how to adapt Blake's prophetic visions to a realistic novel form.

That Cary had *Billy Budd* in mind while he was writing *Mister Johnson* we may be sure from two specific verbal allusions. When Billy is accused of disloyalty to King and country, he replies: "I have eaten the King's bread and I am true to the King."[51] Johnson uses similar words when Waziri asks him for access to confidential government documents: "I belong to de King—I 'gree for de King" (p. 35). Similarly Billy blesses Capt Vere when he is about to be hanged:

At the penultimate moment, his words, his only ones, words wholly unobstructed in the utterance were these—"God bless Capt Vere!" Syllables so unanticipated coming from one with the ignominious hemp about his neck—a conventional felon's benediction directed aft towards the quarters of honor; syllables too delivered in the clear melody of a singing-bird on the point of launching from the twig. (p. 729)

Johnson directs the same benediction toward Rudbeck on the morning of his execution: "Good morning Mister Rudbeck. God bless you . . ." (p. 222).

Cary's recourse to Melville is not, however, merely a matter of verbal echoes. In both novels, the hero is conceived as a child type, a noble savage, on whose innocence and guileless simplicity of heart Melville, in his own case, lavishes every device of poetic praise. Both heroes have prelapsarian selflessness despite which they evince, when roused, a manly fury to kill the villains of their stories with a single blow. Both are tried and executed by their best friend and helper, the man who stands symbolically in the position of a father to the prisoner. Both are free of the fear of death, Johnson because "I no fit know nuffing about it—he too quick" (p. 224), and Billy because he sees death with the thoughtless eyes of children, "who yet among their other sports will play a funeral with hearse and mourners" (p. 725).

Two cycles of episodes are implied in the plot of both novels. Billy starts his career on a friendly merchant ship where he is a great favorite and is nicknamed "the handsome sailor." He is then transferred to a battleship whose repressive military routine renders fictionally the suggestions Cary found in the second phase of "The Mental Traveller." Billy's tragedy is played out on the scrubbed gundeck of H.M.S. *Indomitable*, where he meets the villain; he is forced to kill just as Johnson is forced to kill Gollup. Arrayed against the young sailor's simplicity of heart and sacrificial selflessness is the aggressive majesty of a great battleship, "ponderously cannoned," with its seventy-five men-at-arms; a Captain who, on hearing Billy's dying benediction, stands "erectly rigid as a musket in the ship-armourer's rack" (p. 727); and a Chaplain who "lends the sanction of the religion of the meek to that which is the abrogation of everything but brute force" (p. 727). *Billy Budd* is the story of the sacrifice of what is divine in human nature, innocence, spontaneous creative joy, and noble simplicity of heart, to the violent imperatives of institutional order. As a parable of Love and Justice it is assimilated metaphorically to the Christian mystery of Good Friday.

The discerning reader will notice that Cary tries his best within the constraints of the resistant realistic form he works in to create an equivalent second cycle of episodes in *Mister Johnson*. On the face of it that should be easy since *Billy Budd* and *Mister Johnson* use the same backdrop of an imperial world order. Cary's second sequence begins with the entrance of Tring, who inaugurates an authoritarian regime. Audu and Johnson are sacked and Rudbeck is severely reprimanded. The office, the treasury, and the prison are closely monitored. On Rudbeck's return, administrative and financial regulations cannot be much relaxed. When Johnson goes to Collup's store as a small boy, Cary sustains the military atmosphere by making Gollup a vigilant old soldier ready at any moment for violence and maintaining strict military routine in his work, his drunkenness, and the beating of his black mistress: "He struts about like a little king and when sometimes he looks round from his back stoop at the swept earth, the bright alleys, the new thatched roofs, all glittering in the sun, he pushes up his lips in what is too dignified to be a grin of satisfaction. At such a moment the two points of his moustache rise as if presenting arms" (p. 122). The military background has its most emphatic statement in the prison sequences when Johnson's warders are old soldiers casually chatting about carbines, parades, and camp life, and submitting themselves to the discipline of the soldier's life. The imperial logic which forces Capt Vere to hang his favorite sailor also weighs on Rudbeck when he decides Johnson's case. In the sacrificial love which Johnson exhibits in these prison sequences, the circumstances in which he gives up his clothes and his precious English shoes, and his blessing of his executioner, we have tokens of the scriptural allusions which enrich the end of Melville's tale.

Freud's remark that recurrent dream symbols are "overdetermined" applies with equal cogency to the haunting images of art. Johnson is not a simple character whom we can fully account for in terms of Cary's African experience. The idea is deeply rooted in the novelist's struggle with himself, his experience of life and art, his reading of other literature, and his total vision of the world. From imperial stereotypes of pre-logical consciousness, Cary derived a comic plot heavily laced with racial smugness and bigotry. But he humanized that plot when, looking into the mirror of his own mind, he recognized, perhaps unconsciously, that he was also primitive; and with that dim awareness a deep current of fellow feeling and compassion entered the stream. Blakean mythology and fin-de-siécle theories of art added a third dimension in terms of which Johnson may be seen as the blank impulse of life in its mythical and tragic confrontation with material circumstances which are both its opposite and its means of realization. Melville re-enforced this mythical dimension and suggested a possible fictional form.

Mister Johnson is not a novel about racial contrasts; nor is it concerned with the disorientation of a charming primitive who suffers culture shock in the harsh intellectual disciplines of an outpost of the empire. Although the novel does deal with the shifting relationship between the clerk and his carelessly patronizing English boss, that relationship is taken up in the larger pattern of man's dependence on the unconscious creative sources of life in himself, and the tragic consequences of that seething caldron of power to the individual who is unable to stand at a rational distance from it.

It is proper to remind reviewers and critics, as Cary himself frequently did, that *Mister Johnson* does not specifically address the African condition. This, however, is merely to say that it is an imaginative statement, not a political documentary. For it is precisely because of its deep-rooted and branching mythical suggestiveness that it will always remain refreshingly novel.

NOTES

1. Andrew Wright, *Joyce Cary: A Preface to His Novels* (New York: Harper and Harper, 1959), p. 57. Page 7 of the author's Foreword says: "I wrote him a good many letters in the year before I was able to go to Oxford, and he was always kind enough to reply fully, thoughtfully and frankly. . . . For nearly six months I went daily to his house in Parks Road. He gave me his study on the second floor to work in; and gave me permission to use anything I found."

2. Arnold Kettle, *An Introduction to the English Novel* (London: Arrow, 1965), vol. II, pp. 179 and 183.

3. Frederick Karl, "The Moralist as Novelist," *Twentieth-Century Literature* V (1960), p. 189.

4. Golden Larsen, *The Dark Descent: Social Change and Moral Responsibility in the Novels of Joyce Cary* (London: Michael Joseph, 1965), p. 52.

5. H. R. Collins, "Joyce Cary's Troublesome Africans," *Antioch Review* XIII (September 1953), pp. 397-406; and H. Barba, "Image of the African in Transition," *University of Kansas City Review* XXIX, iii (March 1963), pp. 215-221.

6. Chinua Achebe, "Named for Victoria, Queen of England," *Morning Yet on Creation Day* (London: Heinemann, 1975), p. 70; see also p. 26.

7. M.J.C. Echeruo, *Joyce Cary and the Novel of Africa* (London: Longman, 1973), pp. 26 and 139.

8. Abdul JanMohamed, *Joyce Cary's African Romances*, Boston University African Studies Center Working Papers No. 5, 1978 (mimeograph), p. 20.

9. All references to Cary's published fiction are made parenthetically to the uniform Carfax edition issued in 1951 and 1952.

10. *Daventry* partly typed MS, folio 21, Box 137, John Osborn Collection of Joyce Cary's Papers, Bodleian Library, Oxford. All references to Cary's manuscripts, notebooks, and letters are made to this Collection.

11. Joyce Cary, *The Case for African Freedom and Other Writings on Africa* (Texas: Texas University Press, 1962), pp. 35 and 133.

12. *Ibid.*, p. 221.

13. *Ibid.*, p. 222.

14. *Ibid.*, pp. 74 and 75.

15. *Ibid.*, pp. 132 and 133.

16. *Ibid.*, p. 213.

17. Cited by Malcolm Forster, *Joyce Cary: A Biography* (Boston: Houghton Mifflin, 1968), p. 293.

18. Cary's Preface to *The African Witch* (London: Michael Joseph, 1951) p. 7.

19. *The Case for African Freedom and Other Writings on Africa*, *op. cit.*, p. 37.

20. Cited by Malcolm Forster, *Joyce Cary: A Biography*, *op. cit.*, p. 294.

21. M. M. Mahood, *Joyce Cary's Africa* (London: Methuen, 1962), pp. 11, 23, 25, 55-58, 170, 177-78, 180, and 196.

22. M. J. C. Echeruo's Introduction to *Mister Johnson* (London: Longman, 1975), pp. xxvii-xxviii.

23. Notebook 73 (unpaginated), John Osborn Collection of Joyce Cary's Papers.

24. Lucien Levy-Bruhl, *Primitive Mentality*, trans. L. Clare (London: Allen and Unwin, 1923), pp. 61-62 especially.

25. Jan Christian Smuts, *Africa and Some World Problems* (Oxford: Oxford University Press, 1930), p. 75.

26. Sir F. D. Lugard, *The Dual Mandate in British Tropical Africa* (London: Blackwood and Sons, 1922), pp. 69 and 70.

27. Sir Charles Elliot, *East African Protectorate* (London: Edward Arnold, 1905), p. 173.

28. Sir H. H. Johnston, *British Central Africa* (London: Methuen, 1897), p. 408.

29. Sir F. D. Lugard, *The Dual Mandate in British Tropical Africa*, *op. cit.*, p. 83.

30. *Ibid.*, p. 71.

31. A. C. Hastings, *Nigerian Days* (London: Bodley Head, 1925), p. 161.

32. Notebook 62, Box 265, John Osborn Collection of Joyce Cary's Papers.

33. Letter to Gertrude Cary dated May 30, 1919, John Osborn Collection of Joyce Cary's Papers.

34. Letter to Gertrude Cary dated October 4, 1919, John Osborn Collection of Joyce Cary's Papers.

35. Cited by Andrew Wright, *Joyce Cary: A Preface to His Novels, op. cit.*, p. 21.

36. *Daventry* , *op. cit.*, folio 9.

37. Letter to Gertrude Cary dated October 6, 1919.

38. Letter to Gertrude Cary dated September 9, 1919.

39. Letter to Gertrude Cary dated January 23, 1919.

40. Letter to Gertrude Cary dated February 9, 1919.

41. "My Religious History," TS, S. 22.K in Box 382, John Osborn Collection of Joyce Cary's Papers.

42. Charles Baudelaire, *The Essence of Laughter and Other Essays, Journals and Letters*, ed. Peter Quennell (New York: Meridian Books, 1956), p. 28.

43. *Ibid.*, pp. 139-40.

44. Culled from Charles Baudelaire, *Les Fleurs du Mâl*; edited by Enid Stackie. London: Gerald Duckworth & Co., 1988.

45. John Middleton Murry, *Rhythm* No. I, ii (Autumn 1911) p. 10.

46. Notebook P51, Box 372, John Osborn Collection of Joyce Cary's Papers.

47. Carl Jung, "Psychology and Literature," *Collected Works,* ed. H. Read, M. Fordham, and G. Graham (New York: Pentheon Books, 1954), vol. 15, p. 261.

48. Joyce Cary's Preface to *Castle Corner* (London: Michael Joseph, Carfax edn. 1952), p. 8; and "The Novelist at Work: A Conversation between Joyce Cary and Lord David Cecil," *Adam International Review* XVIII (Nov./Dec. 1950), p. 20.

49. Enid Starkie, "Joyce Cary: A Personal Portrait," *The Virginia Quarterly Review* XXXVII (Winter 1961), p. 121.

50. Notebook 16 (Borgu Notebook), folio 48r, John Osborn Collection of Joyce Cary's Papers.

51. Herman Melville, *The Portable Melville,* ed. Jay Leyda (London: Penguin Books, 1976), p. 709. All subsequent references are made parenthetically to this edition.

2

"I, Okigbo, Town-Crier": The Transition from Mythopoeic Symbolism to a Revolutionary Aesthetic in *Path of Thunder*

Chukwuma Azuonye

There is a clear pattern in the development of the poetry of Christopher Okigbo. As has been shown in my earlier essays,[1] there are probably two major phases in this development. The first phase, stretching from *Four Canzones*[2] to *Distances*,[3] was dominated by a symbolist aesthetic of the kind ritually re-enacted in *Heavensgate III*.[4] Here, the poet-hero, in the romantic solitude of a beach, plants the "secret" of his muse in beach sand, completely unconcerned about "name or audience." This ritual symbolism of covering up a unique vision of reality in utter disregard of overt statements epitomizes the symbolist attitude. Okigbo's poetry up to *Distances* presents various dramatic moments of this ultra-romantic attitude. *Lament of the Masks*[5] marks a turning point in the development of the poems. In this poem, dedicated to W. B. Yeats, on the occasion of the centenary of his birth, Okigbo now assumes, as it were, the mantle of prophecy, having evolved a new person after the attainment of full individuation at the close of *Distances*.[6] No longer the songbird singing "tongue-tied ... among the branches," he speaks of "thunder," "cannons," and "battle" and gives clear promise of more open statements about his crisis-ridden country.

The roots of the development described above were already present in *Fragments out of the Deluge*, *Silences*,[7] and the closing strophe of *Distances*. Even in *Heavensgate*, the "Initiation" poems move from the intensely esoteric explorations of subconscious reality through the archetypal pictographs of the cross, the triangle, the square, the rhombus, and the rectangle (the full implications of which I have ventured to discuss elsewhere),[8] to open invectives, first, against

> the moron,
> fanatics and priests and popes,
> organizing secretaries and party
> managers
> and, subsequently, against
> brothers and deacons,
> liberal politicians,
> selfish selfseekers—all who are good
> doing nothing at all.

Later, within the overriding oracular symbolism of *Fragments out of the Deluge*, we have a thoroughgoing tirade against cultural alienation, philistinism, Christian vandalism, and sentimental literary fads such as "negritude." In *Silences*, we can see in the "Who can say No in thunder" passages presentiments of war arising from the despoiling of the "Great River" (Nigeria) by "her pot-bellied watchers." And, amid the beatific experience of mystical union with the goddess, in *Distances*, we are confronted with "the taste of ash in the air's marrow." It is, however, in *Lament of the Masks* that the tendency toward direct and open political statements clearly declares itself. The mythical mask of the early sequences now begins to tear asunder and we get a faint glimpse of the face behind the mask, a man who, in many ways, would be identified with the Yeats of the later years. In *Path of Thunder*,[9] the mask falls off completely and the poet reveals himself and unequivocally declares his revolutionary options.

This essay will examine, through a detailed analysis of the six poems which make up *Path of Thunder*, the highlights of the remarkable transition from the mythopoeic symbolism of the early phase to a largely unfulfilled revolutionary aesthetic of the second phase. The examination invites a look back into the future of Okigbo's poetic career which was prematurely cut short by the civil war. Nevertheless, it is hoped that by doing this, we rationalize the poet's direct involvement in action and appreciate certain moot tendencies wrapped up in the myth and symbolism of the earlier phase. A good starting point in this investigation seems to be the second strophe of *Path of Thunder*, "Elegy of the Wind," which is by far the most coherent and categorical statement of the main principles of the revolutionary aesthetic of the unfulfilled second phase. Here, the poet describes himself as "Man of iron throat"—a man forced by the prevailing circumstances to "make broadcast with eunuch-horn of seven valves."[10] Then he declares:

> I will follow the wind to the clearing,
> And with muffled steps seemingly out of breath break
> the silence the myth of her gate.

The allusions contained in these declarations must be clear to anyone who is familiar with Okigbo's poetry preceding *Path of Thunder*. The "wind" of the title of the elegy and of the lines quoted above is clearly the political turbulence and upheavals of the middle sixties in Nigeria: it is one and the same with Harold Macmillian's "wind of change" blowing through Africa, but which in the mid-sixties had become a vicious harbinger of "mere anarchy." Okigbo, in the ivory tower of the earlier phase of his poetry, had charted the movements of the wind at "various stations of his cross,"[11] in his progression from *Four Canzones* to *Distances*. The symbolist poetry of these earlier sequences had been as good as silence. We should notice how this is suggested in the unpunctuated collection, "the silence the myth of her gate." What the new situation of crisis requires is poetry of action. The poet, so to speak, must now take to the soapbox with a microphone: he must speak directly to the people. The idea of making broadcasts: the poet of action explores the same area as the broadcaster. He is like the traditional spokesman, the oral artist, who interprets communal experience and fore-warns of dangers ahead. He speaks directly to the masses in the public square, "the clearing." But the erstwhile ivory poet is unused to this mode of communication. That is why he approaches "the clearing" with anxiety and caution: "with muffled steps seemingly out of breath." Later, in the third strophe of the sequence, we see him in person, unmasked, like the town-crier, warning the nation of its follies, despite his awareness of the risks of taking such a course of action:

> If I don't learn to shut my mouth I will soon go to hell,
> I, Okigbo, town-crier, together with my iron bell.[12]

And in the fourth strophe, "Elegy for Slit-drum," in which we are drawn into a dance of condolences, there is, paradoxically, public rejoicing in the new solidarity between the poet and the masses, for the masses need the oracular insights of the mythmaker in their moments of doubts and uncer-tainties, as in the fabulous darkness which provides the backdrop to "Elegy of the Wind":

> The mythmaker accompanies us (the Egret had come and gone)
> Okigbo accompanies us the oracle enkindles us
> the Hornbill is there again (the Hornbill has had a bath)
> Okigbo accompanies us the rattles enlighten us—

The poet of action enjoys this approchement with, and acknowledgment by, the masses that recognize him and rejoice in the insights that they receive from him in times of trouble. It is in the poetry of action alone that the poet can make active, for the benefit of the masses, the special knowledge which he, as the medium of the goddess, is alone privileged to receive.

Every poet who begins his career as a "mythmaker," like Okigbo, comes to this kind of knowledge at a certain point in his career. Yeats, faced with "responsibilities"[13] similar to that which now faces Okigbo, repudiates his earlier poetry as a "coat / Covered with embroideries / Out of old mythologies"[14] and then he realizes "There is more enterprise in walking naked." Poetry of action is "naked poetry," one that does not rely on the tapestry of myth for its effects but on the sincerity and force of the poet's direct questionings and doubts. That is why Okigbo now wants to break "the silence the myth of her gate." In "Elegy of the Wind," therefore, we have a new poetic manifesto, a revision of the old mode, such as every serious, committed poet makes in the face of violence and anarchy. The realization that the old oracular mode will not now suffice to meet the challenges of the times is clearly stated: "I have lived the oracle dry on the cradle of a new generation." Breaking with the restriction of the old mode, the poet must now embrace larger causes and deal openly with issues of wider dimension:

> O Wind, swell my sails; and may my banner run the
> course of wider waters.

There is, here, a Shellyian Paradox[15] in the image of destructive wind which is also the activator of the poet's dead thoughts, the destroyer which is also the preserver, quickening a new birth and scattering the poet's insights throughout the universe.

I have begun this analysis with the second strophe of *Path of Thunder* because the declarations contained in it assure us of the poet's purpose in the sequence and enable us to take the reading we shall record in the rest of this chapter, a reading which involves a closer sociopolitical interpretation of the images and symbols in the sequence than would be possible in any analysis of Okigbo's poetry: "the myth of her gate" or "the oracle" of the past mode. The declarations of purpose seem clear enough and the new mode already beginning to assert itself ("the chant, already all wings") is here before us actively following "the thunder clouds." All these seem to us clearly stated, but to reassure ourselves lest we fall into grievous error, it is perhaps necessary for us to attend more closely to these declarations through a paraphrase of the elegy; and perhaps, it may also be necessary for us to go further to show how these declarations are consistently made all through *Path of Thunder* and how they develop from statements of artistic purpose made elsewhere, not only in *Labyrinths* but also in the preceding and intervening poems.[16]

"ELEGY OF THE WIND"

It might be stated right away that "Elegy of the Wind" is informed by the poet's visions and revisions, his fears and expectations, and his doubts and questionings as he considers what his proper role should be in the "new generation," on the "cradle" of which he finds himself. It is, in essence, a record of his past efforts and failures and an anticipation of the new active role he must now fulfill with all its dangers and challenges.

First, in the opening stanza, he invokes the heavenly muse, "White light ... the milky way"; perhaps once again, but in a different situation, he finds himself a suppliant at Heavensgate. The first time he is discovered in this attitude of ritual supplication before Idoto, in the overture to *Heavensgate*, he is "the young bird at the passage," a child, "lost in the legend" of the mother-goddess of the stream whose worship he had abandoned in the pursuit of strange gods. There, "at *Heavensgate*," he is "watchman for the watchword," waiting under her power, for the goddess to inspire and make him worthy. Now, he has attained manhood, and after his excruciating experiences, he feels he can take the initiative: "let me clasp you to my waist." The phallic overtones are unmistakable; and here, as in the opening strophe of the Watermaid monologues in *Heavensgate III*, images of sexual union combine with those of plant growth to suggest the exfoliation of art. The same attitudes enacted in that first strophe of the Watermaid sequence are repeated here. I have elsewhere dealt with this at length.[17] The unique poetic vision of the poet is a secret akin to the secret which burdens King Midas's barber and which he can declare only at the pain of death or suffering of some sort. Even where the poet invents a clever means of unburdening himself of the secret without telling it into any ear, burying it in beach sand, he does not escape the consequences. King Midas's barber suffers death; Okigbo's prodigal is wounded, when the secret breaks into blossom. The same twilight setting is here again invoked and the poet boldly conjures "the burden of the centuries" (the insights and archetypal modes of perception which he has shared with other poets over the centuries) to break into plumule, disregarding the dangers:

> And may my muted tones of twilight
> Break your iron gate, the burden of several centuries,
> into twin tremulous cotyledons

Here is a passionate plea for liberation from the strictures of mythic imagining. In the second stanza, we have the declaration of his intention to come out in the open, speaking with microphonic audacity, making public statements. Then follows, in stanzas three, four, and five, a look back into the future. Stanza three recapitulates and alludes to the kind of growth recorded in *Limits II*, where the "shrub among the poplars," after the unification in solitude of voice and soul with the selves, becomes the "green cloud above the forest," the crown of its own glory. It had been a unique and spectacular rise for which there is cause for pride:

> For I have lived the sapling sprung from the bed
> of the old vegetation;
> Have shouldered my way through a mass of ancient
> nights to chlorophyll

Next, in the following stanza, he summarizes his progress as a suppliant, beginning from *Heavensgate* to his first close encounters with the maid in her bedchamber, in *Distances*:

> Or leaned upon a withered branch
> A blind beggar leaning on a porch.

These two lines which form stanza four are difficult to interpret. But the first line seems to refer to the poet's posture "at Heavensgate," where he is discovered, early in his prodigal state, "leaning on an oilbean," before mother Idoto. The second, on the other hand, probably refers to the later encounters of the poet as the importunate hero in the bedchamber of his muse, the intractable maid. The lines, however, clearly summarize the progress of the poet: his psychological journey from innocence to experience. *Path of Thunder* then is a sequence in which the poet accepts the responsibilities which come with experience and in which he rejects "the errors of the rendering" in the oracular first phase of his career. The rejection of the "errors" of the earlier phase is explicitly stated in the fifth stanza:

> I have lived the oracle dry on the oracle of a new
> generation. . . .
> The autocycle leans on a porch, the branch dissolves
> into embers,

Here, the inadequacy of the old mode to deal with the challenges of the "new generation" is announced, and the collapse of these modes described. The "autocycle" leaning "on a porch" may refer to the vehicle which the poet now abandons, and the dissolution of "the branch" may refer to the final dissolution of the poet's principal poetic figure—the female figure (the *anima*) which dominates his adventures in the unconscious[18] throughout the first phase of his poetic career. This dissolution of the *anima* figure signifies maturity or individuation through the unification of the opposite tendencies in the poet's psyche and the arrival at a "still-point"—the "motion into stillness" of the sixth stanza, a stanza replete with images of regeneration, manhood, and the pains of maturation. Here the poet, having abandoned his old mode of operation (stanza five), emerges like a phoenix from the ashes of his past and attains full poetic manhood with all its responsibilities and pains, the latter symbolized by the pains of circumcision—the traditional symbol of manhood in African rites of passage. But some aspects of "the child" linger in manhood, just as there are some aspects of manhood in childhood:

> The man embodies the child
> The child embodies the man

We are here confronted with a familiar cyclical pattern in African mythology, a pattern well illustrated by the eternal cycle of "returning to the world" as child (*ilo uwa*) and "returning to the spirit sphere" as man (*ila mmuo*) in Igbo mythology. The man "returning to the spirit sphere" at death will be reborn in the land of spirit as a child, and the child "returning to the world" at birth is a man reborn from the spirit sphere. But apart from this reference to the cyclical interrelationship between the man and the child in Igbo mythology, the idea of the man embodying the child and the child embodying the man is reminiscent of one of the key archetypes in Jungian psychology, namely the child as a symbol of the fully individuated self.[19] We are thus here presented with an image of the fully individuated self who, amid a painful initiation rite, contemplates the bloodshed and suffering of his full involvement in the adult responsibilities ahead of him.

But the bloodshed and suffering notwithstanding, the poet is undeterred. He relishes his emergence from the ivory tower into "wider" social responsibilities:

> O wind, swell my sails; and may my banner run
> the course of wider waters. (stanza seven)

Meanwhile, he reflects on the limitations imposed on his full realization of the wider responsibilities by the opposing forces of innocence ("the child") and of experience ("the man") in him, the former making it difficult for him to reach out for "the high shelf on the wall" (possibly high political office) while the latter draws him toward "the narrow neck of a calabash" (possibly narrow ideological commitments).[20] But amid these reflections, he is suddenly overwhelmed by the winds of the prophecy—"the chant, already full wings"—which it is his duty to transmit to the nation. This chant, of course, is "Come Thunder," the third poem in *Path of Thunder*, in which the poet forewarns of the dangers inherent in the political crises of the period before the January 1966 military coup in Nigeria. We shall return to this poem presently; but first, let us look at the antecedent to "Elegy of the Wind," namely "Thunder Can Break," the first poem in *Path of Thunder*, which forms the background to the manifesto presented in the "Elegy of the Wind."

"THUNDER CAN BREAK"

" Thunder Can Break," as the title implies, is a warning. It sums up in succinct images and symbols the implications of armed revolution of January 1966 in Nigeria and its inescapable consequences. "Thunder" is, of course, a traditional symbol for divine wrath and justice. Only the innocent can escape the wrath of "Thunder" (the Igbo god, Amadioha or Kamalu): it is the only hope of the ordinary man against the tyranny of his rulers. Thus, for example, amid the festive excesses of the decadent civilian regime in Achebe's *A Man of the People*, Odili declares: "I wished for a miracle, for a voice of Thunder, to hush this ridiculous festival and tell the poor contemptible people one or two truths. But of course it would be quite useless. They were not only ignorant but cynical." (p. 2) Nevertheless, at the end of *A Man of the People*, Odili's wish is answered in the form of the military coup which topples the civilian government whose members patronize such ridiculous festivals. The coup at the end of *A Man of the People* which has been described as "a terrifyingly accurate prophecy" is essentially the same as the coup (the "miracl . . . of Thunder") which toppled the ridiculous Balewa regime in January 1966. It is the same "Miracle of Thunder" that is celebrated in "Thunder Can Break":

> This day belongs to a miracle of Thunder;
> Iron has carried the forum
> With token gestures. Thunder has spoken
> Left no signature broken
> Barbicans alone tell one table the winds scatter

Two kinds of "thunder" are here implied: the man-made thunder of cannons and guns and the thunder of divine wrath, the former being the instrument of the latter in this particular context. The idea of describing the "thunder" of January 15, 1966, as a miracle arises from the general feeling, before the coup, that the Balewa regime was far too entrenched to be toppled, an illusion of a kind from which inept but oppressive regimes everywhere in the world suffer from time to time. But "the voice of the people is the voice of God," and no matter how deeply entrenched an evil regime may be, it is bound to collapse one day before the wrath of thunder.

"Thunder Can Break" beings with an image of a "fanfare of drums" and of "wooden bells," an image suggestive of celebration:

> Fanfare of drums, wooden bells: iron chapter;
> And our dividing airs are gathered home.

The occasion is the dawn of a great new chapter of national history, an "iron chapter" which is expected to bring about an end to the "dividing airs" (or the perennial disunity) of the nation. The key idea here is "iron chapter," the military force of cohesion for which the celebration is being staged. The word "iron" appears to be used in, at least, three distinct but related senses. First of all, it seems to signify armed revolution; second, it seems to allude to the name of the man, General Ironsi (nicknamed "Ironsides"), who emerged as Head of State as a consequence of the coup; and, third, it would appear that there is a pun here on the idea of "iron" in "irony," for it is, indeed, an "ironic chapter" of Nigerian history. There is something ironic about the coup, not only because of the sudden popularity of an unelected potentially totalitarian regime but also because of the contradictions between the hopes of the masses and the actions of the new military rulers which soon emerged. In "Thunder Can Break," the poet is particularly concerned with the supreme irony of the January coup—first, the assumption of "the forum" by Ironsi (Iron), a man who does not share the revolutionary ideals of the coup leaders, and, second, the unjustifiable imprisonment of the coup leaders, the instruments of thunder: "For barricaded in iron handiwork a miracle caged."[21] The poet then appeals to the Ironsi regime to release the imprisoned heroes:

> Bring them out we say, bring them out
> Faces and hands and feet,
> The stories behind the myth, the plot
> Which the ritual enacts.[22]

Quite literally, there is a call here for the heroes of the coup to be released unharmed so that the general public can see and honor them. There is no doubt in the poet's mind that the heroic act of the coup leaders has already earned them a place in history and popular myth. The general public is entitled to share in the stories of their heroic exploits and to understand more fully the manner in which the revolution was accomplished.

The poem then ends on a note of warning: The new regime is still suffering from the disease of the ousted civilian regime (symbolized by the elephant); its "obduracy" in refusing to heed the commonweal may call down thunder on it:

> Thunder can break—Earth, bind me fast—
> Obduracy, the disease of elephant.

This warning is repeated in "Hurrah for Thunder" (the fourth poem in the sequence), where the new military regime is accused of tending toward the repetition of the excesses of the "fallen elephant" (the ousted civilian government):

> Alas! the elephant has fallen—
> Hurrah for thunder—
> But already the hunters are talking about pumpkins:
> If they share the meat let them remember thunder.

Okigbo's personal and ideological involvement on the side of the leaders of the coup of January 15, 1966, is now well known, and his later role and death in action on the side of Biafra in the civil war are perhaps better known. He is obviously partisan here, defending the course of the young majors whom he had supported in the belief that they were an instrument of divine wrath but who had now fallen into the hands of a new elephantine iron force likely to repeat the follies of the past and plunge the nation into war. It is this situation that gives rise to his decision, in "Elegy of the Wind," to "follow the winds to the clearing" and "make broadcast with eunuch-horn of seven-valves" of "what is past, is passing, and to come."

This prophetic role attains its full maturity in "Come Thunder," the third poem in the sequence. Discarding all obscurantic mythical and oracular imagery, the poet speaks directly to his people:

> Now that the triumphant march has entered the last
> street corners
> Remember, O dancers, the thunder among the clouds.
> But that the laughter, broken in two, hangs
> tremulous between the teeth,
> Remember, O dancers, the lightning beyond the earth. . . .
> The smell of blood already floats in the lavender-mist
> of the afternoon.
> The death sentence lies in ambush along the
> corridors of power;
> And a great fearful thing already tugs at the cables of
> the open air,
> A nebula immense and immeasurable, a night of
> deep waters—
> An iron dream unnamed and unprintable, a path of stone.

This, clearly, is the new Okigbo—a new voice in the "new generation" of "Elegy of the Wind." Its appeal is direct and its imagery seems to derive from the oral tradition. Chants of the same tone, imagery, and rhetorical vigor can be found in the repertoire of many an African contemporary oral poet in like situations.

"HURRAH FOR THUNDER"

In the next movement, "Hurrah for Thunder," the image of "the elephant" as the symbol of the brutal destructiveness of Nigeria's first republic is further developed:

> The elephant, tetrarch of the jungle:
> With a wave of the hand
> He could pull down four trees to the ground;
> His four mortar legs pounded the earth:
> Wherever they treaded
> The grass was forbidden to be there.

Here, "the jungle" is unmistakably Nigeria of the turbulent early sixties and the "four trees" are decidedly the four regions—East, West, Midwest, and the North—whose unity and progress were ruthlessly devastated by the elephantine forces which dominated the center. Perhaps, more specifically for Okigbo, these destructive elephantine forces were represented by "the tetrarch of the jungle" (the Sardauna of Sokoto, who was killed in the January 1966 coup) and the dominant Hausa-Fulani elite (which has now metamorphosed into the "Kaduna Mafia"). "Hurrah for Thunder," as its title and overriding tone of cynical celebration imply, is an approval of the coup of January 1966—the thunder—which brought about the fall of the brute forces:

> Whatever happened to the elephant—
> Hurrah for thunder—
> . . .
> Alas! the elephant has fallen—
> Hurrah for thunder—

But there is no facile approval here. As has been pointed out, hardly is "the miracle of thunder" fully realized than there are suggestions that the new military leadership ("the hunters") may be succumbing to the temptation to "share" the resources (the meat) of the nation among its members as the ousted civilian leadership did. Okigbo's position on this is clear and simply stated: it was the scramble for the sharing of the national cake that brought down the thunder on the civilian government; if the new military leaders indulge in the same kind of excesses, they too will be visited by thunder. What is needed under the new dispensation is not the sharing of meat but fair play, responsibility, and the fitting of the right pegs in the right holes. Token gestures and promises alone will not do in the circumstances:

> The eye that looks down will surely see the nose;
> The finger that fits should be used to pick the nose;
> Today—for tomorrow, today becomes yesterday:
> How many million promises can ever fill a basket. . . .

In the midst of these homiletic reflections, the poet suddenly realizes the danger of his outspokenness:

> If I don't learn to shut my mouth I'll soon go to hell,
> I, Okigbo, town-crier, together with my iron bell.

But, of course, he does not shut his mouth and even goes further to match his words with action for which he ultimately pays the supreme sacrifice, while fighting for Biafra in the Nigerian civil war.

What happens in "Elegy for Slit-drum" is hard to pin down; but here, there are close references to events immediately arising from the coup of January 1966 and clear presentiments of the outbreak of war. To begin with, the poet reveals his dissatisfaction with the myopic and indecisive conduct of the regime of General Ironsi:

> The General is up . . . the General is up . . . Commandments . . .
> the General is up the General is up the General is up—
> Condolences for our twin-beaks and feathers of condolences:
> the General is near the throne
> an iron mask covers his face
> the General has carried the day
> the mortars are far away. . . .
> Condolences to appease the fever of a wake among
> tumbled tombs

Okigbo's misgiving about the performance of General Ironsi is that, despite the popular reception of his regime throughout the country, his policy of appeasement toward the North as if to mollify its elite over the loss of its leaders (The Sardauna and Balewa) was a position of weakness which undermined the force of his decrees. By harping repeatedly on the idea of "condolences," the poet forces the reader to perceive the irrelevance of the General's insistence on continued appeasement in the face of the numerous challenges before him. At this point, he begins to entertain doubts as to the propriety of the fate of the elephant which he had earlier celebrated in "Hurrah for Thunder":

> the elephant has fallen
> the mortars have won the day
> the elephant has fallen
> does he deserve his fate
> the elephant has fallen
> can we remember the date—

But these doubts and questionings are soon resolved in favor of the revolution. The destruction of the elephant is seen as a blast on "Britain's last stand"—a frontal onslaught on neo-colonialism which, for the poet, has "cut a path" in a jungle situation. Then comes a picture of the pre-revolution jungle situation of the first republic, a state of fulsome anarchy which was unfortunately repeated in the second republic (1979-83):

the elephant ravages the jungle
the jungle is peopled with snakes
the snake says to the squirrel
I will swallow you
the mongoose says to the snake
I will mangle you
the elephant says to the mongoose
I will strangle you

Having painted this picture of the savagery of the first republic, Okigbo returns to his defense of the revolutionary significance of the January 1966 coup and its leaders. In the two lines which carry the central image of the sequence, he presents the coup leaders as thunder which has cut a path through the fabulous darkness of the jungle:

Thunder fells the trees cut a path
thunder smashes them all

The picture is especially that of Nzeogwu. The poet cannot see why Nzeogwu and other heroes of what he regards as a revolution should not be honored rather than punished:

Thunder that has struck the elephant
The same thunder should wear a plume

The same argument is pursued in the image of the roadmarker and the road:

a roadmarker makes a road
the road becomes a throne
can we cane him for felling a tree.

Something has clearly gone wrong. The heroes of the coup who made the road by felling the trees that constituted an obstacle have now been relegated to the background by someone else (General Ironsi), who, it is suggested, sees the road as a throne. Once again the poet warns that "the same thunder" that has struck the elephant "can make a bruise" in this kind of situation.

At the end of "Elegy for Slit-drum," Okigbo's ideological position with regard to the events of 1966 stands out clearly. His death, if nothing else, is proof that when he has come to accept a cause, he does so with unflagging commitment and can unabashedly defend it both in his poetry and in real life. The entire sequence, *Path of Thunder*, merely gives a hint of what would have matured into the most robust, modern committed poetry from the black world.

"ELEGY FOR ALTO"

The closing movement of *Path of Thunder*, "Elegy for Alto," is ironically also Okigbo's swan song—his farewell to poetry and, indeed, to life. In retrospect, the opening lines sound ominously accurate:

> And the Horn may now paw the air howling goodbye. . . .
> For the Eagles are now in sight:
> Shadows in the horizon

There is, here, a clear anticipation of war as in the other images which dominate the poem: "giant hidden steps of howitzers, of detonators," "Bayonets and cannons" with which the Eagles descend, and "iron dances of mortars, of generators." In the end, the poet takes his leave:

> An old star departs, leaves us here on the shore
> Gazing heavenward for a new star approaching;
> The new star appears, foreshadows its going
> Before a going and coming that goes on forever . . .

So much is wrapped up here in what is essentially an adaptation of lines from other sources that the interpretations will certainly be many and varied. The lines may refer to the cyclical pattern of Okigbo's own poetry and the succession of Okigbo by a new generation of poets who share his mythopoeic imagination; they may also refer to the idea of progressive revelation in which every poet-prophet represents a point of illumination in a process of progressive illumination that goes on forever. But negative interpretations of the pattern are also possible.

CONCLUSION

Although the poems that make up *Path of Thunder* were written separately (like everything else in Okigbo's poetic output) they are organically
related and, in the form in which they are published in *Labyrinths*, they
even evince a coherent logic. We may summarize the plot as follows:

First Movement ("Thunder Can Break"): There is general rejoicing. A
revolution (the "miracle of Thunder") has taken place. A new (iron/mili-
tary) leadership has emerged. But the leaders of the revolution have been
imprisoned, despite public clamor to see and honor them. The poet pleads
for the release of the jailed heroes ("miracle caged") and warns against the
dangers of obduracy in flaunting the weal of the masses.

Second Movement ("Elegy of the Wind"): The new situation demands
neither silence nor muffled oracular statements of the poet but open public
statements and direct participation in public affairs. The poet, therefore,
declares his resolve to abandon the old mode of oracular communication
and to address his public more directly on wider issues.

Third Movement ("Come Thunder"): In his first public prophecy, the poet
draws attention to the danger of war breaking out in the midst of a general
atmosphere of euphoria.

Fourth Movement ("Hurrah for Thunder"): The poet returns to the "miracle
of thunder" presented in the first movement. He celebrates the destruction
of the elephant (brute, destructive force) by thunder (a revolution representing divine wrath). But he goes on to warn the new regime about
relapsing into the excesses of the old order, a relapse which, if it happens,
must be visited by thunder.

Fifth Movement ("Elegy for Slit-drums"): The failures of the new military
government are decried; but the poet reasserts his belief that, despite these
failures, the military coup that had brought the government into power was
the right action to break what amounted to a law of the jungle in the country.
In the end, the poet renews his plea for honoring rather than punishing the
heroes of the coup.

Sixth Movement ("Elegy for Alto"): The poet takes his leave amid visions
of war and general violence.

As has been pointed out, Okigbo's *Path of Thunder* occupies a position
in the poet's corpus similar to that occupied by the "responsibilities" poems
of the final phase of the works of most great poets, such as Blake, Eliot, and
Yeats. This involves the abandonment of earlier obscure symbolism for
mere direct statement of faith and ideology. A definitive statement of the
exact complexion of Okigbo's ideology and the relation of his ideology to
his role in the Nigerian crisis and civil war is yet to be attempted. The
present chapter has merely sketched out the framework for such inquiry.[23]
Path of Thunder is not a fulfillment but a promise of the revolutionary
direction of the unrealized future of Okigbo's poetry. Had he survived to

realize that future, it is conceivable that he would have shed the remnants of obscurity in imagery and allusion, which, despite his new poetic manifesto, can be found still lingering in this essentially transitional piece.

NOTES

1. See Chukwuma Azuonye, "The Secret of the Watermaid: Dramatization of the Symbolist Process in *Heavensgate III*," unpublished paper, Nsukka, 1973; "Memories, Initiations and Geometrical Symbolism in Okigbo's Poetry," English Departmental Seminar Paper, University of Ibadan, May 1979; "The Organic Unity of Christopher Okigbo's Poetry," English Departmental Seminar Paper, University of Ibadan, March 1980; and "Christopher Okigbo and the Psychological Theories of Carl Gustav Jung," *Journal of African and Comparative Literature* no. 1 (March 1981), 30-51.

2. *Black Orpheus* II, 1962.

3. *In Labyrinths with Path of Thunder*, London: Heinemann African Writers Series, 1971.

4. *Ibid.*

5. In *W. B. Yeats: 1865-1965: Centenary Essays* (Ibadan: Ibadan University Press, 1965).

6. In *Labyrinths*, op. cit.

7. *Ibid.*

8. Chukwuma Azuonye, "Memories, Initiations and Geometrical Symbolism," *op. cit.*

9. Labyrinths, *op. cit.*

10. The precise meaning of "eunuch horn with seven valves" has not been ascertained. But, apart from its other possible meanings, Okigbo may be using "eunuch" here by analogy to the adjectival use of "virgin" to suggest a horn that has never been put to use before.

11. The phrase is from Okigbo's Introduction to *Labyrinths, op. cit.*

12. Okigbo is here the traditional town-crier calling attention to his message by the beating of the "iron bell," actually the Igbo metal gong, *ogene*. The use of *bell* here instead of *gong* is, however, probably deliberate. It forces the reader to call to mind a modern, urban type of the town-crier, the evangelist who parades the streets, often before daybreak, crying forth his homilies and warnings about the imminent destruction of the utterly sinful world.

13. Cf. W. B. Yeats, "Responsibilities" poems (1914) in his *Collected Poems* (London: Macmillan, 1933, 1950, etc.).

14. See W. B. Yeats, "A Coat," in *Poems of W. B. Yeats*, selected with an Introduction and Notes by A. Norman Jeffares (London: Macmillan, 1963), p. 58.

15. See Shelley's "Ode to the West Wind," in *The Poems of Percy Bysshe Shelley* (London: Collins, 1966), p. 514.

16. These include *Lament of the Masks, op. cit.*, and *Dance of the Painted Maidens, In Verse and Voice: A Festival of Commonwealth Poetry*, ed. Douglas Cleverdon (London: Poetry Book Society, 1965).

17. Chukwuma Azuonye, "The Secret of the Watermaid," *op. cit.*

18. See Chukwuma Azuonye, "The Secret of the Watermaid,"*op. cit.*

19. *Ibid.*

20. In an obituary on Christopher Okigbo published in *Black Orpheus*, shortly after the end of the civil war, the impression is given that Okigbo wasted his life in pursuit of narrow sectional or ethnic interests. The same argument runs through Ali Mazrui's unfortunately ill-informed so-called novel of ideas, *The Trial of Christopher Okigbo* (London: Heinemann, 1971). Anyone who met Okigbo in his lifetime would recollect that he was one of the most de-tribalized Nigerians, the last person to sacrifice his life on the altar of sectionalism or ethnicism. Okigbo's self-sacrifice can be understood better if it is seen from the point of view of ideological commitment or of the kind of romantic fascination for new experiences which, in other countries, has led many sensitive young artists like him to the same kind of adventure.

21. The "miracle caged" here may refer specifically to the leader of the revolution, Major Chukwuma Nzeogwu.

22. There are close echoes in these lines of the mythic pattern described by John Speirs in his "A Survey of Medieval Verse," in Boris Ford, ed., *The Age of Chaucer* (London: Pelican Books), p. 39: "The young god slays and supplants the old; yet he *is* the old renewed, become young again". In the original ritual—for *a myth is the story of a ritual, the story the ritual enacts*—the old divine king and the young king who supplanted him evidently impersonated one and the same god. "The implications of this mythic pattern become clearer when, in "Thunder Can Break" Okigbo perceives certain genotypal relationships between the new military regime and the ousted civilian regime in their predilection to scramble for the national cake.

23. See also Ime Ikiddeh, "Iron, Thunder and Elephants: A Study of Okigbo's *Path of Thunder*," in *New Horn* I, ii (1974), p. 46, and Sunday Anozie,*Christopher Okigbo: Creative Rhetoric* (London: Evans Brothers, 1972), for earlier contributions to the discussion of the text.

3

The Ogun Consciousness in Modern Creative Man: A Reading of Wole Soyinka's "Idanre"

Edward C. Okwu

That Soyinka is one of Africa's most accomplished writers and easily its most versatile is no longer in doubt. Although that view has always been held by some, it took the highly prestigious Nobel Prize in Literature which he won in 1986 not only to give that assessment of Soyinka a seal of authority, but also even to rank him as one of the most distinguished writers in the world today. In doing that, the Nobel Award has lifted Soyinka criticism from the "bolekaja" alleyways in which it appeared to be mired for some time and deposited it in the more dignified arena of sober reflection and critical exegesis.[1] It is as if almost overnight he has been transported from the ranks of the famous to the ranks of the immortal.

At the same time, this ennobling event has also re-awakened old fears about Soyinka's alleged elitism, fears that a full understanding of his works demands a degree of literary sophistication that might exist among members of the Nobel jury but ordinary people in Nigeria and Africa clearly lack. Without trying to re-open the old debate about obscurity which usually generated more heat than light anyway,[2] we can note that in Soyinka's case it centers around two concerns: concern with his subject matter (whether or not it has any relevance to the African predicament), and concern with his artistry (especially his language) which even his most ardent admirers acknowledge as not being within easy reach.

It has been relatively easy in discussions of Soyinka's drama to exonerate him or, at least, plead mitigation on both counts. For one thing, drama is unquestionably a peopleoriented medium in ways that poetry is not. The total dramatic idiom can often transcend more verbal communication in conveying meaning and significance to an audience, and many of Soyinka's plays (especially when skillfully staged) are noted for being able to do just that. For another thing, the sheer quantity of his output in drama (from occasional satirical sketches to comedies and tragedies) is such that there is something for everybody, both for entertainment and for reflection.

Of far greater importance, however, is the now generally accepted fact that virtually all his plays (and, indeed, all his works) explore in various ways what one critic recently described as "a central antagonism between two forces, one pursuing revelation, the other consistently denying, rejecting, or negating that pursuit."[3] Abiola Irele has put it this way: "No attentive appraisal of Soyinka's work can fail to grasp the fact that it has been marked by a special concern for the moral issues involved in the unfolding process of our communal existence." Pointing out that Soyinka's work is centered on the African experience, Irele argues that it "enacts the drama of ambiguity and the conflict of moral choices which confront the awakened consciousness in the contemporary African situation."[4]

That this Africa-centered theme has a universal significance is, of course, the point made in the Nobel Citation, which praises Soyinka as a writer who "in a wide cultural perspective and with poetic overtones fashions the drama of existence,"[5] thereby acknowledging for a worldwide audience a point made much earlier by one of Soyinka's earliest and most consistent admirers, Professor Eldred Jones: that in using his Yoruba cultural background, Soyinka has depicted the plight of man on earth as both creator and destroyer.[6]

As I said earlier, this sweep of artistic vision that radiates from a central theme has been relatively easy to demonstrate in Soyinka's drama (as both present and accessible to an audience), while the fact that much of his poetry is sustained by the same vision has not been as widely proclaimed or demonstrated. It is significant that a book of essays that was originally intended to mark Soyinka's fiftieth birthday but which was later revised and issued as a tribute to him as a Nobel Laureate contains not one discussion of his poetry.[7] Whatever the reason for this unfortunate omission, the fact still remains, as Isidore Okpewho states it, that in his drama, his poetry, and his prose fiction, "Soyinka has pressed the Ogun essence into service in his examination of the painful dualisms of human existence—life and death, creation and destruction, etc.—and the need to constantly explore the potential for a resolution."[8]

The aim of this chapter is not to redress the imbalance in the book mentioned. I do not think that it will diminish Wole Soyinka's stature as a poet to admit that he deserves an even greater stature as a dramatist. In fact, in much the same way that William Shakespeare's reputation as a poet rests largely on the poetry of his drama, much of the poetry of "our own W.S." (Eldred Jones's pun) can be found in his poetic drama. Yemi Ogunbiyi has pointed out, "*Death and the King's Houseman* has the 'sweetest' poetry in Soyinka's drama. Its incantatory lyricism, so superbly close to original Yoruba poetry, is breathtaking."[9]

At the same time, there is need to set the record straight and show that his poems derive from the same wellspring that nourishes his plays. In this connection, it is the argument of this chapter that if we accept that Soyinka's central artistic concern is a continuing attempt to show the significance in human terms of the Ogun archetype, then we must acknowledge the central position which the poem "Idanre" occupies in his scheme. In his many-sided nature, this Yoruba god of iron, war, creativity, and harvest is Soyinka's prototype of modern creative man burdened by his own complex personality in an even more complex existential reality and striving to achieve a unified consciousness.[10]

I believe that "Idanre" is Soyinka's most significant treatment in one poem of the major themes in his works. In this essay of interpretation, I hope to show that, far from being the failure that some people thought it was,[11] "Idanre" is a major poetic accomplishment that deserves a place in Soyinka's corpus that is roughly comparable to that enjoyed by "The Waste Land" in T. S. Eliot's. Also, I hope to show that the poem demonstrates why a certain quality of character which the creative individual possesses (and of which Ogun is the exemplar) is often held up in Soyinka's works as man's best answer to the circumstances of his flawed existence.

One aspect of this quality of character is that by which someone dares to seek answers to a difficult or significant contemporary problem while all else wait in faith. It is this impulse that moves the poet in the first instance to go out on a stormy night when most people merely sit to await the dawn of harvest, and attempt to probe the mystery and the background of Ogun's place as the presiding deity:

> And no one speaks of secrets in this land
> Only, that the skin be bared to welcome rain
> And earth prepare, that seeds may swell
> And roots take flesh within her, and men
> Wake naked into harvest-tide.[12]

Such a move shows the artist as an explorer and corresponds to a similar quality of Ogun's character by which, alone among the gods, he undertook to subdue primordial chaos and "clear a path to man." Another important aspect of this character shows how the artist, again like his divine patron, is able, through profound selfknowledge, to maintain willed control over the warring contradictions in his nature. Without such knowledge, man would blunder through life as the victim of an uncontrolled nature that is prone to perversity. With it, however, he can turn the conflict in him into a principle of constructive behavior. At any rate, knowing that he *can* be perverse will function as an important mechanism of control. "Idanre" is, therefore, an important attempt by the poet to seek in the archetypes of myth the place where a major aspect of the creative temperament was forged.

Given the tragic consequences to man and to society of a lack of this creative and balanced orientation, it is not surprising that Soyinka has said of "Idanre" that, as public affairs in Nigeria took a turn for the worse, he recognized it as part of a pattern of awareness which began when he wrote *A Dance of the Forests*. This, of course, is the play he had written and staged in 1960 for Nigeria's Independence celebrations (an occasion when most nations create myths of a glorious past) in which he warned that without a full recognition of the total national character, its good and its bad, and without a corresponding effort to make such recognition the basis for national conduct, the country might embark on a shallow, blind, and ultimately counterproductive course of selfdeceit. With the events that subsequently led to a bloody civil war clearly in his mind at the time he prepared the poem for publication, Soyinka says, therefore, that "in the human context of my society, 'Idanre' has made abundant sense. . . . And since then, the bloody origin of Ogun's pilgrimage has been, in true cyclic manner, most bloodily re-enacted. Still awaited is that postscript image of dawn, contained even in the beginning, the brief sunled promise of earth's forgiveness."[13]

Soyinka has described "Idanre" as a passion poem.[14] Its basic framework is that of an actual pilgrimage to Idanre, a hill that is sacred to Ogun (something analogous to the Christian Stations of the Cross as an Easter rite) on the night before harvest by a devotee, who hopes to do more than merely wait for harvest, but to seek the true meaning of it in the mysteries of its presiding deity.

The first section, "Deluge," recounts the stormy nature of the night just before the protagonist sets forth. The violence of the storm and the powerful forces at work are described in terms that suggest an analogy between this setting and the equally tempestuous chaos of the beginning, when "the skymen of void's regenerate Wastes" might have been seen "Striding vast across / [a] still inchoate earth," and when Ogun's tale of conquest of chaos may be said to have properly begun. As the storm lessens, the atmosphere begins to look like a vast undifferentiated gray laced with flickers of lightning from the forge of Sango, the god of lightning ("the axe-handed one"). A sensitive observer looking on and seeing human dwellings and the iron rods that shield them from lightning might see through his mind's eye Ogun the god of iron poised "on such combatant angles" that "He catches Sango in his three-fingered hand / And runs him down to earth." Such a frame of mind induces the protagonist to seek the protection of him he describes as "my god" who is well endowed for the task—with a "large creative hand" and a "savage round" of "rebel mane" like a fierce lion:

> Safe shields my eaves
> This night, I have set the Iron One against
> All wayward bolts.

In the manner of an epic tale, therefore, this first section of the poem is like an invocation to the hero's divine protector before he sets out on his journey.

The start of the pilgrimage itself occurs in the second section and is to be made in the company of the god who, as "the first of reapers," would be expected to make his rounds this harvest eve. The protagonist knows this and so describes this night as the appointed time of their meeting ("our tryst") when, because of his association with iron, Ogun's movements are quite pronounced: "when sounds are clear / And silences ring pure tones as the pause / Of iron bells." But first, an important Bacchanalian ritual has to be enacted—in the five indented stanzas.

As the poet-protagonist reaches the foot of the hills, he stumbles across what I believe is an act of sexual intercourse. He notices "the wine-girl" described as "dazed from divine dallying." Partly on the strength of Soyinka's notes to the poem, she is generally accorded a symbolic role in the poem. She is not only an ordinary wine-girl (one recognizes that Ogun would surely drink wine on a night like this); she is also a girl recently killed in a motor accident, as well as Oya "once the wife of Ogun, latterly of Sango." The ambiguity of the line, "dazed from divine dallying," must also have been deliberate. It can refer to either a fatal accident that happened because the gods got careless (or demanded pre-harvest human sacrifice) or a sexual encounter with a god whose vigor has worn her down to a frazzle and left her dazed.

While one would not wish to deprive the poem of its wealth of associations, it seems to me that the text provides ample support for reading the girl's function in the poem precisely as a sexual one. Her aspect, as she lies there in the rain and appears to look up questioningly at the intruding protagonist, suggests not the look of death but post-coital tranquillity. (This is not to deny that lovemaking is sometimes taken as a form of dying.) First, she "felt her limbs / Grow live" when "a gourd [a phallic image and a pun on god] rose and danced between," and she took and "held it to her womb." After, she felt calm "beyond interpreting" and sat "in her grace" sharing wine with the now seated men to the obvious delight of Ogun, who "smiled his peace upon her." We are told that in the meantime "the night awaited celebration of the crops"; and it becomes clear that the coital process is being shown here as a paradigm of Nature's growth / harvest cycle. As the prototype of male virility and the lord of the harvest, Ogun presides over both. And it appears likely that the girl, indeed, functions symbolically as an earth goddess, an incarnation of the female principle, receiving pre-harvest tribute both from the rains and from Ogun, whose footprints will now make "future furrows for the giant root." In either case, the effect is to help restore calm.

In fact, this is the traditional role of Oya as mother and wife. Later in this section, we see her as a madonna, a "sacred leaf whose hallow gathers rains" (rightly read by someone as a reference to the hallowed nature of the female pudenda),[15] and as an agent of peace with tempering qualities who, because she was married in succession to both deities, can be seen as a link of friendship and reconciliation between the fearsome Ogun and the volatile Sango.

It is significant that, in contrast to Ogun's combative and wrestling stance in the first section where he "catches Sango . . . and runs him down to earth," their relationship after this reference to Oya is now described in terms that suggest friendship and cooperation. As Ogun walks among palm towers and power cables, they "danced / In writhing ecstasies, point to point, wart to wart / of electric coils." Sango can now send his "captive bolts" of lightning "on filaments / Spun of another's forge." It would seem evident, therefore, that the significance of the encounter with the wine-girl is that it helps to establish that atmosphere of calm and celebrative communion which is an intrinsic aspect of the harvest ritual.

As the walk continues in this apparently peaceful setting, we are shown evidence of other aspects of Ogun's nature: he can be demanding and bloodthirsty. There are signs of construction and mining work going on in the area as well as wreckage and death therefrom. To presume that we can follow in the footsteps of the god of metallurgy and mine the earth for its treasures is to have to pay "with wrecks of year's suppers" and pave his roads with shells and "milestones of breathless bones." Man may be resourceful and constructive, as the artifacts of his civilization attest, but only at a cost.

Furthermore, the signs of accidental deaths remind one that a rainstorm is, indeed, one of Ogun's elements, presaging as it does the dawn of harvest, but it is, also, a time when the roads (whose guardian he is) prove to be most treacherous; and to walk even through forests is to pass through "endless safety nets" that "prove a green deception."

> Fated lives ride on the wheels of death when,
> The road waits, famished.

At such a time both "cave and castle, shrine and ghostly grottos" for poor and rich become alike "playthings . . . of children, shades / For browsing goats." The paradoxes of life and of Nature are a recurrent theme in Soyinka's poetry. In the present poem, the inherent duality in the "wheels of death" is accentuated in the fact that the same agent of death happens to support the lives of others:

The wheels have fallen
To looters and insurance men, litigant on
Spare part sales and terms of premium.

The tragedies of life are their own sources of sustenance, as the wheels turn full circle.

At any rate, the present occasion is one of thanksgiving and ritual communion between the living and the dead; and the latter are now seen rising to accept the sacrificial fruit and oil left for them "on doorstep shrine and road," their lips "moist from the first flakes of harvest rain." However treacherous the circumstances of their deaths may have been, Ogun remains the "godfather of all souls who by road / Made the voyage home"; and as the protagonist watches, his senses heightened in such company, they drift away together to join "the gathering presences" for the next day's reunion. There they will preside, "guests unseen / To whom the rams will bow, and the open throats / Quench totemic thirsts."

The six stanzas beginning with "Vast grows the counterpane of nights since innocence / Of apocalyptic skies" are something of a pause for reflection in the poet-protagonist's harvest-minded train of thought. Their strong and evocative language would seem intended to imagine what primal disorder must have looked like when earth was inhabited by "pachyderms of myth." In his notes to the poem, Soyinka describes these stanzas as "apocalyptic visions of childhood and other deliriums"; but I am not sure that this part of the poem is as illogical as those notes suggest. The details of the picture painted—thunderous shields clashing across heights, bulls leaping cloud humps, armored beasts and cavalcades of awesome hosts springing in the night—do look like the outpourings of a fevered childhood imagination. And in the second of the six stanzas, the poet has added the qualifying remark that only the wisdom of hindsight has termed it the apocalypse; otherwise, at the time the vision was experienced, "it stayed / Portents in unquiet nights."

If this is so, then the troubled mind of the protagonist as a child deserves credit for the prophetic significance of the portents it has conjured because this vision of cosmic disorder is paralleled in the next stanza by a more contemporary record of worldly disasters—"whorls of intemperate steel" (destructive and bloody warfare), "triangles of cabal" (groups of self-serving and scheming politicians), "crusades, empires and revolution / Damnations and savage salvation." Later, when as an adult his mental horizon has widened, the figures he now sees have conversely diminished in size. They no longer appear threatening and are even portrayed in a mock-heroic tone. Rather than armored beasts, there are now "diminutive zebras" racing on track edges; the cavalcades of awesome hosts have been replaced by dwarfs blowing on royal bugles; and in place of banners of saints there is a sorry looking *ogboni* (a figure of political and religious authority) mounting a zebra's back and galloping "up a quivering nose."

The point being made in all this would seem to be the same one that recurs in Soyinka's works: how little and seldom the world deviates from an established and recurrent pattern. The actors might change, but the same disorder (even on a lowered scale) prevails. Only the observer's perspective changes with time, and in a more mature and less easily frightened age one might take refuge in irony from which vantage point such disorderly events take on the aspect of a farce. Otherwise, the world that now chokes in the "wet embrace" of its tail-devouring serpent (Soyinka's symbol of history's doom of repetition) would simply wait for such auspicious events as "Ajantala's rebel birth." Like Atunda, Ajantala (described in the notes as an iconoclast and as virile essence in opposition to womb-domination) is one of the poet's figures of history and myth whose non-conformity leads society out of the jaded cycle of history and reveals new vistas of creative and meaningful existence. At the head of this band of path-finders is Ogun "the god that ventures first," who returns now to the poet's immediate consciousness in the last two stanzas of section two. The rest of the poem will re-enact the process by which he as emerged as the prototype of creative man, the man whose fingers "drew warring elements to a union of being."

The next two sections of the poem traverse the rock formations of Idanre hills and recall some of the major events of myth buried in the fossil remains. "This road," Ogun says as he sets out to relive those events,

> have I trodden in a time beyond
> Memory of fallen leaves, beyond
> Thread of fossil on the slate, yet I must
> This way again. Let all wait the circulation
> Of time's acrobat, who pray
> For dissolution: the chronicle abides in clay texts
> And fossil textures.

First to be recalled is the time when there was the single undifferentiated essence of the creator god, an essence that eventually suffers a split in Atunda's rebellious rock-throwing act. It would appear that this event is paralleled by the subsequent alienation of man from divine company and is to Soyinka the heart of tragic dilemma; remembrance of it leaves Ogun "grieved." Because of this dilemma whereby man is torn between the desire to be reabsorbed into a womb essence, and the desire to remain uniquely individualized and self-willed, the poem talks of man's passage through life as both "re-ordained" (in consequence of a shared primal essence that asserts or acts out its nature in spite of man) and "self-ordered" (because of the directing force of individual willpower).

Ogun's achievement is in being able to overcome the anguish of severance and alienation, and in going on to act in a manner that shows how individual will may be put to a use that is both self-fulfilling and beneficial to a common cause. When all the gods, "defeated in the quest to fraternise with man," gather to lament the growth of a primeval forest that has distanced man from the gods, it is Ogun who rises to make the pledge "I will clear a path to man," refusing to accept that "a mere plague of finite chaos / Stood between the gods and man."

> He made a mesh of elements from stone
> Of fire in earthfruit, the womb of energies
> He made an anvil of the peaks, and kneaded
> Red clay for his mould. In his hand the Weapon
> Gleamed, born of the primal mechanic.

The significance of Ogun's role is that it shows both his inventive genius and his readiness to act in an otherwise difficult situation. While everybody else sits in apparent awe of the forces of chaos, it is he (like a true culture hero) who undertakes to bridge the gulf for his companions to follow—an act considered by Soyinka as a hubristic one that implicitly challenges the power of those forces. So that even though the hero emerges wiser and more powerful "from the draught of cosmic secrets," he also pays a penalty: "Ogun not only dared to look into transitional essence but triumphantly bridged it with knowledge, with art, with vision and the systematic creativity of science—a total and profound hubristic assertiveness that is beyond any parallel in Yoruba experience. The penalty came later when, as a reward and acknowledgement of his leadership of the divinities, gods and humans joined to offer him a crown."[16] Not inclined to accept such a role, he retreats to the mountains to meditate until the "diplomatic arts" of the Ire elders "laid skilled siege to divine withdrawal" and he consents to be crowned king.

From this point, we begin to see a variation on a common Soyinka theme of how man can harness the power of natural phenomena. Since this power can be used for good as well as for evil, it takes the proper frame of mind and skill to prevent it from getting out of hand. Unfortunately in this case, the men of Ire are about to let loose the extraordinary power of a god not for something constructive but for the petty and selfish purpose of overrunning a rival town (a sad indication of how their "diplomatic arts" have been wrongly channeled). They want Ogun to lead them in battle. But as the narrator ruefully notes, "We do not ask the mountain's /Aid to crack a walnut." The immensity of the force now abroad is effectively captured in the picture we get in section five of Ogun's battle-ready appearance:

> Storms strain his mighty chest, his nipples
> Glow the blackness, from hair-roots
> Spit black jets of flames. Tall he rises to the hills
> His head a rain-cloud had eclipsed the sun
> His nostrils blow visible
> Exhalations as twin-flues through clouds
> There are myriad lesser motes in flight
> And leaping mists.

Earlier, the poet had warned of the consequences of letting such a supernatural force free to roam a mere terrestrial range:

> O let heaven loose the bolts
> Of last season's dam for him to lave his fingers
> Merely, and in the heady line of blood
> Vultures drawn. Merely,
> And in the lungstreams of depleted pastures
> Earth is flattened.

Such is the disproportionate power of the warrior god measured on a human scale that his sword ("this blade he gorged") cuts a path of carnage that does not discriminate between friends and enemies. A force has been unleashed that the people cannot now control—a force that was constructive in the past but whose potential for massive and unsparing destruction the elders of Ire either had not anticipated or thought they could use selectively against others. In a sense, therefore, their folly (considering that they are elders who should have known better) may be seen in agricultural terms as a lack of the farmer's sense of proportion and forethought; and what they reap is a perverted harvest of "falling ears of corn" and ripe melons tumbling "from the heads / Of noisy women." What might have been a celebrative feast of communion and friendship between two factions becomes, instead, a surfeit of human flesh:

> To bring a god to supper is devout, yet
> A wise host keeps his distance till

> The Spirit One has dined his fill. What mortal
> Brands a platter with an awesome name,
> Or feeds him morsels choice without
> Gauntlets of iron. A human feast
> Is indifferent morsel to a god.

Indeed, a feast is a feast to a god even if it is a feast of human flesh. But it is also, for the god, an act of error for letting the fumes of wine he had imbibed at that onset of battle cause him loss of control as "his hands cleave frenetic" to his iron implement. This is the penalty he now has to pay for that strength of character that had emboldened him to challenge the chonic powers; and the lesson is that the hand that molds to create can also slash to kill. Ogun the "path maker . . . who goes fore where other gods / Have turned" has now become a common butcher (a "lust-blind god" and "monster deity"). As Eldred Jones notes: "As the poet watched the god relive his day of error, understanding—the harvest of his daring—came to him: 'understanding came / Of a fatal condemnation.' The scales fell from his eyes the same moment as in his dramatic agony, the blood scales fell from the god's eyes, and once again restored to sanity, he saw the error of his deed."[17]

When the truth of what havoc he has caused dawns on him, Ogun is filled with profound sorrow and pained awareness, the kind from which self-knowledge (and the resolve it brings to exercise self-control) originates:

> He recognised the pattern of the spinning rock
> And passion slowly yielded to remorse.

In other words, he sees in his action the consequence of that individuating process that had started with Atunda's act. And the penultimate section of the poem becomes, in fact, a celebration of individuality. As the poet-protagonist sees it, in articulating his new awareness, it may well be that human beings have been cut tragically adrift from a reassuring union with primal essence; but the alternative to this going of our separate ways is to be eternally buried in the comatose existence of a "protoplasmic broth." Insofar as the stressing of his individual will amounts to a claim of self-sufficiency in the management of his destiny, man must be prepared to pay a price with a proneness to make mistakes. But only through such conduct (however risky and given to excess) can man open up his own latent creativity. Ultimately, therefore, the lesson to be learned from the facts of our human condition is the determination not to be weighted down to inaction by grief over our first severance but to celebrate through acting the liberation of creative potential that came with it:

> Rather, may we celebrate the stray electron, defiant
> Of patterns, celebrate the splitting of the gods
> Cannonization of the strong hand of a slave who set
> The rock in revolution—and the Boulder cannot
> Up the hill in time's unwind.

This way, Atunda will be recognized as the first in a line of revolutionaries whose actions have opened up fresh pathways for society, new "kinks" in the tail-devouring loop of time:

> All hail Saint Atunda, First revolutionary
> Grant iconoclast at genesis—and the rest in logic
> Zeus, Osiris, Jahweh, Christ in trifoliate
> Pact with creation, and the wisdom of Orunmila, Ifa
> Divining eyes, multiform
> Evolution of the self-devouring snake to spatials
> New in symbol, banked loop of the "Mobius Strip"
> And interlock of re-creative rings, one surface
> Yet full comb of angles, uni-planet yet sensuous with
> Complexities of mind and motion.

The linking of the name of Atunda with those of Zeus, Osiris, Jahweh, and Christ is significant in suggesting that the principle of revolutionary action is a universal and recurrent one. Zeus, it will be recalled, was the son of Cronus (the then ruler of the Greek pantheon) who attempted to defeat a prophecy that he would eventually be overcome and replaced by one of his sons by swallowing each of them as he was born. Zeus was the only one who saved himself from this fate, and he did go on to overcome his father and take over as the ruler of the pantheon.[18]

Described as "the most popular of all Egyptian deities," Osiris was born out of an illicit affair between the earth-god Seb and the sky-goddess Nut. Later on, as a king on earth, he reclaimed the Egyptians from savagery, gave them laws, and steered them away from cannibalism by teaching them to farm.[19]

The name Jahweh or Yahweh is one of the attempts at creating a pronounceable Hebrew substitute for the ineffable name of God. Others include Jehovah, Elohim, and Adonai. As Jahweh or Jehovah or whatever other name, God, of course, remains the Supreme Artist and Creator, the

First Being to create order out of chaos. Christ we know too well to need reminding. Not only did his revolutionary teaching (directed at changing the individual from within) change the face of the earth, but by willingly paying the supreme sacrifice, he was able to heal the breach between God and man.

In their different acts of iconoclasm, of breaking with tradition or the status quo and thereby fashioning new ways of doing things (in other words, of really creating a new culture or civilization), these prototypes teach a universal lesson—the lesson that a step forward is rarely achieved until someone with the right combination of "mind and motion" comes along to lead society out of its old rut. Such an individual has the will to dare, the boldness to act, and the courage (if necessary) to suffer immolation.

Needless to say, this lesson has significance not only for the society but also for the individual sojourner who, if only to save himself from existential despair, desires to achieve self-apprehension and a state of heightened consciousness. As one scholar has put it,

The traveller who is fortunate enough to survive the dangers of the road may be rewarded by attaining the goal of the Quest, which is essentially the Boon of understanding. According to his capacity, he learns what is enduring and life-sustaining in a time-bound world; ideally, his individual being merges with and participates in the inexhaustible energy of the source of life. The discovery which crowns the Quest cannot, by definition, be passed along to others like a body of factual knowledge or a skill. It must be experienced to be known.[20]

It is precisely this sort of experience (at the symbolic level of ritual) that the protagonist of "Idanre" has lived through; and with the insight gained from his pilgrimage he goes on to assert in a measured cadence, "Night sets me free." He feels light like one from whom a burden (of ignorance) has been lifted; and the dawn of the harvest day that now breaks matches his own dawn of a new consciousness. Ogun himself, his night of passion behind him, ushers in the harvest dawn by rinsing "the sunrise of his throat in agile wine." He has once more lived through his harvest of excess so that in the new spirit of a crisis resolved (and of men and the gods in a state of harmony) mankind may reap a more fitting harvest:

> He who had dire reaped
> And in wrong season, bade the forests swallow him
> And left mankind to harvest.

The harvest procession, which the poet now witnesses, is a bountiful one whose fullness and vitality are symbolic of a new spirit in the community. Most of its members (like those who merely sit and wait, hoping to "wake naked into harvest-tide") may not know it, but the regenerative principle in the community has been preserved by the private and self-effacing agony of a few. Those few are the strong breed whose actions not only compensate for the lethargy of the rest but also preserve the vital flint of creativity that illuminates the whole society.

> And Harvest came, responsive
> The first fruits rose from subterranean hoards
> First in our vision, corn sheaves rose over hill
> Long before the bearers, domes of eggs and flesh
> Of palm fruit, red, oil black, froth flew in sun bubbles
> Burst over throngs of golden gourds.

This is the ideal harvest whose meaning the poet had set out to discover in the Ogun ritual. As a process that embodies some of the paradoxical truths in Nature, the harvest cycle can be seen as an appropriate image of man's growth cycle. Only through self-knowledge and the stress of will by which the individual keeps the contradictions in his own nature under harness and exploits them for constructive purposes can we reap the harvest of an enlarged consciousness and a fruitful life. In the facts of his drama, Ogun is the embodiment of this growth process and has, therefore, become Soyinka's ideal type of the creative man as a culturehero.

My aim in this chapter has been to demonstrate that, given the nature of Soyinka's creative vision and the themes with which he has been preoccupied in his writings, "Idanre" occupies a pivotal position in his scheme and so deserves greater recognition and critical acclaim than it has enjoyed so far.

There is, of course, no doubt that it is a difficult poem. Apart from what may be described as a few visible props in the poem's narrative structure, which a reader can barely hang on to, it is possible to lose one's bearing in the shifting scenes of the poem's action. Similarly, its numerous and not always familiar allusions, the swift and subtle shifts in tone and perspective, and, in particular, the complex vocabulary and tortuous syntax can overwhelm a reader.

But how, except by what Molara Ogundipe-Leslie describes as the sort of manipulation of language that "breaks the semantic barrier to poetic efflorescence and linguistic newness"—the type of manipulation through which "the artist dares to break the rules to create new ones"[21]—how, except by such a wrestling with words, does one give form and expression to an entirely subjective and almost numinous experience without trivializing it? How does a poet state or imply the need for us to break our entrenched habits of thinking and acquire new ones except by assaulting and breaking our entrenched habits of language?

Soyinka is not always this difficult or this profound; but he is clearly a complex and learned poet who has no false modesty about the extent of his erudition. The profundity of his perception and his thinking is matched only by his "arresting imaginative power" over the language.[22] That is why many of his works, especially the poems, are not for the occasional reader in search of surface-level entertainment; not even for the serious literary critic who lacks patience or whose pride is wounded when he fails to comprehend a work on first reading.

I hope that the present discussion has at least brought out the fact that the seeds of virtually all the major themes in Soyinka's works can be found in "Idanre," thereby making the poem deserving of whatever number of readings a serious reader requires to come to terms with it.

The most dominant themes in Soyinka's works of which all others are but variations are the nature and experience of the ideal heroic temperament. It seems fairly certain from the literary evidence that Soyinka's heroic ideal (and the testimony of those who know him well suggests that he may well have modeled his own personal life after this ideal)[23] is of someone who is both an artist or creative man and a man of action.

It will be recalled that in his early essay "And after the Narcissist?" this was the point on which he based his criticism of Senghor's Chaka, whom he saw as being too much of a brute in strength, lacking the tempering qualities of the artist.[24] At the opposite end of the Chaka type of temperament is one in which the urge to act has been so completely suppressed that the artistic essence becomes "degenerate, decadent . . . effete, homosexual" (consider Joe Golder of *The Interpreters*).

The ideal artist / warrior is not like Obatala, who, because he made a mistake when he was drunk (by creating deformed and other handicapped human beings), swore never to drink intoxicating wine again and forbade his worshippers to touch it. He is like Ogun, who, despite his own drunken mistake, continues to drink with undiminished relish (and encourages any of his devotees who wishes to do likewise) but in the full awareness of the risks and the conscious resolve never again to lose self-control. It is for this reason that Soyinka has described Ogun as a combination of the Dionysian and the Apoleonian (the festive and the serious) as well as the Promethean (the will to act). "Obatala is the placid essence of creation; Ogun the creative urge and instinct, the essence of creativity."[25]

The source of Ogun's creativity, we come to realize, is a conscious and skillful exploitation by him in his conduct of his paradoxical qualities. But first he has to know the type of person he is; and then as he acts he neither denies nor tries to falsify it. The Bacchanalian in him makes him something of a man of the people; the Apoleonian sets him apart from the common run by giving him a vision of and commitment to ideals (which vision it tempered and humanized by a Bacchanalian and popular social conscience); while the Promethean gives him the will to dare to translate his vision into reality.

These are the attributes that make up the ideal heroic temperament of Ogun, whose drama is re-enacted in "Idanre." It is he who, as an archetypal figure, innervates the consciousness (sometimes is the outright prototype) of the major heroic characters in Soyinka's works. And the innate paradox in his character, from which his creative orientation has been forged, is only one example of the workings of a universal principle of paradox in nature (such as in the coexistence in one object of contrasting elements and the dialectic of growth from one state to its opposite) which provides thematic variations in the creative works of Wole Soyinka.

NOTES

1. The term *bolekaja* (Yoruba for "come down and let's fight," sometimes heard among touts as an exasperated invitation to an exchange of blows in order to settle differences) is now commonly used to refer to the sort of strident and polemical criticism typified by the critical writings durng the 1970s of Chinweizu, Onwuchekwa Jemie, and Ihechukwu Madubuike which provoked equally spirited responses especially from Wole Soyinka himself, who in one such response dubbed them "The Troika." See in particular their "Towards the Decolonization of African Literature," *Transition* 48 (1975), pp. 29-37, 54-57, a considerably enlarged version of which appears in their book, *Towards the Decolonization of African Literature* (Enugu: Fourth Dimension, 1980), pp. 163-238. See also Soyinka's "Neo-Tarzanism: The Poetics of Pseudo- Tradition,"*Transition* 48 (1975), pp. 38-44, and "Aesthetic Illusions: Prescriptions for the Suicide of Poetry," *The Third Press Review* 1, no. 1 (1975), pp. 30-31, 65-68.

2. In addition to the preceding references, see in particular: Ali Mazrui, "Abstract Verse and African Tradition," *Zuka* 1 (1967), pp. 47-50; Roderick Wilson, "Complexity and Confusion in Soyinka's Shorter Poems," *The Journal of Commonwealth Literature* 8, no. 1 (1973), pp. 69- 80; Donatus Nwoga, "Obscurity and Commitment in Modern African Poetry," *African Literature Today* 6 (1973), pp. 26-45; Bernth Linfors, "Wole Soyinka: When Are You Coming Home?" *Yale French Studies* 53 (1976), pp. 197-210; and Chinweizu, "Shamanist Mystifications: The Social Cost" (fifth of a six-part series of "Reflections on Nigeria's Literary Culture"), *The Guardian* March 5, 1986, p. 5.

3. Brian Crow, "Soyinka and the Romantic Tradition," in *Before Our Very Eyes*, ed. Dapo Adelugba (Ibadan: Spectrum, 1987), pp. 163-64.

4. Abiola Irele, "The Significance of Wole Soyinka," *The Guardian*, November 1, 1986, p. 17.

5. See the cover story in *The African Guardian*, October 30, 1986, p. 11.

6. See the following works by Eldred Jones: "Naked into Harvest Tide: The Harvest Image in Soyinka's *Idanre*," *African Literature Today* 6 (1973), pp. 145-51;*Wole Soyinka* (New York: Twayne, 1973); "Wole Soyinka: Critical Approaches," in *The Critical Evaluation of African Literature*, ed. Edgar Wright (London: Heinemann, 1973), pp. 51-72; and "The Essential Soyinka," in *Introduction to Nigerian Literature*, ed. Bruce King (New York: Africana, 1972), pp. 113-134.

7. Dapo Adelugba, ed., *Before Our Very Eyes* (Ibadan: Spectrum, 1987).

8. Isidore Okpewho, "The Mythic Essence," in *The African Guardian*, October 30, 1986, p. 11. See also Margaret Folarin, "The Poetry of Wole Soyinka," *The Guardian*, November 2, 1985, p. 11.

9. Yemi Ogunbiyi, "Toast to Our Own W. S.," *The Guardian* (Sunday Supplement), July 15, 1984, p. B4. This essay appears in a slightly revised form in *Before Our Very Eyes*, pp. 48-55.

10. See Soyinka's interpretation of the Ogun myth in his fascinating essay, "The Fourth Stage: Through the Mysteries of Ogun to the Origin of Yoruba Tragedy," in *The Morality of Art*, ed. D. W. Jefferson (London: Routledge and Kagan Paul, 1969), pp. 199-234. A slightly revised version of this essay appears as an appendix in Soyinka's *Myth, Literature and the African World* (Cambridge: Cambridge University Press, 1976), pp. 140-60. For more general comments on Ogun's place in Yoruba mythology, the following works may be consulted: Anon., "Ogun: A Yoruba Masque," *Transition* 47 (1975), pp. 38-39; S.A. Babalola, *The Content and Form of Yoruba Ijala* (London: Oxford University Press, 1966), pp. 3-18; and Harold Gourlander, *Tales of Yoruba Gods and Heroes* (Greenwich, Conn.: Fawcett, 1973), pp. 47-51.

11. In their *Transition* article referred to earlier, the Chinweizu et al. claim that "'Idanre' is a failure. At best it is a private cipher meaningful to no one but the poet himself perhaps," p. 32. See also *Towards the Decolonization of African Literature*, pp. 187-88.

12. Quotations from this poem are taken from the text in *Idanre and Other Poems* (New York: Hill and Wang, 1967), pp. 61-85.

13. "Preface," *Idanre and Other Poems*, pp. 57-58.

14. See the Acknowledgement in his translation of "The Bacchae" of Euripides in *Wole Soyinka: Collected Plays I* (London & New York: Oxford University Press, 1971), p. 234.

15. Femi Fatoba, "Idanre: An Appreciation," *Nigeria Magazine* nos. 107-9 (1971/72), p. 104.

16. "The Fourth Stage," *Myth*, p. 157.

17. Eldred Jones, *Wole Soyinka*, p. 152.

18. See Michael Grant, *Myths of the Greeks and Romans* (New York: New American Library/Mentor, 1962), pp. 86 ff.

19. See Sir James George Frazer, *The Golden Bough: A Study in Magic and Religion*, abridged (New York: Macmillan, 1963), pp. 420 ff.

20. John Alexander Allen, ed., "Preface," *Hero's Way: Contemporary Poems in the Mythic Tradition* (Englewood Cliffs, N.J.: Prentice-Hall, 1971), p. xxiv.

21. Molara Ogundipe-Leslie, "Reflections on the 1986 Nobel Prize," *The Guardian*, October 27, 1986, p. 9.

22. Jane Brown, "Playwright Who Indicts the Tyrants," *The Guardian*, October 27, 1986, p. 12.

23. See cover stories in *The African Guardian*, October 30, 1986, pp. 11-17, and *African Concord*, December 23, 1986, pp. 6-24. See also the contributions in part I of *Before Our Very Eyes*.

24. Wole Soyinka, "And After the Narcissist?" *African Forum* 1, no. 4 (1966), pp. 53-64.

25. Soyinka, "The Fourth Stage," in *Myth*, p. 141.

4

Nigerian Drama and the Theater of the Absurd

Chinyere Nwahunanya

One important feature of modern drama is the propensity toward experimentation. This propensity involves an iconoclastic attitude which has led to attempts by some dramatists to break away from the formal requirements of Aristotelian dramatic theory and move toward new forms of drama by adopting a revolutionary attitude toward dramaturgy.

Despite local sociocultural differences, international interactions have made it possible for people from different geographical locations to see the similarities in the economic, political, or social problems that exist in their various societies and the pressures they exert on men. These problems are often responded to by artists in similar ways, and their responses often find expressions in their art.

The dramatic trend referred to as "the Absurd" is one of such responses to contemporary experience that have cut across international geographical boundaries. From Eugene Ionesco's *The Bald Suprano*; through Sartre's existentialist philosophy expressed in various fictional, semi-fictional, or non-fictional works; to the plays of such masters as Samuel Beckett and Camus, we see a link which derives from a common way of looking at man's predicament in the contemporary world.

The characteristics of the Theater of the Absurd have been outlined and analyzed by various critics and commentators. Martin Esslin, who it is said coined the term, takes a strictly literary approach in his monumental book *The Theatre of the Absurd* (1961), and his analysis has provided the definitive description from which many subsequent analysts have taken off or continued.

In his preface to the Pelican (1968) edition of his book, Martin Esslin laments that the term Theater of the Absurd "has been treated as though it corresponded to an organized movement," instead of being looked at as a term "coined to describe certain features of certain plays in order to bring out certain underlying similarities."[1] Such similarities are what Esslin then

goes on to discuss as the characteristics of this theater. The "sense of
metaphysical anguish at the absurdity of the human condition" is what
Esslin considers the theme of dramatists of the Absurd. But, according to
him, one important difference between Absurd dramatists and other dramatists who might pursue similar themes is that "The Theater of the Absurd
strives to express its sense of the senselessness of the human condition and
the inadequacy of the rational approach by the open abandonment of
rational devices and discursive thought": that is, a "striving for an integration between the subject matter and the form in which it is expressed."[2]
Also, this theater "tends towards a radical devaluation of language."[3] In
essence, the thesis of Esslin's analysis is hinged on the stylistic and
thematic tilt of Absurd drama.

Writing as recently as 1979, Gene Blocker adopts a philosophical approach to the subject and analyzes the metaphysical background to the
dramas of Sartre, Ionesco, Camus, and Beckett. Blocker rephrases Esslin
and states that Absurd literature refers to "the divorce of thought from
reality, or as it is variously expressed, and split of word and object,
meaning and reality, consciously and the world. It is, in short, the perceived distance between man as the source of meaning and intelligence and
a thoroughly distinct reality."[4] Blocker's latter comment in his book is
worth quoting at some length: "So long as absurdity is perceived privately
as the absence of something which ought to be present, whether reason,
meaning, knowledge, or whatever, the perception of absurdity is tragic and
heavy. The light side of absurdity consists in removing the hope, or
expectation that the world ought to be reasonable, meaningful, knowable."[5]
This comment encapsulates the general belief among critics of Absurd
drama that its origins are traceable to existential philosophy. Shakespeare,
whom I consider the first dramatist in whose work one could trace elements
of the Absurd, had made a successful foray into existentialism with his
Hamlet. Hamlet is possibly the earliest existentialist hero in literature not
only because of his concern with the presence and removal of evil, but also
for his preoccupation with the problems that plague man in society. Hamlet's
ruminations on man's existence, his nature, and his gradual moral deca-
dence and dissolution in existential flux, which is embodied in the "To be
or not to be" soliloquy, make him the precursor of the modern absurdist
hero in the existentialist tradition. After all, modern man, like Hamlet, is
involved in a search for identity and security, in his attempt to define and
come to terms with his existence.

The high priest of existentialism, J. P. Sartre, sees man as alone in a
godless, meaningless universe. Later thinkers in this tradition agree with
him and go on to suggest that to shape (or reshape) his destiny in this
chaotic, insecure, and uncertain universe, man must act. After all, "To
cease to act," to quote Sartre, "is to cease to be."

Like these Western dramatists and thinkers, some Nigerian dramatists have been experimenting with new forms under the influence of new ideas. This chapter sees the Absurd tradition as one main area of attraction for our dramatists and will argue that an Absurd tradition, manifested so far in some plays of Soyinka, Clark, and Rotimi, is gradually taking root in Nigerian theater and dramaturgy. It is perhaps no accident that it is these established dramatists who have branched off from their traditional sources and forms into the experimental mainstream of modern drama. After all, experimentation takes off when custom becomes stale. It might of course be doubtful whether these dramatists can be said to have turned as pessimistic as, say, Beckett; yet there are in the plays we shall consider here indications that these playwrights have absorbed or identified with the intellectual tradition that gave rise to Absurd drama.

Unfortunately, the Absurd plays in the African repertoire have hardly been seen as such and have therefore not received attention as Absurd drama. Odun Balogun has, in a non-dramatic context, pointed at how unusual it has been to speak of Africa as having a literature in the tradition of the Absurd. This unusualness, he notes, is "indicative not of the non-existence of such a phenomenon but of the lack of attention" to it.[6] In fact, because of this lack of attention, some critics even deny outright the presence of any Absurd elements in such plays as *The Raft*, *The Road*, and *Madmen and Specialists*; some others deliberately keep silent on the matter, while yet others make comments which suggest limited vision. D. S. Izevbaye, for instance, sees the journey in *The Raft* as just "a series of anecdotes and local gossip loosely strung together." And to him "The *Raft* suffers from the fragmentary nature of Clark's vision."[7] (We shall deal with the question of Clark's vision in this play later.) Oyin Ogunba altogether dismisses the possibility of including *The Road* within the Theater of the Absurd.[8] Eldred Jones on his own part finds it easier to see the differences rather than the similarities between Soyinka's *Madmen and Specialists* and the plays of the dramatists of the Absurd: "One way in which the play seems to differ from the plays of, say, Beckett, and other practitioners of the Theatre of the Absurd is that though insulated from everyday reality, with *Madmen and Specialists* the connection with this reality is fairly readily made."[9] In his 1974 doctoral thesis on West African drama, Osofisan declares in respect of *The Raft*, "The four Lumbermen isolated by Clark are not surrounded by a background of a stress, anguish or sin which could be called profound." He goes on to state that "Clark cuts his characters adrift without profound motivation"[10] Except that Osofisan attaches any special non-dictionary connotation to the notion of profundity, one would insist that the kind of complaints which the Lumbermen in The *Raft* articulate and the circumstances surrounding their precarious existence make it doubtful whether these men are not surrounded by a background of anguish and stress, even if we cannot see profound sin.

Furthermore, to suggest the absence of "profound motivation" in Clark in his creation of these characters as Osofisan does is like accusing Clark of "fragmentary . . . vision" (Izevbaye), both of which statements reveal a surprising degree of misunderstanding. For, is Clark not highlighting the predicament of the likes of these men in society, an essentially existential problem?

A few critical comments, however, recognize and admit the presence of the Absurd in Nigerian drama. Femi Osofisan, for instance, in a more recent study mentions in passing the attempts of Old Man in Soyinka's *Madmen and Specialists* "to raise a cult of the absurd as a counter to a painful moment of history in which the ascendant element is absurdity itself."[11] But he does not amplify the character of this absurdity in the play. On his own part, Martin Esslin has identified in *The Raft* "a very ambitious objective—he raft as an image of human life and man's dependence on his fellow men and sheer chance," which is "very boldly and imaginatively pursued."[12] Dan Izevbaye, in his comment on *The Road*, appeals for a balancing of what he calls "the image of Professor as an absurd character with the tragic figure of the condemned man, who speaks the word of truth in the end;"[13] while Annemarie Heywood submits that in *The Road*, "We are in a world of absurd clowns."[14] Unfortunately, none of these critics explores the nature of the absurdity he prods at. Only Elaine Fido,[15] Clive T. Probyn,[16] and Catherine Acholonu[17] have taken any pains to do some analysis in depth. Yet, Probyn's study of *The Road* is only "a comparative approach to *The Road* by way of examples of the Absurd genre" that "offers resources of meaning and interpretation which *neither* limits its meaning *nor* reduces it to an imitation of a European mode."[18] Probyn in fact warns (rather unnecessarily, and mistakenly too) that "the consciousness of absurdity and futility which marks the characters in *Waiting for Godot* and *Endgame* (for example) is not present in Soyinka's play."[19] The contrary is in fact the case: the consciousness of absurdity and futility which we find in *Waiting for Godot* and *Endgame* is present in *The Road* as well as in a few other plays of Soyinka. It is this fact that makes Catherine Acholonu's study the most insightful analysis of the Absurd in African drama so far. But she concentrates on Soyinka only. It is our contention here that Soyinka, Clark, and Rotimi have elements of the Absurd in their writings, for there are definitely present in Soyinka's *The Road* and *Madmen and Specialists*, as well as in J. P. Clark's *The Raft* and Ola Rotimi's *Holding Talks*. They contain many of the characteristics which are the hallmarks of the plays that have traditionally come to be classified as the Absurd.

Most of the earlier analyses of *The Road*[20] concentrate on Professor's search for the Word, what Soyinka refers to in his prefatory production note on the play as "the part psychic, part intellectual grope of Professor towards the essence of death"; but such analyses do not feature a corresponding emphasis on the existential implications of that search. Only O. R. Dathorne has come close enough. While acknowledging the centrality of Professor's search to the play, Dathorne sees Professor's preparation for a grand ritual sacrifice which will engulf him in revelation as involving "skirting delicately the borderline between futile existence and sudden glorious disaster."[21] But, again, the nature of this "futile existence" is not explored. Yet, this indeterminate borderline in Professor's search comes very close to what Adolph Wegener calls "the enigmatic aspect of being"[22] with which many writers in the Absurd tradition are preoccupied.

Professor, to say the least, is an enigma; but his enigmatic posture derives from the kind of enterprise he is engaged in, and the way he fashions his mode of survival within the social milieu in which he finds himself. Apart from his often cryptic statements, his enigmatic nature is most pronounced in his relationship with the layabouts who just cannot penetrate him.

There is a general reluctance in characters in Absurd drama to abandon the actions or activities they find themselves engaged in. Such activities come to be regarded almost as a vocation, the abandonment of which would amount to abdication of responsibility. As Professor states with regard to his waiting for the Word, "it is a painful thing to desert one's calling" (p. 94). One wonders whether Professor does not see his whole quest as ultimately meaningless when he admits, "I have despaired again and again" (p. 94). But it is despair interspersed with hope. Professor's attitude to the matter is one of eternal vigilance (of his instructions to Samson on page 70) since he believes that the revelation of the object of his search could come at any moment. One cannot resist the temptation to compare Professor's wait for the Word with Vladimir and Estragon's wait for Godot. We understand their general patience borne out of optimism, if we realize that Professor imagines the Word as something "Trapped . . . in demonic bondage" (p. 35), encapsulated in a cyst, "the slumbering chrysalis of the Word" (p. 45). The word, for him, is not dead; he optimistically believes that it only slumbers, and will rise from slumber "when the crust cracks" to meet those who patiently wait for its germination from its "kernel." And so he waits. The Absurd dimensions of *The Road*, therefore, result mainly from the activities the characters engage in while they wait for the revelation of the Word.

Professor is of course aware that "Life is difficult for the faithless" (p. 36) and therefore encourages Samson and his fellow layabouts not to despair. Of course, Professor himself "can wait. Continue the search with patience" (p. 35) until the final revelation. For he sees the revelation of the Word as "the key, the moment of [his] rehabilitation" (p. 63), just as the tramps in *Waiting for Godot* rely on the saving potentials of Godot for their eventual liberation from a life of boredom, stagnation, and want.

His beliefs and hopes notwithstanding, it is perhaps the height of illusion for Professor to call his preoccupation a "calling." But the point he makes about the pain of desertion is central to the experience of the Absurd. It explains the reluctance of Vladimir and Estragon, the two tramps in *Waiting for Godot*, to leave each other; it underscores the symbiotic relationship of Ham and Clov in *Endgame*; it accounts for the closeness of the Lumbermen in *The Raft*, despite their petty quarrels and differences. And the mendicants in *Madmen and Specialists* as well as the barber and the apprentice in *Holding Talks* face a similar predicament. For if they desert each other, their last link with humanity is broken. Therefore, they cling to each other as the bugs cling to the raft in *The Raft*.

Idleness is an index of the experience of the Absurd, and in each of these plays we see the characters engaged in no meaningful activity, idly waiting, yet filling their vacancy with all kinds of verbal games and unnecessary physical activity. This idle life is accompanied by unusual patience. As Professor tells Samson and Kotonu in *The Road*, "Like you all I also wait but you do not hear me complain" (p. 60). Indeed, shortly after the play opens, when one of the layabouts starts singing, "The others hanging by the fence join idly." Idleness, for characters in Absurd drama, is thus integral to the waiting which represents the transitional phase between the reality of their immediate predicament and their anticipated realization of their aspirations.

Professor's search for the Word is of importance to the metaphysical and existential aspects of the play; but what places the play firmly in the mainstream of the Absurd is the apparent waste of intellectual and physical energy through word play and verbiage in the course of the long unending wait for the revelation of the Word. This lexical gymnastics by Professor (and the waste of valuable time by the layabouts through their engagement in apparently meaningless and valueless activity) compares favorably with the activities of characters in earlier Absurd dramas. Salubi, on one occasion, drives home a vital point when he reminds Samson, who has been busy narrating Professor's life history, that they have wasted the whole morning: "De whole morning done vanish for your cinema show" (p. 18). Absurd drama is a show with the potential for spectacle and entertainment like the cinema, but it lacks the excitement of the latter. It is this feature that makes it sometimes boring to the audience, even when, as in *The Road*, the playwright effectively exploits humor. We never see the layabouts in *The Road* engage in meaningful activity, except waste their time discussing irrelevant matter, or going over over-discussed topics all over again. Perhaps the subjects and pattern of their discussions are inevitable, since those involved are unemployed. But the point is also that such unemployed people, whose minimal existence has been made dependent on accident wreckages, are mere human wrecks that cannot but dramatize absurdity in their everyday life. Men like these living on the income from accidents have been brought to a reconciliation with the experience of death, an experience that destroys a vital aspect of the meaning of life, since the premium placed on life has been removed in the first place. And what meaning can be found in debris as improperly mixed as accident wreckage?

Professor's movement from the church to the bar and to the road represents the existential search for meaning characteristic of the literature of the Absurd. He is one of the questers, the unsatisfied wanderers, usually seen as itinerant madmen who die without finding the answers to the problems they seek to unravel. As a quester, he is highly sensitive and responsive to the minutest details that he thinks might lead him to a revelation of the ultimate meaning he is looking for. Characteristically, as he himself confesses, Professor does not accept all manifestations as truth. He is down-to-earth in his search for the Word even in football coupons; but despite what looks like desperation in his search, he is circumspect and discerning enough to know what is not the Word, believing as he does that "eventually the revelation will stand naked, unashamed" (p. 12) and that "the subterfuge will be over," his cause vindicated. This is a typical existentialist hope characteristic of the Absurd.

But Professor's search is decidedly meaningless, as is suggested at various points in the play. His predicament as an Absurd hero is partly encapsulated in his disillusioned address to Samson: "Have I spent all these years in dutiful search only to wind up in meaningless statements?" (p. 56). This reality is possibly too startling for Professor to reconcile himself with it. But, in fact, Professor winds up in meaningless statements, as a strong case for meaning or comprehensibility cannot be made for his maledictory dying statement which constitutes the epilogue to the play. The ultimate message of *The Road* as an Absurd play would then seem to be that life is meaningless, especially as our desperate efforts to unravel its secrets and use such secrets to exercise undue influence over people often culminate in a boring existence that ultimately frustrates even a scheming pseudointellectual like Professor.

It cannot be contested that Professor achieves nothing tangible beyond this realization and perhaps a confirmation of his belief that the Word and whatever it represents can be found companion not to life but to death. This open-endedness of *The Road* confirms Eldred Jones' observation "There will probably always be some questions as to the ultimate value of whatever it is Professor finds at the end of his search for the Word in *The Road*."[23] As we have seen, like most Absurd heroes, Professor achieves nothing; so we need not even bother with raising questions.

The Absurd dimensions of *Madmen and Specialists*[24] center on the life of the mendicants, and on "The pattern of violating audience expectations"[25] which Ann Davis has identified in the play. This is present in *The Road* as well, though it is more prominent in *Madmen*. In both plays it manifests in wordplay, which Ann Davis sees with reference to *Madmen* as the abstraction of morphological units from the context of value-laden words, units that are given meanings which contrast with those of the original words.[26] The Old Man's speech best illustrates it:

You cyst, you cyst, you splint in the arrow of arrogance, the dog in dogma, tick of a heretic, the tick in politics, the mock of democracy, the mar of marxism, a tic of the fanatic, the boo in buddhism, the ham in Mohammed, the dash in the criss-cross of Christ, a dot in the i of ego, an ass in the mass, the ash in ashram, a boot in kibbutz, the pee of priesthood, the peepee of perfect priesthood, oh how dare you raise your hindquarters you dog of dogma and cast the scent of your existence on the lamp-post of Destiny you HOLE IN THE ZERO of NOTHING! (*CP II*, p. 275)

It would be interesting (if one had the time and space) to compare the morphological structure of this speech with Lucky's speech, or some of Vladimir's dialogues with Estragon in *Waiting for Godot*. If we just go back to the beginning of *Madmen,* we cannot but see a similarity between the openings of these two plays. The discussions of the mendicants encapsulate the feeling of vacancy and boredom we find in *Waiting for Godot*. This boredom leads to a certain amount of loquaciousness which serves to reduce their boredom, but with the consequence that those characters start to drift mentally. The victims of the road in *The Road* reincarnate in *Madmen* as "broken bodies or wandering souls" (*CP II*, 260), and these "Creatures of As" are presented in "the timeless parade" (*CP II*, p. 218) which one must take to mean the repeated enactment of unending human suffering that is so rife in contemporary society. Collectively, they represent "Humanity, the ultimate sacrifice to As" (*CP II*, p. 255). Aafaa refers to the mendicants as "vultures" who "clean up the mess made by others" (*CP II*, p. 220), suggesting that theirs is an imposed function. He tells us: "We are not here because we like it. We stay at immense sacrifice to ourselves" (*CP II*, p. 221). Like Professor, the mendicants (if we must believe Aafaa) "are all seekers after truth" (*CP II*, p. 223), although the character of this truth is as indeterminable as the character of the Word. Whatever truth Aafaa and the other mendicants seek must be different from that which Bero seeks, since they have different philosophies, despite their belonging to the cult of As. Bero, in fact, comes near to Professor as a power monger, since he believes that "power comes from bending Nature to your will" (*CP II*, p. 237).

Soyinka captures the isolation of the mendicants in *Madmen* in a statement which echoes Beckett. The Cripple in *Madmen* observes, "The lane is deserted. Nobody comes and goes anymore" (*CP II*, p. 219). Similarly, Beckett's Estragon laments: "Nothing happens, nobody comes, nobody goes, it's awful" (*Waiting for Godot*, p. 41). If these characters are so deserted, then their life is a frustrating one, and they must find some occupation to save themselves from total mental collapse. These mendicants even make noise to attract the attention of sympathetic people like Si Bero, for fear of being forgotten.

Like the characters in *Madmen* and *The Road*, the lumbermen in J. P. Clark's *The Raft*[27] are lowly placed men who subsist on the strenuous occupation of floating log rafts down the river for a small fee. But unlike in the earlier-treated plays, the emphasis is neither on a search for meaning nor on the institution of a cult. Rather, the play focuses on the cosmic and social forces that keep such lowly placed men perpetually in a low station and stifle their efforts at self-fulfillment. Clark therefore sets the play in a tidal flow and symbolically represents the journey of the lumbermen as a journey through life, with its attendant problems. The monotony and unfulfilled nature of life on the raft and the kind of dialogues and petty quarrels between the lumbermen all add to and underline the absurdity of the play. But most important of all perhaps are the existential questions which the play directly raises.

Absurd literature since *Hamlet* has always raised questions about the state of man, that little kingdom which, like the mind of Brutus, suffers insurrection while under the pressure of various social forces. In his concern with the state and fate of man, J. P. Clark opens *The Raft* on a rather fearsome note that points almost inevitably to tragedy. The lumbermen discover that the moorings on their raft have disappeared and they are adrift. Kengide's comment that theirs is an "accursed raft" (p. 91) cannot be false, even though we are not told who cursed it. The mysterious circumstances surrounding the disappearance of their moorings immediately place them in a situation similar to those of Synge's Irishmen in *Riders to the Sea*, exposed as they are to hostile marine and cosmic forces. Man has been cut adrift in a hostile world. Can he survive? Does he deserve his fate?

Amid all kinds of speculations, existential questions begin to crop up. Olotu, for instance, is made to ask, "How / is it we have gone adrift like this?" (pp. 93-4). Their questions and their desperate attempts to establish their spatial location within what is apparently a hostile marine environment call for sympathy for the human condition. For, at various points, they are said to be in "darkness" (p. 95), "waterlogged" (p. 104), in a "wilderness," in "this waste" (p. 116), all of which images underline their marooned state and elicit sympathy for them. Their life is so miserable that Kengide, despite Ibobo's complaints, munches away at kolanuts with the consolation that kolanuts are "not as bitter as life" (p. 126). The immensity of the forces against them is suggested in Ibobo's comment that, if the combined current of the eight rivers which empty into the whirlpool in which they are trapped sweeps them out, it will not stop until they are past Age and right in the ocean (p. 105).

We would recall that the four men are only part of a party of seven men who set out on the journey. This party of seven, which is reduced to two men toward the end of the play, suffers progressive decimation at the hands of some malevolent forces. Their world is one in which they have for company snakes and stakes, swarming bedbugs, scorpions, mosquitoes, sharks and starfish, fog, inclement tides, barges, tugs, and ocean liners all poised to prevent them from achieving their aspirations. These are the various manifestations of "the enemy that sucks [them] pale and leprous" (p. 129). The other "blood suckers" of whom they are also victims are the timber merchants because of whose attitude Kengide laments that "Making money for some other" has been his fortune in life (p. 130). Their problems are so numerous in fact that once they overcome one, another presents itself. In their helplessness, it seems as if they are waiting for death, and they buoy up their spirits by becoming tirelessly talkative, in order to distract themselves from the disconcerting awareness of boredom and stagnation. It is significant that the lumbermen are very conscious of the reality of death, hence most of them talk about it. Kengide thinks Ogro dwells "on the one theme of mud." Ibobo accuses Kengide of having stood between Ibobo "and his destiny, certain doom" (p. 114). All this becomes clearer, if we link it with Ogro's own comment about the life and death cycle: "Each day some poor fellow is either / Going out with a hiss or making his brief / Entrance with a howl, and the women Wail / Going to bed and wake up wailing, for their seeds / are eaten up by the black beetle" (p. 113). Despite the apparent echo of Eliot's "The Hollow Men" here, it seems that Clark's real debt is to Beckett's articulation of the cycle of life and death expressed as an almost pessimistic epiphany in *Waiting for Godot*: "One day we were born, one day we shall die, the same day, the same second, . . . they gave birth astride of a grave, the light gleams an instant, then it's night once more" (*Waiting for Godot* [Faber, 1956], p. 89).

Thus *The Raft* (like *Waiting for Godot*) raises crucial questions about man and his environment, man and the forces which condition his existence in the milieu in which he finds himself. It is suggested that men placed in the kind of world represented in *The Raft* are no more than mere drifters, vaguely aware of their destination, but never getting there because of limitations placed on them as mortals. If man is as doomed as Clark suggests, then *The Raft* has to be classed with other Absurd plays that "question the whole state and destiny of man, proclaiming the irrationality and apparent meaninglessness of existence."[28]

What strikes the lumbermen in *The Raft* is said to be "Death that has nothing to do with God" (p. 114). Ogro goes on to link their plight with Ozidi, "the all-strong / Who's come to strike down man." Gerald Moore has made what I believe is an impressive attempt to explain the place of Ozidi in the fate of the lumbermen, based on a link he establishes with the Ijaw saga of that name. He comes to the conclusion "It seems at least likely that Ozidi is the dealer of that death which has 'nothing to do with God,' which strikes down the seven lumbermen, and that the parting of their moorings prefigures the severing of their lives."[29] He then goes on to work out the permutations of numbers which point to Ozidi's responsibility.

Despite the fact that the role of Ozidi has mythic origins, and could therefore be dismissed as originating from Ogro's superstitious conscious-

ness, the point raised focuses on one preoccupation of existential literature—the concept of a dead or hidden God. God is a reality in the world of
The Raft, but at this point God has hidden himself, and therefore given free
rein to the malevolent forces which Ozidi would seem to symbolize. At this
level, the conceptual link of *The Raft* and an Absurdist play like *Waiting for
Godot* becomes obvious, for Beckett too expresses God's apathy when he
makes Pozzo in his inarticulateness mock or bemoan God's "divine apathia
divine athambia divine aphasia," all of which suggest indifference.

Near the end of the play, when the reality of their predicament dawns on
them, when "fog has stuffed its soot and / smoke in [their] eyes, has shut
up the world" (p. 133), Kengide suggests that they "shout / to the world."
As the two men hold each other, we have a pathetic picture, for the
spectacle suggests an awareness of the potential pain of further isolation
that would necessarily attend their separation. When they shout for help,
their shout is only a "long squeal," and is thus ineffectual, especially as
they shout *"into the fog, over the waters,"* both forces of which have been
shown to be insensitive to (and have been largely responsible for) the
sufferings of the lumbermen from the beginning. The "long hooting of
horns" and the noise of "men crying and calling out to one another in fear
in the distance" suggest a secular Armageddon, a complete catastrophe for
doomed man.

If there is any sense in which we can talk of the achievement of Soyinka
and Clark in their plays just discussed as accidentally Absurd plays, we
cannot call Rotimi's *Holding Talks* (University Press Ltd. 1979) an
accident; for this is the only play so far in which he, through his subtitle,
indicates obvious intention to write an Absurd drama. I have earlier on
pointed out Martin Esslin's observation that the Theater of the Absurd
"tends towards a radical devaluation of language," a feature he considers
"one of the revolutionary concepts of an art beyond the theatre itself."[30]
Rotimi aims at this kind of language in *Holding Talks*, and he admits to
writing in deliberate deviation from his usual style, for he meant the play
to be of universal applicability. The anonymous characters, the vague
setting, and the "un-African" language are some of the tools with which he
strives for his own kind of universalism.[31]

Basically, *Holding Talks* is about the unnecessary dissipation of energy
and waste of time on insignificant issues, and the neglect of serious issues
that demand immediate and serious attention. Significantly, the action of
the play is built around an argument between a barber and a man who comes
in for a shave. The argument is on whether or not the barber's hand shakes
while he works. The barber is hungry, almost to the point of death, and
what stands between him and instant death from hunger is his finishing the
job at hand and going for a quick meal. But the argument which ensues
between him and the Man engulfs him, since he believes that he should not
compromise his integrity by admitting that his hand shakes.

As far as the man is concerned, the barber's hand shakes while the latter
works; and the barber's admission of the fact would have saved everyone all
the embarrassment that sets in later. Man states the problem the play
explores:

> Now what was the point? I saw his hand shake.
> With my own two straight from-the-mother's womb
> eyes. He should have confirmed my suspicion,
> ratified my powers of observation, sanctioned the
> powers of my penetrating insight. But no. Argument.
> Spent over seven minutes on who was right—my
> wide-open eyes, or his hand. By the time we had
> settled that, life had gone. (p. 12)

Before the barber collapses he still maintains that his hand does not shake,
while Man believes the opposite. The matter has to be decided by a bet since
each man believes his honor is at stake. Funny enough, Man can afford the
bet—with one pound; whereas the hungry barber bets with all he has—
fifteen pence. Man wins the bet as the barber's hand is proved to shake. Not
long after, the barber collapses from hunger and dies. The rest of the play
concerns the efforts made and the problems involved in conveying the
barber's corpse to the hospital and contacting the police.

One major feature of this play is the play on words which characterizes
Man's speech. Here is an instance: "I bet you by the time we get this man
to the hospital, he'll be dead as mud. You know what I mean? Dead-dead.
Iron dead. Door-knob dead. Dead-wood dead. Stone floor dead. Dead-
weight dead. Rock-bottom dead. I mean: dead" (p. 10). These variants of
"deadness" through which Man tries to drive home the fact of the termina-
tion of the barber's life serve no other function apart from imbuing Man
with a certain degree of garrulousness. When the apprentices ask him
whether he is a reverend, he goes on to make his "point" in a deliberately
structured verbiage that ironically places a question mark on whatever point
he believes he is making: "That's the point. That exactly is the whole point.
You have just put your finger neatly on the tip of the point. . . . The head of
the nail has just been dexterously hit by the head of your hammer, man" (p.
10). All this gibberish is only a preface to his "point" that his rejection (by
whom, we are not told) is due to his having no religion.

Given this kind of language, we are sometimes not sure whether to take
Man and his verbiage seriously or not. Occasionally, however, he is given
lines which must be taken seriously, given what one must suppose are the
author's intentions. For example, Man laments the death of Barber because
the barber gave him no opportunity to demonstrate his magnanimity, his

"sense of service to [his] neighbour" (p. 12). Such a gesture is invaluable in a world riddled with problems. It is his realization that kindness toward one another no longer exists that forms the basis of his lament: "The world stinks, you mean; . . . Nobody cares for anybody anymore. Gone are those days, mothers caring for fathers, sister-in-law smiling at mothers-in-law and all that" (p. 13). The loss of this kind of humanism is partly due to distrust of the type that makes the barber keep back three pence during the bet. Such distrust does not attract help, but rather aggravates suffering.

Just as human relations have been soured (possibly by materialism), so are lives that could have been saved lost because of bottlenecks in the bureaucratic process. With the barber dead, the next thing for those around to do should be to take the corpse to the hospital and report to the police. But the play suggests that beyond the problem of getting a taxi to carry a dead man there would be the embarrassment of the good samaritan associated with police investigations. For it is such dialogues with the police that involve "talks" which are invariably a waste of valuable time and energy.

These anomalies in contemporary social behavior are, the play suggests, perhaps the reason for the withdrawal of God. If "no man's to be trusted these days" (p. 33), it is "no wonder the big man himself [God] doesn't listen much these days" (p. 38). So, men like the apprentice and the barber "permanently atrophied . . . by a daily diet alarmingly rich in protein deficiency" go on wasting time in irrelevant discussions littered with unnecessary "expositions, definitions, terms of reference, promises, assumptions, axioms, data, postulates, etc" (p. 25).

It is probably too early to evaluate Absurd drama in Nigeria, but the plays we have looked at demonstrate sufficiently not only the potentialities of experimentation in Nigerian drama but also the fact that the Absurdist experiment in Nigerian drama is the direct result of the influence of established Absurd dramatists, such as Beckett and Ionesco, within the philosophical assumptions of existentialism. There have also been stylistic lapses, but an examination of these has not been the thrust of this chapter. But we must ask the question ultimately, Has the kind of experiment which Absurd drama represents a place in Nigeria or elsewhere for that matter?

Arnold Hinchliffe has expressed the opinion that "Absurd theatre does not . . . appear to have a social aim."[32] Hinchliffe here raises a question that touches on the relationship between literature and life, that is, the function of literature in society. To suggest as he does that Absurd drama does not appear to have a social aim, only to state in the next sentence that it "seeks to express the feeling that the world cannot be explained or reduced to a system of values,"[33] is self-contradiction. Granted that the world is so elusive and disordered that its values cannot be systematized; if the playwright tries to articulate this fact, then a social aim emerges. If Professor is on a quest for the essence of death which is unrevealable to the living; if Clark's lumbermen are doomed to inevitable suffering and death because they are under the control of overwhelming cosmic forces; if valuable time is wasted and life is lost as uncaring men are engaged in useless discussions and argument; if these various subjects constitute the concerns of these playwrights, then we must assume that a social aim underlies these concerns. For these plays that posit these realities are in the process of fortifying man to whom these messages are addressed thereby enable him to come to grips with these phenomenal realities of his existence.

Only a misunderstanding of the basic existential assumption that gave rise to Absurd drama can make a critic dismiss it as socially valueless. The following perceptive comment by Adolph Wegener is worth bearing in mind: "The writers of the absurd re-establish an awareness of man's situation and project truths that reach a profound universality to express modern man's endeavour to come to terms with a world in which the dice are loaded against his ability to survive."[34] Beyond this relevance of Absurd drama to contemporary Nigerian society vide the nature of the themes these plays explore, the method in which existential themes are handled in them exhumes once again the polarization of contemporary Nigerian writers into reactionaries and revolutionaries, an intellectual position adopted by many of the younger writers who have socialist sympathies. This accounts for the fatalism that we find in the plays analyzed in this chapter, a fatalism that manifests as the playwrights' creation of superstitious characters, who are willing to link their predicament to some god or malevolent supernatural force. The plays thus seek to explain (or even justify) the world, instead of seeking to change it.

The fatalism which pervades these plays and other works by these dramatists demonstrates the basic difference between them and others like Femi Osofisan and Bode Sowande who in their plays propose a radically revolutionary approach to social problems as a way of reordering society. Unlike these latter dramatists who look up to Brecht as their intellectual mentor (especially in their adoption of the techniques of Brecht's epic theater), mainly because Brecht usually aims at provoking his audiences out of their fatalism, the Nigerian dramatists of the Absurd adopt the existential fatalism of a Beckett, a Camus, or an Ionesco. This is probably why Andrew Gurr sees the Absurd as "in many ways the most substantial current alternative to a revolutionary creed."[35] The Absurdist vision may, therefore, seem statist.

But the playwrights' anguish portrayed in the anguish of Absurd characters also implies a realization of the need to change the world. It could therefore be seen as a progressive call for a rejection of the fatalistic attitudes expressed in the self-pity of Absurd characters, which arises from their belief that their condition is not only hopeless but also unchangeable. The audience is called upon to shed the fatalistic attitudes that lead them into anguished resignation, for they can, through their own efforts, bring about changes in their lives. This is probably the most significant relevance of these Absurd plays to contemporary Nigerian reality.

NOTES

1. Martin Esslin, *The Theatre of the Absurd*, 3rd edn. (Penguin, 1980,) p. 13.

2. *Ibid*, pp. 24-25.

3. *Ibid*, p. 26.

4. Gene Blocker, *The Metaphysics of Absurdity* (Washington, D.C.: The University Press of America, 1979), p. 1.

5. *Ibid*, p. 160.

6. Odun Balogun,"Taban Lo Liyong's *Fixions*: A Study in the Absurd,"*Journal of the Literary Society of Nigeria* no. 2 (1982), p. 28.

7. D. S. Izevbaye, "The Poetry and Drama of J. P. Clark," in Bruce King, ed., *Introduction to Nigerian Literature* (Lagos University of Lagos: Press, 1971), p. 169.

8. See Oyin Ogunba, *The Movement of Transition* (Ibadan: Ibadan University Press, 1975).

9. See Eldred Jones, *The Writing of Wole Soyinka* (London: Heinemann, 1973), p. 91.

10. Femi Osofisan, "The Origins of Drama in West Africa" (unpublished Ph.D. thesis, University of Ibadan, 1974), p. 482.

11. Femi Osofisan, "Tiger on Stage," in Oyin Ogunba and Abiola Irele, eds., *Theatre in Africa* (Ibadan: Ibadan University Press, 1978), p. 164.

12. Martin Esslin, "Two Nigerian Playwrights," in Ulli Beier (ed.), *Introduction to Nigerian Literature* (1967), 2nd impression (London: Longman, 1980), p. 286.

13. See D. S. Izevbaye, "Language and Meaning in the Road," in Eldred Jones, ed., *African Literature Today* no. 8, p. 65.

14. Annemarie Heywood, "The Fox's Dance: The Staging of Wole Soyinka's Plays," in Eldred Jones, ed., *African Literature Today* no. 8. p. 49.

15. Elaine Fido, *"The Road and the Theatre of the Absurd," Caribbean Journal of African Studies* vol. 1, no. 1, (1978).

16. Clive T. Probyn, "Waiting for the Word: Samuel Beckett and Wole Soyinka," in *ARIEL* vol. 12, No. 3, July 1981.

17. See Catherine Acholonu, "A Touch of the Absurd: Soyinka and Beckett," in Eldred Jones, ed., *African Literature Today* no. 14, (London: Heinemann, 1984).

18. Clive Probyn, *op. cit.*, p. 37.

19. *Ibid.*, p. 38.

20. Wole Soyinka, *The Road* (London: Oxford University Press, 1965). All page references inserted in the text of this chapter are to this edition.

21. O. R. Dathorne, *African Literature in the Twentieth Century* (London: Heinemann, 1976), p. 336.

22. Adolph Wegener, "The Absurd in Modern Literature," *Books Abroad* vol. 41, no. 2, (spring 1967) p. 150.

23. See Eldred Jones, *The Writing of Wole Soyinka* (London: Heinemann, 1973), p. 61.

24. Wole Soyinka, "Madmen and Specialists" in his *Collected Plays*, II (London: Oxford University Press, 1974). All references are to this edition and are indicated in the text of the essay as *CP II*, followed by page number.

25. Ann B. Davis, "Dramatic Theory of Wole Soyinka," in James Gibbs, ed., *Critical Perspectives on Wole Soyinka* (Washington, D.C.: Three Continents Press, 1980), p. 155.

26. *Ibid.*

27. J. P. Clark, *The Raft*, in *Three Plays* (London: Oxford University Press, 1964). All page references are to this edition.

28. Adolph Wegener, *op. cit.*, p. 151.

29. Gerald Moore, "Symbolism in African Drama," unpublished paper presented at the First Ibadan Conference on African Literature, July 6-10, 1976, p. 7.

30. Martin Esslin, *Theatre of the Absurd*, p. 435.

31. See Margaret Folarin's interview with Ola Rotimi in *New Theatre Magazine*, vol. XII, no. 2 (n.d.), p. 6.

32. Arnold Hinchliffe, *Harold Pinter* (London: MacMillan, 1976), p. 27.

33. *Ibid.*

34. Adolph Wegener, *op. cit.*, p. 156.

35 . Andrew Gurr, "Third World Drama: Soyinka and Tragedy," *JOLISO* (Nairobi) vol. 2, no. 2 (1974), p. 19.

5

The Burden of the Dramatic Experience: A Synoptic and Comparative Analysis

Afam Ebeogu

One basic fact which the student of literature learns quite early in his or her academic career is that there are three genres of this verbal art, which, like every other art, is an imaginative selection and interpretation of life experiences. These branches are poetry, prose, and drama. This categorization is so deceptively convenient that many a student of literature in no time proceeds to create three compartments of the discipline in the brain, and proceeds further to slot into each compartment only those genres expected to inhabit it. The student goes on to lock up each compartment with its own key, then stores the keys in a mnemonic veranda through which access to any of the three compartments must be gained. Then each time the student is confronted with any piece of the literary experience, he has to subject himself to a mental ritual of selecting the right generic key, unlocking the right generic door, examining the contents of the generic compartment, and deciding to which genre the literary experience that confronts him belongs. While this mental exercise is occurring, the literary experience waits in the mnemonic veranda, in agony and bewilderment, to be admitted into the apartment to which it has an inherent disposition and right of entry without the need for any mnemonic mechanism of mediation.

This perhaps labored metaphoric explanation is an attempt to show how often a futile, even if mechanically necessary exercise it is for one to insist on rigid demarcations between these three major genres of literature. The fluid relationship between poetry, prose, and drama has, from the time of the development of theories of literary criticism, tended to upset the neat theories of literary critics who appropriate specific genres as their specialties. Part of the major preoccupation of this chapter is to use the dramatic experience to illustrate how complex the linkages among these three genres can be.

The *Chambers 20th Century Dictionary* defines drama as "a string of life and action to be represented on the stage"; the *Chambers Universal*

Dictionary defines it as "a play for acting on the stage"; and the *Longman Dictionary of Contemporary English* calls it "a serious work of literature that can be acted or read as a play." These definitions are aimed at what one might generally call the layman. But dictionaries also usually strive for some basic truth in whatever they define, and the basic truth common to the three definitions is the idea of "acting." Robert Sharpe rightly says that "impersonation, the actor ostensibly pretending to be a character is the very heart of the dramatic experience."[1] Both Sharpe and the dictionaries echo Aristotle, who defined Poetry, his general name for "epic and tragic poetry, comedy, dithyrambic poetry, and most music composed for the flute and the lyre," as *mimesis,* or "forms of imitation of representation" of life.[2] Aristotle's theory of poetry, especially as it relates to tragic drama, is too well known to occupy our time, but we observe that he uses literary models from the Greek written tradition to illustrate his views on the art of poetry.

Most other critics of drama have followed the footsteps of Aristotle, and certain formal elements have come to be recognized as the constants of drama.[3] These elements include action, plot, character, dialogue, audience, stage, and conflict. It has thus been the convention for both teachers and students of drama to assess plays in the light of these constituent elements of drama.

The tendency to split drama into its various components for purposes of formal analysis is, of course, another compartmentalization syndrome, necessary no doubt but often exasperating. For drama, like every literature, is an attempt to give some order to human experience, in order to interpret that experience. Any creative literary exercise bases its authenticity and uniqueness on some kind of wholeness, a unity of being that may, paradoxically, be an articulation of disparate and divergent experiential factors. To subject a play to the anatomical relationship of its components or the so-called elements is always a crude kind of surgery, for after the exercise, the atoms and molecules of the dramatic piece reassert the indivisibility of their mold. A play forever insists that if we must experience its wholeness, the totality of its being, the indivisibility of its elements, then we must accompany it, willy nilly, to the theater, and observe it in the context of the ambience of performance.

It is the play's insistence on performance for the realization of the dramatic experience that distinguishes drama from the other genres. One can pick up a novel any time, anywhere, and read it for as long as one wants. It is at the end of the dumb exercise called reading that one is in a position to assess the novel as a whole. As for poetry, its experience may be immediate, an experience that is often inexpressible and indefinable; a feeling of a remote or close brush with that elusive knowledge that passes all understanding. But the poetic experience, though rare, does not need the particularity and selectiveness, in terms of locale, and yet the ubiquity, in terms of affirmation of the human condition, of the dramatic experience.

(We are by no means ignoring the fact that poetry and prose can be turned into performance, and the issue will be discussed later.)

For the dramatic experience to be derived from a play, one would need a particular locale, a bounded spatial definition identifiable as stage and auditorium, and a particular time when the play is being presented, after many days of tedious rehearsals and trials. The play, then, mounts an often suffocating pressure on time and space, and it is this compactness of the event, the compression of diverse elements into a theatrical configuration, that is often responsible for the capsular, one-dose effect of the dramatic experience. For, whether or not a play is faithful to the Aristotelian unities of time and place, the point remains that the producer or director of the play has no more than three hours to present (it) before an audience, and in such a way that that audience goes home with a feeling of acquaintance, or re-acquaintance, with some significant aspects of human experience.

The historical events of Bertold Brecht's *Mother Courage* span a period of one hundred years, and in that play, Mother Courage traverses country after country in Europe in her coach. And yet that play would not, ought not, last for more than three hours on the stage. The events of Shakespeare's *Antony and Cleopatra* span a period of three years, during which the key actors shuttle between Rome and Egypt, and yet that play does not last up to three hours on the stage. Even Wole Soyinka's play *The Road*, which takes place absolutely in one place, with events which last for just twelve hours, has to be compressed to a period of two hours or so on the stage. The Japanese theater has been said to last for more than ten hours,[4] with the audience never getting bored in an almost-all-day event, but the events of that theater may carry the audience even into their mythical past.

The point being made is that the dramatic experience often plays interesting games with time and space, both of which are physically limited on the stage but can be subjected to unimaginable malleable dimensions. Time can indeed be arrested, and the core of a people's whole life experience subjected to one explosive moment of reenactment, as Athol Fugard does in *Sizwe Banzi Is Dead,* a play in which the audience is confronted, against the background of painful humor and sardonic satire, to the unfathomable horrors of apartheid. Here, the dramatic experience is an intensity of emotion magically conveying, in a most concentrated idiom of farce that evolves almost into pathetic ritual action, an unimaginable ideology of racial superiority which one would have thought too primitive anywhere and anytime in our generation. The concentrated impact one experiences from watching this play may not be gained in a lifetime spent scanning all the volumes that have been written in the world on fascism, racial bigotry, and the most callous forms of inhumanity.

The dramatic experience is thus an intensity of feeling, a concentration of emotion captured in the context of an action in which the intellect is at peak point, locked up in the art of interpreting human values against the background of a given experience or a rapid succession of experiences. The formal, well-written play, with its overriding unit of plot, is an attempt to recreate a pattern of experiences that constitute a significant wholeness, and the impact of this wholeness is only realizable, as drama, in the context of stage action. But even within the larger framework of the whole plot of a play, made up of a collocation of well-patterned experiences, a significant experience can be extracted, and the test of its effectiveness or ineffectiveness as an extract from drama is to subject it to some of the crucial criteria with which any good piece of drama is assessed.

Any Shakespearean play, for example, does not cease to be drama, notwithstanding the fact that most people these days read rather than watch Shakespeare. *Othello* remains a most remarkable piece of literary work, but what is responsible for the remarkable effect it has on an audience or reader is neither Iago's Faustian rhetoric of self-justification of motives nor Othello's poetry of majestic and martial rhythms. Instead, it is that intensity of condensed action, in which very short strides propel characters across a wide expanse of sea and land, compressing expansive space into a telescopic focus and giving urgency to every moment of time. In this kind of situation, there is a dissolution of every utterance into action, and Othello's ritualistic liturgy at the moment of Desdemona's killing confirms his earlier observation that "sorrow's heavenly / It strikes when it does love." And thus the vocal set (of expressing sorrow and agony over an apparent faithless world) culminates into the physical action (of murder, made to assume the grand ritual of sacrifice). No wonder T. S. Eliot insists that dramatic verse is not ordinary speech: it must justify itself as poetry in a play. Says Eliot:

Let us avoid the assumption that rhetoric is a vice of manner, and endeavour to find a rhetoric of substance also, which is right because it issues from what it has to express.[5] . . . We should expect a dramatic poet like Shakespeare to write his finest poetry in his most dramatic scenes. And this is just what we do find: what makes it most poetic. No one ever points to certain plays as being the most poetic, and to *other* plays as being the most dramatic. The same plays are the most poetic and the most dramatic, and this is not by a concurrence of the two activities, but by the full expansion of one and the same activity.[6]

Any speech from any war scene in any Shakespearean play would illustrate the point Eliot makes here. No one reads them without forming a visual image of galloping horses, and a concrete impression of military formations. Shakespeare was of course no common dramatist, and in an age with little advancement in theater techniques, it was inevitable that the great dramatist had to rely on words alone in order to evoke action and create a powerful sense of concreteness, space, and time. Only a man of such talents is able to use words to evoke sunshine, daylight, thunderstorm, darkness, the noises of battle, where, in modern times, the dramatist would probably rely on electricity, sound effects, and other mechanisms for creating a naturalistic setting.

But this is not to say that the modern theater can afford to ignore the fact that the dramatic experience is an intense feeling deriving from the inevitable interplay of action, sight, and sound. Wole Soyinka is a playwright who has revolutionized the African theater. His is a literary invasion which has upset conventions and reformulated dramatic theories. Obsessed with action even as an individual, Wole Soyinka, not surprisingly, perceives the world only essentially in the context of dramatic associations. His logic appears to be a simple one: in a universe in which human conduct is characterized by an overpredictable course; in which history repeats itself in a most sordid pattern, and human beings—wretched hens that feed on their own chicks—do not seem to learn from experience; in a world in which fatalism has chained the human psyche in manacles of desperation; in that kind of world, it is only the Promethean instinct—embodied in the irascibility and irrepressibility of Ogun, the Yoruba god of war—that holds a possibility of creating a kink somewhere along what Soyinka has called "the cyclical pattern of human stupidity."[7] And the Promethean instinct is an instinct of action, where even the phonic exercise is a deliberate catalyst to visible manifestation, a reminder that the universe exists as a result of an artistic impulse in which, in the days of Genesis, God created by word of mouth.

It is not surprising that where scholars, who claim authority on African religion and metaphysics, have spent ages and volumes trying to explain the relationship between the physical world of the African man and his supernatural world, Soyinka has proceeded to illustrate his understanding of the concept through the medium of drama. The playwright propounds a theory of the Fourth Stage and the total theater and proceeds to organize dramatic situations in which men, spirits, and godheads interact as easily as if they had always been aware that the cosmos belonged to all entities. And it is not that Soyinka is determined to reduce the religious to the profane, the profound to the banal. Rather, it is that he attempts to achieve understanding through an act of interfactional juxtapositions of disparate entities, where gods nevertheless remain gods, the gnomic elements remain in their domain, and man remains essentially man in his human environment. The complexities involved in the exercise are quite overwhelming, and it is only the kind of dramatic experience which Soyinka creates that is capable of bearing this burden of extending human vision and awareness beyond the limitations of time and space; an experience one would have thought belonged exclusively to the very few men of mysticism who, once in a while, by either spiritual or "cocaine" inducement, experience the mysteries of the supernatural world. Soyinka says that when *A*

Dance of the Forests was staged several times in the 1960s, it was the common, unsophisticated, unready masses who kept on attending the play night after night, apparently because the dramatic experience enabled them to have a more intimate knowledge of what had hitherto remained abstract and mysterious in their cosmology.[8]

What Soyinka does is to reduce every human experience to its dramatic denomination. It is only such a creative exercise that makes a play like *The Road* retain its miraculous balance between human melodrama and human tragedy. It is a play in which dialogue does not merely always precipitate action; dialogue becomes action when the evolution from dialogue to action becomes overcharged with the dramatic spirit. Mime then takes over and at this level the play operates on a cultic zone of transition between the mundane and the metaphysical. Murano is the symbolic character transmitting this charged dramatic experience. Astride the two worlds of the living and the dead, the cultic zone of transition, Murano possesses knowledge of the otherworldly which he is forbidden to reduce to phonic proportions for the benefit of humanity. But that humanity, both those, like the Professor, who recognize the dramatic moment ever present in Murano, and the uninitiated layabouts who, however, always commune with Murano's palm wine—catalyst to the Promethean urge for action—always pay him obeisance. Professor, who literally keeps Murano the way an astronomer keeps his observation lenses, for constant watch for the most minute developments, says to Sampson of Murano: "Deep. Silent but deep. O my friend beware the pity of those that have no tongue for they have been proclaimed sole guardians of the Word. They have slept beyond the portals of secrets. They have pierced the guard of eternity and unearthed the Word, a golden nugget on the tongue. And so their tongue hangs heavy and they are forever silenced."[9]

What the Professor recognizes is the ritual value of Murano, and, essentially, ritual is myth recreated, often in silence, through a stylized pattern of action. Ritual action is sacred movement, dramatically charged, highly potent with religious meaning, and it is the inability of the characters that people *The Road* to maintain the dichotomy between mere mimicry and religious ritual that culminates in the explosive external dramatic conflict on which the unresolved resolution of the play hangs. Even a very mundane character like Sampson recognizes that there is a boundary between the trivial and the spiritually significant, between life and death. He is an acolyte at parody and mimicry, but when his mimicry of the character of Sergeant Burma slides into a parody of the dead and of death itself, Sampson suddenly recoils, feeling terrified at a near sacrilege which he commits. For a mimickery of death is akin to the act of masking, and masking in the African context is a serious ritual event involving an interaction between the two worlds of the living and the dead.[10] Therefore, when the layabouts in Professor's shanty soak themselves in palm wine, the sacred product of Murano's proletarian energy, and use the medium of song and music to create a charged atmosphere in which any incident, including entrancement, is a possibility, they are initiating a course of events which will obviously run out of their control. This last scene of *The Road* is the play's most dramatic moment, and it is in this atmosphere in which mundane action is inadvertently allowed to assume ritual dimensions that the fight between Say Tokyo Kid and the masked, possessed Murano takes place.

Professor, ever vigilant in observing dramatic moments which are also moments of profound truth, espies a possibility of a fruitful end to his Faustian search for the Word, the ultimate meaning of death, which would reveal the mysteries and uncertainties of living. In other words, he, a living mortal, wants to gain perfect knowledge of the nature of the gulf of transition without himself being subjected to the experience of death. This is the most serious of all his sacrileges, and for Soyinka to make him succeed would have reduced this very profound drama to mere farce. So, Professor has to die, after re-affirming the bond between human conduct and that of the winding road which, waiting forever famished, evenly preys on human life. And the message of Professor remains a profound experience because it is a message communicated through the medium of drama. Soyinka's success as a dramatist confirms an observation by Granville-Barker: "Language in the theatre . . . is not simply verbal language. The artist . . . thinks in terms of his material. The dramatist, then, must think in terms both of speech and action; and in terms of his structural or pictorial background besides. The artist thinks also of the proportionate importance of each item of his material to the particular piece of work he has in hand, its use for the effect he wants to make."[11]

That effect which Granville-Barker talks of is the dramatic effect, a most effective medium for transmitting human experience. Really to appreciate the vital difference between, say, ordinary narrative performance, where language as a communicative art is essentially sequentially ordered along the patterns of logical relationships, and the dramatic, where the significance of language is really only in context of accompanying action, let us give one more illustration with the art theater: the literary or conventional drama, this time of Efua Sutherland, a successful playwright who has demonstrated an immense awareness of the singularity of the dramatic experience. Sutherland's *The Marriage of Anansewa* has become a kind of classic in African theater, and if it is a play which lends itself easily to repeated performance, it is because Sutherland elevates a communal experience that is essentially comic to a level in which it becomes a dramatization of certain existential problems of man. The play, which Sutherland classifies as belonging to what she has called the *Anansegoro* in the Ghanaian tradition of theatrical evolution, is based on pure narrative performance among the folk.[12]

The *Anansegoro* was originally a folk art in which families used percussive instruments and dance to imbue a dramatic touch to what is otherwise folktale, narrative experience. But later the narrative performance became so popular as to turn into a communal affair. At that level, its significance to the community was basically due to the fact that it became a medium for satire.

But in *The Marriage of Anansewa*, a formalization of the *Anansegoro*, the folk dramatic version of the narrative *anansemsem*, into the status of the literary drama, the experience of Ananse is more than mere satire. This Everyman suddenly assumes the dimensions of the average African who is essentially a victim of a politicosocial system of immense cheating, corruption, worship of wealth, and hypocrisy. The Ananses must survive in this kind of system, and in order to survive, to break off from the perpetual circle of the victim, they have to play the game of the spider or Ananse, the trickster animal in Akan narrative tradition akin to the Tortoise, symbol of wisdom and cunning and the will to survive in a hostile environment. The problem of Ananse then becomes an existential problem: philosophical, serious, and urgent; transcending the narrow confines of the comic. Watching the play on stage, in context of the operatic ambience of dance, music, and song, the audience becomes suddenly aware of the large dilemma facing Ananse, aware that they could be Ananse, and that the character on the stage is using every means available to him to make sure that he exists in the society. The audience feels the inadequacy of the social system and the fortuitous nature of the circumstances that determine human motivations and choices. Man is suddenly seen not only as being a victim of forces in society but also as being right at the center of his destiny; indeed, man is in a position to manipulate the tragic circumstances that tend to undervalue his significance. Our contention is that it is only the dramatic experience of the Ananse phenomenon, rather than the narrative quasi-dramatic, that effects this feeling of the large and finer dimensions of life.

What this chapter has so far done is to draw evidence from formal, literary drama to illustrate what we regard as the burden of the dramatic experience. But we are very much aware that this burden extends its antennae into other genres of literature, adding greater significance and meaning to the very essence of these genres. Often literary critics, while enumerating some of the admirable qualities in a piece of poetry or prose, would use such expressions as "dramatic immediacy, ritualistic, verisimilitude, three-dimensional, eidetic, graphic, vivid, climactic, tragic, comic, Melodramatic, epiphanic, heroic, mock-heroic, resolution of conflict, rhetorical, satirical," and other such expressions that now constitute the repertoire of the literary register. A good many of these expressions deal with either qualities that are associated with visual perceptions or other impressions that often arise from the dramatic experience—an experience that suggests the realities of human action and character. Is it then surprising that many great poets and novelists have gone out of their way to use words in a way that suggests the desire to subject ordinary literary experience into haloes of dramatic enactment?

For illustration, a good deal of Elizabethan poetry has been described as being the product of a dramatic imagination in which the reader not only sees, this time in the mind's eyes, the faces of the poet-persona and poetic characters, but also "hears," in his inner ears, the voices of these characters as they talk. Discussing the essential characteristics of metaphysical poetry in an introduction to her volume of the same title, Helen Gardener writes:

The greatest glory of [the decade of the 1590s] is that it saw the flowering of the drama. . . . [Donne's] strong dramatic imagination of particular situations transforms the lyric and makes a metaphysical poem more than an epigram expanded by conceits. . . . The strong sense of actual and often very ordinary situations which the metaphysical poetry convey makes us agree . . . that words such as "conceited" or "fantastic" do not sum up their quality at all. A reader may at times exclaim: "Who would ever think such a thought in such a situation?" . . . Dryden praised Donne for expressing deep thoughts in a common language. He is equally remarkable for having extraordinary thoughts in ordinary situations.[13]

Gardener's assessment (and notice that she also makes references to other great critics who have shared her views) is hinged on three elements: ordinary situations, ordinary language, and profound thoughts. These are what evoke the strong sense of the dramatic in the poetry of the metaphysical poets, as is typified in the poetry of John Donne.

We may add that it is not surprising that English poets of succeeding generations have never ceased casting their glance on the metaphysical poets. T. S. Eliot, one of the world's acknowledged modern poets, whose possible influences have generated a great debate even on the African literary scene, thought the metaphysical poets significant enough in the mainstream of the tradition of English poetry to devote an essay to them. Eliot's poetry itself is a poetry in which words always conjure visions of action, gestures, movements, situations, and the "living voice," as in the following extracts:

I shall *rush* out as I am, and *walk* the street
With my hair down, so.[14]

Or

And if it *rains*, a closed car at four
And we shall *play* a game of chess,
Dressing lidless eyes and waiting for
a knock upon the door.[15]

Or

HURRY UP PLEASE; IT'S TIME[16]

Or

At the violet hour, the evening hour that *strives*
Homeward, and *brings* the sailor home from sea.
The typist home at tea-time, *clears* her breakfast, *lights*
Her stove, and *lays* out food in tins
Out of the window perilously spread
Her drying combinations *touched* by the sun's last rays,
On the divan *are piled* (at night her bed)
Stockings, slippers, camisoles, and stays.[17]

Or

Wipe your hand across your mouth.
The world is like a lonely woman
Gathering fuel in vacant lots.[18]

Eliot's poetry is a poetry of echoes of uncoordinated actions (as revealed in the italicized action verbs:) solitary gestures of impotence and indecision, purposeless movements, screaming and unenthusiastic voices. They are, of course, poetic metaphors of the broken monodies, the shattered harmonies, the sense of hopelessness, the broken communication, and the uprooted-ness that characterize the wasteland of our contemporary world. It is significant that only dramatic experiences evoke this feeling which Eliot communicates very powerfully and effectively. We can understand why this great poet also experimented religiously on literary drama.

Let us take one more illustration of the dramatic experience conveyed in other genres of literature, this time from Achebe's prose. A passage in *Things Fall Apart* reads thus:

Umuofia kwenu! }
                 } 3 times.
Yaa!   }

There was immediate silence as though cold water has been poured on a roaring flame. Okika sprang to his feet and also saluted his clansmen four times. Then he began to speak.

(The Speech)

At this point there was a sudden stir in the crowd and every eye was turned in one direction. There was a sharp bend in the road that led from the market-place to the White man's courtyard and to the stream beyond it. And so no one had seen the approach of the five court messengers until they had come round the bend, a few paces from the edge of the crowd. Okonkwo was sitting at the edge.

He sprang to his feet as soon as he saw who it was. He confronted the head messenger, trembling with hate, unable to utter a word. The man was fearless and stood his ground, his four men lined up behind him.

In the brief moment the world seemed to stand stilly waiting. There was utter silence. The men of Umuofia were merged into the mute mackcloth of trees and giant creepers.

The spell was broken by the head messenger.

"Let me pass!" he ordered.

"What do you want here?"

"The White man whose power you know too well has
ordered this meeting to stop."

In a flash Okonkwo drew his matchet. The Messenger crouched to avoid the blow. It was useless. Okonkwo's matchet descended ice, and the man's head lay beside his uniformed body.

The waiting backcloth jumped into tumultuous life and the meeting stopped. Okonkwo stood looking at the dead man. He knew that Umuofia would not go to war. He knew because they had let the other messengers escape. They had broken into a tumult instead of action. He discerned fright in the tumult. He heard voices asking: "Why did he do it?" He wiped his matchet on the sand and went away.[19]

Now, this is Achebe at his best. This is the creative sensibility of a laconic man writing about a laconic people; a people gifted in the art of rhetoric, but who do not always say it all; who recognize that certain things are better left unsaid. Like Okonkwo, the Igbo take refuge in action where there is the danger of their feelings overpowering them. Achebe is a writer whose thoughts are essentially in the form of images of action, and when he describes things, he operates strictly within the requirements of the descriptive ethos in which the senses that assert themselves are the visual, the auditory, and the tactile. The reader—I almost said the audience—sees the mass of the people of Umuofia in this crucial meeting, hears the thundering voice of Onyeka's *"Umuofia kwenu!"* hears the rhetorical masterpiece of Okika, then sees the road that leads to the white man's court, and beyond the stream, and the four messengers as they emerge from that road's bend. Even the silence that engulfs Umuofia on the appearance of the court messengers is appreciated dramatically: a silence felt to the bones for what real silence is: the absence of noise. Then the reader—I almost said the audience—watches, breathless, the drama between Okonkwo and the head messenger. We see the gleam of Okonkwo's knife against the sun, as it rises in a flash and cuts down the head of the messenger. And the pandemonium that ensues almost deadens our eardrums. But in spite of that, we never take our eyes off Okonkwo, and we experience his sense of disappointment at the futility of action, captured in his final gesture of wiping his matchet on the earth and walking away. It is a pathetic gesture of surrender, and it overwhelms us. The experience is purely dramatic, even though the medium is that of narrative prose. No wonder *Things Fall Apart* has readily attracted the attention of the film industry, for the fact is that that industry, which is a complex exploration of the sophisticated possibilities of the dramatic experience, has always had a vigilant eye for the novel with dramatic potentialities.

The reason why the non-dramatic genres of written literature cannot really exist independent of the dramatic experience is that experience is rooted in humanity, a humanity that has ever existed before literacy became an event.[20] It is generally known that before what we know today as language ever existed, men interacted through signal codes. Mime has always preceded words. This explains why ritual has remained a significant factor in human life, has always been a very concise pattern of expressing human emotions and convictions. And ritual is dramatic.

In pre-literate society, literature was oral. But oral literature was more expressive than written literature is today, because it was more serious and more embracing of life values. It was less pretentious, and, therefore, less amenable to prostitution and cant. Oral literature was something that was part of the substructure of society; it indeed expressed that substructure. This is something we tend to forget these days, when it is fashionable to extract the literary experience from the rest of life, and quantify it as just one of the superstructures of the human society. Because oral literature has always justified itself only in performance, in enactment and reenactment, it has always been dramatic, whether it is an organized literature, like the secular and religious festivals, or whether it is a spontaneous but regular festival, like the women birth songs, or an organized but very routine festival, like the daily kolanut ritual among the Igbo. Here we use the word "festival" both in the sense of a ceremony with an overt or covert religious import, which reenacts some communal myth and reaffirms humanity's bond and communion with the supernatural forces believed to order human experience, and in the more symbolic sense of gesture or experience that simply reaffirms faith in human life.

Let us illustrate our argument. Among the Igbo, there are very many formal festivals. There is, for example, the "Ufiejioku" (or "Ifejioku" or "Njoku"), festival which is dedicated to the Igbo yam god, yam being the major staple food among the people, their source of physical strength and endurance. This is an annual harvest festival, and like most annual harvest festivals, it celebrates the communities' bond with *Ala,* as the source of the agrarian sustenance of the community. All the rites, therefore, that are involved in the festival, both strictly religious and essentially entertaining, are unpretentious performances which constitute part of living. The dramatic experience of the festival is, therefore, that which is part of the process of living. Even oral "poetry" is performance literature: songs realized in the context of dance and music, themselves a celebration of life. Nor need we forget the prose genres, like folktales, which are light, less specialized in rendering, overtly more entertaining than educative. These two are a dramatic experience which the people live in the course of their everyday life.

The tendency among scholars of oral literature in Africa has been to emphasize more of the serious festivals in our societies, which have always embodied the communities' serious view of life. Often, when scholars want to prove that there do exist non-religious festival performances in our communities, the admission is grudgingly made as a concession, and the scholars usually proceed to adduce other evidences of the functionality of these arts.[21] But more recent research in the area[22] reveals that the entertainment quotient in traditional African performances is much higher than surface observation is prepared to acknowledge. And the evidence is really all around us, even in the Igbo society, where, it is generally agreed, people take life rather too seriously.

In Umuoji, a community in Idemili Local Government of Anambra State of Nigeria, there is a festival called Mbajekwe, organized usually after harvest when the rains are almost gone, and there is little farming activity still on, with the result that the community has more time for recreation. The culmination of the Mbajekwe festival is a one-day masking event, in which all types of masquerades people the special communal square in the thick grove, shaded all round by the foliage of tall trees and luxuriant shrubs. Each masquerade is a kind of stock character, representing either some significant events in the history of the community, or the way of behavior of particular kinds of people, or of particular kinds of animals which in themselves are a representation of particular human attitudes.[23] Most of these masquerade characters move about the very large square, miming the actions or behavior or nature of people, things, phenomena, or attitudes they represent. Thus one could find the *agu* (tiger) masquerade character, properly attired in the natural colors of the tiger and making amazingly agile springs characteristic of the tiger as it stalks and surprises its victims. The miming of the attitudes and actions of the tiger is so expertly done that one wonders whether the person in the mask, costumed also in a head that one would have sworn was that of the tiger, is human at all. When the issue is broached with an informant, he smiles knowingly, and assures you that the person in the mask may be human, but not ordinary. And it is not just that he is a good actor who has done his homework well, but that he does possess special supernatural powers, special *ogwu*, which enables him to be possessed by the spirit of the tiger and to act exactly like it. The only difference is that he will not tear to pieces the victims, wary or unwary human beings who are the spectators of the festival, whom the tiger catches each time it springs from its lair.

Among the other characters in this galaxy of masquerades, one finds the big-for-nothing elephant, the amphibious rhinoceros, the crafty and wise tortoise, the policeman in colonial police uniform attempting to make some arrests, the colonial court messenger asking for bribes, the white colonial Divisional Officer in his perpetual pipe, obviously speaking through the nose and nodding with condescending understanding, and many other types of masks. These masquerades move about and act their types, while the mass of human beings, who have traveled from far and near, also move about in the square, wary and alert, so as to avoid being victimized by any of the "animals."

Now, the Mbajekwe masquerade event is, no doubt, purely an entertainment festival, and the masks do not suggest what masks usually do in Igboland: ancestors come back to life to commune with the living.[24] Rather, their masks suggest the other meaning of mask as disguise. The Mbajekwe ceremony, which in modern times is being revitalized with creativity, its stage being modernized and converted into a strongly fenced stadium so that spectators cannot gain entrance into the arena without paying the due fees, is a conglomeration of dramatic experiences with episodic and undeveloped plot structures, attempting to capture in one panoramic sweep various dimensions of human life and attitudes and significant instances in the history of a people. The impression the performance creates is strong and enduring, and its illumination of segments of animal and human action deep. It is only the medium of drama that can make such a deep impact.

There is a popular and thrilling heroic war dance in Igboland whose origin is usually traced to the Ohafia clan. This performance is now featured on many occasions, such as communal festivals, burial ceremonies of important people, state festivals of arts, launching of political parties and rallies, or regular television performances celebrating our culture. The lead dancer, usually bearing the oblong basket of *juju* and human heads, is an acolyte in his art; a product of many dramatic experiences as a war dancer, and obviously a man who understands the cultural and historical background behind the war dances and is, therefore, in a position really to enter into the spirit of the performance, as it were.

The performer moves with concentration; his demonstrations are obvious recollections of war exploits. He would make a sudden forward movement constituting a number of swift steps; then he would suddenly stop on his track, stand still briefly, shake his shoulders, make as if to move toward his left, shake his head in the act of rejecting an idea; attempt to move toward his right, again reject the idea by shaking his head, get involved in a complex leg movement of withdrawal from a possible target or an enemy, reassess his aim and objective, take another spurtive move forward, and then check his advance. All these movements are in rhythm with the music provided by scanty percussion. And all this time he utters no sound, for in between his lips and teeth is a strip of *omu* (fresh palm frond) which ensures that he does not open his mouth. The oblong basket remains balanced on his head, and his hands are occupied in the bicepal muscular demonstration of his art of heroism. He is a warrior come back from one of the wars; he has gotten human heads—you can see them in the basket. He is celebrating his heroism in the community, being initiated into the title cult reserved only for men who have come back with human heads after a war.[25] This dancer understands the essence of the war dance; he is a product of a community in which a man's worth is determined by his heroic acts of courage and bravery, and his dramatic performance must bear the import of this celebration of some cherished communal values. He is not a pretender; he is reliving, within the context of music and dance, realistic experiences. For such is the burden of the dramatic experience. As Meki Nzewi observes in "Dramatic Moments in Igbo Traditional Life Style":

Generally, organized drama occasions or displays without traditional music presence and upliftment of some sort are rare. On the other hand, incidental or spontaneous dramatic events do occur as traditional patterns without organized music presence. Even in ordinary traditional ceremonies, the active participants traditionally act their functions—i.e. people generally act that way through the events of life; after all the world is a play according to folk thought—and therefore give dramatic import to other ceremonial situations or occasions. . . . Drama amongst the Igbo is an essential component in their art of living and social interaction. This may be why they are not transparently straight forward and predictable. They have tortuous and emotionally stretched approaches to simple issues of life. Diplomacy for them is not calculated deceit either. It is involved in their choice of words and mode of expression.[26]

The conclusion, which our argument inevitably leads us to, is the affirmation that the dramatic experience is the living of life itself. This is why we think that the argument as to what constitutes drama,[27] especially as it applies to the modern African situation, is essentially an academic argument in which the verbal combatants do not really disagree on the essential fact that the dramatic denominator is action either per se or in dialectics with language. And we know that behind every language is its motivator, which is thought. When M.J.C. Echeruo argues that the Igbo should, like the Greeks, force myth out of their ritual, reducing myth to its story and giving ritual plot, and ultimately creating the secular out of the religious,[28] the point he makes, though obliquely, is that the process of evolution of the art theater, or literary drama, implies an inevitable textualization which gives drama a stylized format. We do not think that Professor Echeruo is denying the authenticity of ritual action and myth, or ascribing limitations to them; rather he is saying that these have their own limited but useful purposes, which are different from the purposes of contemporary art theater. The ritual experience, as we understand it, is a dramatic experience, just as the secular theater is also a dramatic experience. Both have different functional purposes; both serve different communities and sensibilities, and both have their own degrees of aesthetic appeal. But there could be, but there need not be, an evolutionary relationship between them.

Behind every dramatic experience is the enactment or reenactment of action, whether the action is stylized mimesis, or spontaneous mimesis. Every action is a representation of some sort, and no human action, whether it is a willful representation or an unassuming, routine gesture and/or utterance made in the course of everyday life, is, strictly speaking, original to the actor. What one may think is unique to one's manner of behavior is no more than an enactment of mannerisms and demeanor of millions of other human beings with whom one shares resemblances and typifications. All humanity shares a common ancestry, and down the line of the Jungian collective unconscious to which our primordial instincts are rooted is a string, forming a repertoire of all human actions and experiences. What human beings do or say in any given generation is only an echo from the unfathomable depths of the collective memory of all humanity. The burden of the dramatic experience is that in which human beings often, even in their most tiny gestures, actions, and utterances, impress on us significantly that literature is always an affirmation of human life and human values. The dramatic experience is a messianic experience, for it is an encapsuled articulation of all genres of the literary experience. Its impact is bold, solid, deep, arresting, lasting, strikingly illuminating, and somewhat religious. George Bernard Shaw meant business when he suggested that it would perhaps be more useful for one to spend three good hours in the theater, watching a good play, preferably a Shavian play, than dozing off most of the hours of service in the church.

NOTES

1. Robert Sharp, *Irony in the Drama* (Chapel Hill: University of North Carolina Press, 1957), p. 4.

2. T. S. Dorsch, Trans., *Classical Literary Criticism: Aristotle, Horace, Longinus]* (Harmondsworth: Penguin, 1965), p. 31.

3. See, for example, J. L. Styan, *The Elements of Drama* (Cambridge: Cambridge University Press, 1980), and Marjorie Boulton, *Anatomy of Drama* (London: Routledge & Kegan Paul, 1960).

4. See Richard Southern, *The Seven Ages of the Theatre* (London: Faber & Faber, 1962).

5. T. S. Eliot, "Rhetoric and Poetic Drama" in *Selected Essays* (London: Faber & Faber, 1934), p. 52.

6. T. S. Eliot, *Poetry and Drama* (London: Faber & Faber, 1951), p. 32.

7. For a fuller exploration of this, see Afam Ebeogu, "From *Idanre* to *Ogun Abibiman*: An Examination of Soyinka's Use of Ogun Images," *Journal of Commonwealth Literature* XV,: I (Aug. 1980), pp. 84-96.

8. See Wole Soyinka, "Who's Afraid of Elesin Oba?" Paper delivered at the Conference on Radical Perspectives on African Literature held at the University of Ibadan, December, 1977.

9. Wole Soyinka, *The Road* (Ibadan: Oxford University Press, 1965), p. 44.

10. See Wole Soyinka, "Drama and the African World View," *Myth, Literature and the African World* (Cambridge: Cambridge University Press, 1976), 37-60.

11. H. Granville-Barker, *On Poetry in Drama* (1937), pp. 16-17. Quoted in Styan, *op. cit.*, p. 28.

12. See Foreword to Efua Sutherland, *The Marriage of Anansewa* (London: Longman, 1975), pp. v-vii.

13. Helen Gardener, *Metaphysical Poetry* (Harmondsworth: Penguin, 1966), p. 23.

14. T. S. Eliot, "A Game of Chess: 'The Waste Land,'" *Selected Poems* (London: Faber & Faber, 1954), pp. 55-56.

15. *Ibid.*, p. 56.

16. *Ibid.*, p. 57.

17· T. S. Eliot, "The Fire Sermon," *op. cit.*, p. 59.

18· T. S. Eliot, "Preludes," *Ibid.*, p. 24.

19. Chinua Achebe, *Things Fall Apart* (London: Heinemann, 1962), pp. 182-84.

20. See Jack Goody, *The Interface Between the Oral and the Written* (Cambridge: Cambridge University Press, 1986).

21. See, for example, Bakary Traore's *The Black African Theatre and Its Social Functions* trans. Dapo Adelupha. (Ibadan: University of Ibadan Press, 1972).

22. See Isidore Okpewho, "The Aesthetics of Old African Art," *Okike* 8 (July 1978), pp. 38-55.

23. This festival has striking similarities with the Owu Masquerade Festival in some parts of Imo State of Nigeria (see Beatrice C. Ezirim, "The Literary Significance of Owu Masquerade Festival in Amauzari," B.A. Long Essay submitted to the School of Humanities, Imo State University, Okigwe, 1987, esp. pp. 25-40.

24. For a full exploration of the mask idiom among the Igbo, see Ossie Enekwe, *Igbo Masks: The Oneness of Ritual and Theatre* (Lagos: Nigeria Magazine, 1987).

25. See N. Uka, "A Note on the Abam Warriors of Igboland," *Ikenga* 1, 2 (July 1972), pp. 76-82.

26. Meki Nzewi, "Dramatic Moments in Igbo Traditional Life Style," *Ugo* 3 (June-November 1976), pp. 32-33.

27. See, for example, M.J.C. Echeruo's "evolutionist" approach to the development of African theater and Ossie Enekwe's opposing "relativist" view in M.J.C. Echeruo, "The Dramatic Limits of Igbo Ritual," pp. 136-48, and Ossie Enekwe, "Myth, Ritual and Drama in Igboland," pp. 149-63, in *Drama and Theatre in Nigeria: A Critical Source Book,* ed. Yemi Ogunbiyi (Lagos: Nigeria Magazine, 1981).

28. Echeruo, *op. cit.*

6

Literature in Indigenous Nigerian Languages

Ernest N. Emenyonu

He is trying to explain the difficulties of writing down African music, for
the notation of African music has not yet been sufficiently developed
and differentiated from that of European music.

–Ngugi wa Thiong'o, *Devil on the Cross*

It would seem, perhaps, out of place to begin a chapter on "literature in
indigenous Nigerian languages" with a quotation from a novel by a Kenyan
author. Permit the indulgence but I hope I shall be able to show the
significance shortly, for I believe that with *Devil on the Cross*,[1] Ngugi
uttered a parable which urgently needs to be pressed home to critics,
scholars, and readers of African literature.

The message of the novel is resoundingly clear, that neo-colonialism (the
exploitation by a country of its own people's sweat and blood, the raping
of its own mothers) is in Africa and in Kenya, and that power still rules and
"the forces of law and order are on the side of those who rob the workers
of the products of their sweat, of those who steal food and land from the
peasants. The peace and the order and the stability they defend with
armoured cars is the peace and the order and the stability of the rich, who
feast on bread and wine snatched from the mouths of the poor" (p. 204).
This is as current and revolutionary a theme as can be found in any African
fiction of the second half of the twentieth century. Ngugi's literary techniques and style are manifest elements of the theme of the novel. The reader
is confronted with the fact that this novel was not originally written in a
European language. Ngugi himself translated it from Gikuyu into English.
This novel draws attention to two major successes of Ngugi. First, he was
able to explore fully and effectively in Gikuyu, apparently without inhibi-
tion, the powerful theme of the obligation of the Kenyan people to overthrow the neo-colonialist powers that dominate their lives. He portrays
effusively such foreign and abstract concepts as imperialism, capitalism,

neo-colonialism, and Marxism in an African language at the level of Kenyan masses. He makes *Devil on the Cross* the first contemporary African novel in an African language to grapple with these issues. This highlights his second success in the novel, that of style and technique. Ngugi's extensive use of proverbs, folktales, songs, dramatic dialogues, flashbacks, foreshadowing, and humor provides the reader with an insight into the vanishing African oral tradition. Songs and cantos are scattered liberally throughout the book. The songs create a rhythm that is reminiscent of sonorous traditional drums. The rhythm provides a pace that moves the story rapidly. The songs are used by the author to achieve an uplifting feeling when necessary and at other times to instigate rebellious action in the characters. Dialogues in the novel are extremely simplified to make the reading easy and continuous. The masses for whom the story was written needed dialogues in plain words for easy comprehension. Throughout the book, the old oral forms persist, however, adapting themselves to the new genre, transforming and being transformed: poems, songs, and anecdotes rush pell-mell; proverbs appear and reappear, as in the tradition of African oral performance, as a mnemonic device, and to assure that they will be heard amid the tumult. As Chinua Achebe states, "Our ancestors are sending us signals from the long history and experience of bygone days. . . . Because they are so far away and we are surrounded by the distractions and tumult of daily life, they have to shout and repeat themselves . . . again and again, until the central message goes home."[2]

Ngugi uses proverbs, anecdotes, and humor which are both exclusive and universal at the same time. Although his Gikuyu and other African readers in general are bound to find it more powerful, the strengths of the traditional elements of style are not lost on the non-African readers. For instance, Muturi's outburst on the way to Ilmorog is a mixture of traditional proverbs and Marxist thought:

"You!" Muturi added. "You are very highly educated. But let me tell you this. When a monkey is robbed of its young, a mouthful of food is given it in return. But you people go too far. You rob us of the produce of our own hands, and you don't throw us even a small portion. You dam the river above us so that not a drop of water gets through to us below. God never has a chance to see how strong your thighs are. I've heard it said that the Earth spins constantly and never rests at any one spot. Life is the circulation of the blood; death is the blood clogged in the veins. Life is the heart beating; death is the heart stilled. We know that a baby in its mother's womb will not be still-born when it plays inside her and moves about. You! Something new may appear at dawn that was not there the night before. Don't despise the masses. The Iregi generation is still alive and rebellious. What did the singer say the other day? That your people had better take care—it's we who were there with Kimaathi."
(p. 80)

How do you write a literature that genuinely records the human voice of the African masses and not the voice of Westerners or black Africans pretending to be Westerners? The answer is a return to African cultural roots. Ngugi's *Devil on the Cross* is in Gikuyu. The setting is Kenya. The characters are Kenyans. The issues in the story are local and dominate the lives of Kenyan masses. As a novel, *Devil on the Cross* was a great success with the Kenyans. Non-Kenyans, indeed the world, subsequently asked for it in a foreign language—English—and got it.

The implications of the preceding scenario, I hope, are clear to everybody. One of the most fatal impediments to the rapid development of modern African literature was the ambiguity that surrounded its definition in the early sixties. Pioneer African critics contributed to this sad situation by clinging to the wrong emphasis. African literature was then defined to the exclusion of any real nationalist outlook. When Obi Wali came up with the definition which restricted African literature to literature in African languages, he was ridiculed by the "experts" and forced into a golden silence. If he had had his way, perhaps the course of modern African literature as we know it today would have been altered for the good of Africans and the world. Critics rejected his stand because if the African writer limited his medium to his mother tongue, he would be limiting his audience and depriving the world of his message and art. Not many realized the reverse consequence that by making his message and art accessible to the world, the African writer was depriving the African masses, his largest possible audience, of his art and message. Ngugi's mechanism may have changed all that.

Literature in indigenous languages is the most neglected in Africa today. Some years ago, it was oral literature. Nowhere in Africa is the retardation of indigenous literature more felt than in Nigeria. Here, among other things, to encourage anything peculiar to one language group is assumed to be a means of sanctioning ethnicity and therefore forestalling national unity. It is taking Nigerians a painfully long time to realize that no matter how much the author denies or disguises it, every Nigerian who writes fiction in English today has his foundation in the oral heritage of his ethnic group. Every Nigerian who tells or writes a story today in whatever language is reflecting consciously or unconsciously something of his past, something of his people's or community's oral heritage. Oral literature and written literature in indigenous languages constitute Nigerian literature. Literature in non-Nigerian languages is only a development and not the origin of Nigerian literature.

Nigeria is Africa's most populous country. Its present population is about 91 million. It is estimated that by the turn of the century it will surpass 150 million and by the year 2030, will reach 533 million, approximately the present population of the African continent.[3] Nigeria speaks a staggering 394 languages.[4] Although not all of these are capable of sustaining creative literature yet, it shows Nigeria as a very fertile ground for literary creativity in indigenous languages and Nigeria could capture great world attention in literary output if it could encourage the development of literature in as many written indigenous languages as possible.

At the present time, in spite of a few scattered publications here and there, a discussion of literature in indigenous Nigerian languages inevitably must focus on literatures in Hausa, Yoruba, and Igbo—the three major languages of Nigeria. Literatures in all three languages have origins dating as far back as the nineteenth century and even earlier in the case of Hausa. In each case, the early European missionaries were instrumental in the reduction of the languages to written alphabets, and instrumental in the production of the first literary creations in the new alphabetic scripts. F. F. Schon, a German missionary, "wrote in Hausa more than ten books on collections of oral traditions, translation of Christian books, compilation of dictionaries and readers, and preparation of the biography of his informant, Dorugo, in a book narrative called *Magana Hausa*. Published in 1885, it can be regarded as the first literary work in prose form in Hausa."[5] Out of this foundation and through such government institutions and agencies as the Translation Bureau (1930), Literature Bureau (1933), North Regional Literature Agency (1953), and the Northern Nigerian Publishing Company Limited (1960) have emerged a variety of impressive literary creations in Hausa as well as a number of novelists, including Mallam Abubakar Iman (*Ruwan Bagaja*), Mallam Abubakar Tafawa Balewa (*Shehu Umar*), Bellow Kagara (*Gandoki*), Mallam Mohammadu Gwarzo (*Idon Matambayi*), and Mallam Tafida with Dr. East (*Jiki Magayi*).[6] These pioneer works had one thing in common, namely, their dependence on and strong attachment to the Hausa oral tradition from which they freely borrowed themes and narrative techniques. In the past decade, creative writing in Hausa has been increasing but without the same strong and deeply committed government support which had historically led to the flourishing of Hausa literature in the three decades preceding Independence as well as the sixties, when the government specifically set up some agencies charged with the sole responsibility of translating books and materials from Arabic and English into Hausa and encouraging indigenous authors to write books in Hausa. Left currently mainly at the whims of commercial publishers, young Hausa authors are not getting the patronage and exposure that their productivity deserves or desires.

Among the Yoruba, the missionary literary foundation produced a remarkable and prolific novelist, D. O. Fagunwa, who began writing in the forties and is today described as truly the father of the Yoruba novel and "one of Africa's most influential writers."[7] Among his works are "five long narratives, two travel books, collected short stories and folktales, as well as a series of graded readers for primary schools."[8] Of all these, only one of the long narratives, *Ogboju Ode* (*The Forest of a Thousand Daemons*, translated by Wole Soyinka), has been translated into English. Fagunwa's influence extended to the fictional arts of Amos Tutuola, Wole Soyinka, and a number of other Yoruba authors.[9] Fagunwa, like his successor and disciple, Amos Tutuola, set his stories in the realm of fantasy and wrote about ghosts, spirits, the world of the supernatural, and the heroic individual who was carried into them by extraordinary adventures. He advocated the indigenization of creative literature in Africa, contending: "We should not merely copy others but should give first consideration to the need of our society. Experience has shown that British humour is not the same as the African's. . . . Besides, there is nothing wrong in making our own kind of writing our special contribution to the literary history of the world."[10] Abiola Irele has said of Fagunwa:

His knowledge of Yoruba life and customs, combined with the particular effect of his descriptive and narrative power, gives vividness to the settings of his novels and lends a strange and compelling quality of truth to his evocations. The world of spirits, the realm of fantasy is made familiar and alive, because it proceeds, in these novels, from an individual understanding of human life and of the varied moral situations in which it takes place. It is this element in Fagunwa's art, the continuous extension of human fate and responsibility beyond the confines of the immediate social world into the spiritual, which lends to his work its total impact.[11]

In spite of Fagunwa's widespread popularity and indisputable success as a novelist in the indigenous medium, and the added distinction of possibly being "the author with the largest reading audience in Africa,[12] contemporary Yoruba novelists would probably look to the Alukos and Soyinka rather than Fagunwa for sustained literary inspiration and artistic model.

Literature in the Igbo language has been the most hampered and the most neglected literature of the three major Nigerian languages, although it had as good a foundation as literatures in Hausa and Yoruba. Because it is the only Nigerian language I can read well and write in, I shall use some of the publications in Igbo language for closer textual analysis and specific statements on the contributions of indigenous writers to the growth and development of Nigerian literature. I shall limit my remarks to the novel. The first major literary creation in Igbo language was an anthology entitled *Isoama Ibo Primer* published in 1925 by the ex-slave-turned-missionary Bishop Ajayi Crowther. It consisted of prayers, Bible verses, folktales, short narratives, riddles, and proverbs. It was revised and enlarged in 1927. It was not until 1933 that an Igbo novel, *Omenuko*, was published by Pita Nwana, who goes down in history as the founding father of the Igbo novel. *Omenuko* was read by generations of Igbo schoolchildren and adults in the thirties, forties, and fifties. Although *Omenuko* was a best seller and a literary masterpiece, nothing else came from the pen of its author. Today, some readers would not even associate the novel with an author.[13] It was to take thirty years after the publication of *Omenuko* before two other novels visibly emerged, three years after Nigerian Independence. They were Leopold Bell-Gam's *Ije Odumodu Jere* (1963) and D. N. Achara's *Ala Bingo* (1963).[14] The next decade witnessed a marked improvement in literary productivity in Igbo. Four noteworthy novels were published: D. N. Achara's *Elelia Na Ihe Omere* (1964), J. U. Tagbo Nzeako's *Chi Ewere Ehihe Jie* (n.d.), L. N. Oraka's *Ahubara Eze Ama* (1975), and Julie N. Onwuchekwa's *Chinaagorom* (1978). The latest and most important novelist to emerge on the Igbo literary scene is Tony Uchenna Ubesie, who with five successful novels—*Ukwa Ruo Oge Ya Odaa* (1973), *Isi Akwu Dara Nala* (1973), *Mmiri Oku Eji Egbu Mbe* (1974), *Ukpara Okpoko Buuru* (1975), and *Juo Obinna* (1977)—is the most prolific creative writer in Igbo language today.

D. N. Achara's *Elelia Na Ihe O Mere*[15] is, as the name implies, an account of the adventures of the hero, Elelia. It tells of his hardships, trials, and tribulations in his quest for the hand of a woman of unmatchable beauty. His heroic and courageous deeds are set out as a kind of testimony of the Igbo philosophy of manhood. A full-fledged man must prove himself by his ability to fend for himself and his household. The story is set in Asan in the Cross River State of Nigeria. The emphasis is not on the physical setting but on the universality of some aspects of human behavior. In any environment, the law of survival at all costs is paramount to every human existence. Thus when there are odds they have the advantage of providing the individual the opportunity of proving his sterling qualities of perseverance, determination, and endurance as a man. The story of Elelia is in effect tailored to illustrate this. Thus, *Site na-ime dikariri ike, ka ndi Igbo ji eziputa na ha etoole dimkpa* (Thus it is by an individual's ability to dare and perservere that the Igbo assess maturity into manhood) (*Ilelia* p.v.). Achara's narrative style is circumlocutory and repetitive. There is a profusion of anecdotes and sub-plots which are constantly recounted at every stage of the action as a device which links events and explains immediate cause and effect. The language often lacks precision and there is little evidence of abundant use of imaginative language. The central idea in the story is the quest for glamour and beauty. When the imagery of beauty is expressed, it is done by extensive comparisons instead of clear-cut figures of speech. For instance, this is how Achara describes the paragon of beauty that Elelia has set his mind on conquering and possessing:

Olu ya di ka nke anigo. Ihu ya na ntutu isi ya dika nke nwayi ahu bi nime miri ana-akpo, "Mermaid," nke ana-ahu ebe ndi Bekee sere n'akwukwo. Ahu ya kworo muru

muru kari enyo Ekwukwara si na nani ile ya anya ga-eme ka madu chefuo iri ihe oriri ruo otu onwa.

Her neck is as erect as the *anigo's*. Her face and her hair are like those of the mermaid seen in European books. Her skin is as smooth and glittering as the mirror. It is also said that the sight of her could make one even forget food for a month. (*Elelia*, pp. 46-47)

The author's artistic design is evident in the ending of the story where Elelia emerges despite overwhelming odds and the underrating of his abilities. His success justifies the truism implicit in his name—*Elelia nwa ite ogbonyuo oku* (if you underestimate the small boiling pot, it bubbles over and quenches the fire). Achara's message comes out clearly, but in the total assessment of the book, it is evident that art has been sacrificed for a moral projection.

Despite the uneven balance between medium and message, *Elelia Na Ihe O Mere* is a better work of art than Tagbo Nzeako's *Chi Ewere Ehihe Jie*.[16] This story is best described as a chronology of rituals and sacrifices with little action. The author's grand design appears to be to acquaint his audience with details of important Igbo customs and traditions, and accordingly he advocates:

Dika nkita siri wee hu onye rijuru afo we sowe ya nazu, buru n'uche ya na oburu na onye ahu anyughi anyu, ogboo agbo, etu ahu ka m choro ka onye obula na esonye n'omenala ndia, nihi na onye na-agaghi akwukwo adighi aga nkuzi.

In the same way that the dog saw a man who had heavily over-eaten and followed him with the thought that eventually the man would either defecate or throw up, I also want everyone to follow these customs, because one who hasn't been to a school cannot be a teacher. (*Chi Ewere Ehihe Jie*, p. 55)

The ending of the story is unconvincing and appears to have been contrived for the sole purpose of creating a diversion for an otherwise monotonous and unexciting plot. There is a profuse use of proverbial expressions, some of which are couched in humor and irony. But the impact of these proverbs is minimal because they read very much like a litany of aphorisms on which a thin veil of a story is unevenly spread. A printing error on page 21 (last line) distorts a popular adage and destroys its designed effect. *Chi Ewere Ehihe Jie*, as the title implies, is a sad tale of the trying experiences of an only child who dies in mysterious circumstances. His parents send him down the grave with lots of precious keepsakes. Some daring robbers exhume the body with the intention of stealing the things in the coffin. In the act, Nonyerem the hero awakes, and the thieves scramble for their lives. The story has two major divisions—Nonyerem's life before and after his "death." Everything else is given significance according to how it relates to this main action. As earlier pointed out, what could have been a good plot was marred by an overindulgence in explications of cultural norms and traditions with little room for the development of the story.

If *Chi Ewere Ehihe Jie* is ruined by cultural digressions which weaken the plot, L. N. Oraka's *Ahubara Eze Ama*[17] suffers from a haphazard and disjointed plot. It is best seen as two different stories loosely held together by invoking the name of the major character at different times in different places. Told with the deliberate purpose of discouraging and punishing avarice, fraud, injustice while upholding and rewarding humility, justice, and innocence, *Ahubara Eze Ama* is lacking in skillful narrative techniques such as imaginative use of language, suspense, and, most significantly, the ability of an author to hold the story together as one coherent entity.

Julie N. Onwuchekwa's *Chinaagorom*[18] combines all the flaws of the plots of *Chi Ewere Ehihe Jie* and *Ahubara Eze Ama* and takes on the additional liability of poor production evident in countless spelling errors of both Igbo and occasionally introduced English words, punctuation, and other language infelicities. But unlike its two counterparts, *Chinaagorom* is partially redeemed by the author's sensitive handling of her theme, a powerful descriptive ability, and a flair for apt and accurate imagery and proverbs.

Chinaagorom is a woman's story told in a manner that highlights the conventional prejudices against the woman in contemporary Nigerian society. The woman is more sinned against than sinning. She is abused, discriminated against, and denied her rights. But, in spite of all these, she must emerge victorious, vindicate her virtues, and exonerate her kind. It is almost as if Julie Onwuchekwa wants to pour out in the ninety pages of the novel all the problems that beset womanhood in Nigerian society. Her scenes are, therefore, crowded, and this adversely affects the plot, the pace of the narrative, and the development of the story. The story is, however, enriched in places by the author's privileged insights into a number of female subtleties, such as when she informs us: *Odighi ihe na ato umu nwayi ufodu ka iritu nri onye ozo* (Nothing pleases a woman as much as eating the food prepared by another person). Similarly, references to sex and sexual symbols are handled with modesty and decorum. Examples include the following: *Nne Chinagoro kwuru na otu o siri muo nwa ka ebe a na-anyu maamiri turu ya ujo ma dikwa ya obi uto* (Chinaagoro's mother said that the way in which her daughter delivered the baby as if she merely urinated pleased and at the same time frightened her) (p. 24); *Oriaku Mazi Chijioke enyidatala n' udo* (Mazi Chijioke's wife has climbed down peacefully) (*Oriaku* literally means "consumer of wealth"; climbing here refers to labor at childbirth) (p. 24); *Agwa oma ya na mma ya mere ka ndi oji okpa ebie okazi wee gbuloo ahu n'ebe di ya no* (Her good manners and charm were the things that restrained wayward girls from snatching her husband from her) (p. 84); and the following song

> *Biam biam ka mma n'ebe?*
> *Biam biam ka mma n'ute.*
> *Biam biam ka mma n'ebe?*
> *Biam biam ka mma n'ute.*
> *Ibiachaa ya gi abiata nwa*
> *Biam biam ka mma n'ute*
> *Ibiachaa ya gi abiata ihe*
> *Biam biam ka mma n'ute.*

> Where is the best place to *rub* the body?
> It's best done on the mat [i.e., in bed]
> Where is the best place to rub the body?
> It's best done on the mat [in bed]
> For, after the *exercise*, there comes a baby
> The mat [the bed] is the best place for rollicking
> After it, you produce something great
> The mat [bed] is the best place to rollick. (*Chinnaagorom*, p. 73)

At the end of *Chinaagorom*, what stays in the mind of the reader is not the thought of a story well told, or an exciting story of incidents that will long be remembered, but a series of incidents which have been strung together without precision. There are visions of suffering and maligned women vindicated, subdued women elevated, idle women gingered into places of action and responsibility; but the author has left her new-found women still clapping and dancing in circles unsure of the value and direction of their new victories. As a social commentary *Chinaagorom* could pass as a masterpiece, but as a novel it leaves much to be desired.

Tony Uchenna Ubesie is in a class by himself. He is the most accomplished author writing fiction in Igbo today. His *Ukwa Ruo Oge Ya O Daa*[19] is a love story without the trappings of sensationalism and hackneyed sentimentality. It is a realistic story of two people in love and their bitter experiences in a bid to attain their heart's desire. It includes parental intrusions, obstacles by outside interests, and the menace of the corruption of the conventional society. It also includes a reaffirmation of the values of education in the battle against out-dated tradition and conservatism. Yet, none of these is given more weight than it deserves to keep the story from

faltering. Ubesie reinforces his thematic realism with sound narrative
techniques through which the functional value of proverbs and witticisms
is brought out to the fullest. He has a dramatic way of opening his stories
and holding the reader to the narrative through a judicious use of suspense
which he gradually builds up to a climax and a convincing resolution. This
is how he reports the death of a village philanthropist to whom everyone
owes a debt of gratitude:

*Umunnanm, ndi Igbo turu ilu si na odighi onye nwuru obodo ghara ino, ma oburu
na ana-ahu onwu, onwere onye o ga-abu onwuo, ndi obodo asi onwu bia horo
mmadu ato ozo ma ya hapu onye ahu. Ma onye onwu choro igbu, odighi ihe ga-eme
ka ohapu ya nara onye ozo.... N'ezi Maazi Obi, mma abaghi ji, Ekwwu esighi ite.
Ahia azughi. Ndi nkwu eteghi, maka na ahu ihe ka ubi, eree oba. Nwanne amaghi
nwanne ya, nke ogo ji ama ogo ya maka na ihe nwamba huru nyuo nsi kpochie ya
aja, anya hu ya, ogbawa obara. Enwe hukwanu ya, o tunye nwa ya n'ohia, were ndu
ya mere ihe, n'ihi na ebe ukukurudimgba dara olulu, anu nwere ukwu gbawa oso
maka na obu ihe ukwu mere mkpu ji ada. Obu gini mere? Baa n'ime ulo ebe Maazi
Obi ka ijiri anya gi hu ebe Madzi Obi dina nelu akwa ka obu ura ka ona-arahu, ma
eziokwu ahu erula odogwu ala.*

My brothers, the Igbo have a saying that there is no one who dies and the town
ceases to be [i.e., no man is indispensable] but if it were possible to meet Death face
to face, there could be a situation where a particular individual would die and the
townspeople would ask Death to spare him but pick any other three people from
among them. Unfortunately, when one is destined to die, there is no way out. . . .
In Mazi Obi's compound that day, there was no cooking, no going to the market,
and no palm wine tapping. When you see something greater than the farm, you
forgo the barn [i.e. a great tragedy or event overshadows everything else]. Brother
did not recognize his brother, nor an in-law his in-law, because whatever causes the
cat to defecate and cover the shit with sand, if the ordinary eyes see it, they would
bleed. If the monkey sees it, she would abandon her child and run for dear life.
Where *ukukurundimgba* (long and strong-legged creature) falls into a pit, any
animal with legs had better run because when there is great tumult and screaming,
something quite unusual has happened. "What is it that happened?" Enter Mazi
Obi's room and see for yourself where Mazi Obi is lying in state as if he is
ordinarily sleeping. The truth, indeed, is that the hero is gone. (*Ukwa Ruo Oge Ya
Odaa*, p. 29)

The rhythm of this passage reminds one of any of the beautiful musical
renderings of the late Igbo musician Harcourt Whyte's choir.
    In general, Ubesie's narrative style is characterized by this sensitive use
of language. It is not peculiar to long paragraphs. It is evident in short as

well as long sentences, in detailed descriptions as well as terse accounts of events. A few examples will serve to illustrate the rhythm, humor, imagery, and verbal dexterity of his anecdotes:

1. *Onye jiiri ihere ghara ikwu ka oha ya, oburu ya gafee n'ama nna ya. . . Ha emeela ka ha huru, n'ihi na ha ahughi ka ha mere. . . . Oso moto ahu na-akpu akpu ka esu, ebe onye oso ruru ka onye ije ga-eru.* (p. 19)

   If a person, out of shyness, does not express how things are with his [i.e., his problems, his difficulties], he might be carried past his father's compound [the admonition is that one should not suffer in silence]. . .. They did what they could because they saw nothing else that could be done. . . . The lorry was going at a snail speed, however, wherever the sprinter reaches, the pedestrian will eventually get there.

2. *Odigh onye na-enye onye na-anya ya mmekpa ahu, n'ihi na odighi onye ahughi tagizi soro.* (p. 19)

   No one bothered the driver [of the slow vehicle], because everyone saw taxicabs before deciding to join the lorry.

One can say of Ubesie's sensitive use of language what he himself says of the utilitarian value of proverbs in the Igbo culture—*Ihe ufodu na-esi ike ikwu, ma ewere ilu bio okwu ka ejiri akwukwo nri bio ji, odi onye na-anu ya uto na nti* —(Certain things are hard to render into words, but if you embellish words with proverbs, the way you season yam porridge with spices and vegetables, they become pleasing to the ear) (p. 21).

Juo Obinna[20] is a novel based on the recent Nigerian civil war. Obinna, the hero of the novel, is afraid of violence and would die at the sight of blood, even that of an animal. Obinna perfected all known devices for evading conscription but once in the midst of the womenfolk in his kindred, Obinna would unwind his endless tales of bravery in the face of advancing armies, armored cars, and war planes.

Despite his tragic theme and the general atmosphere of suffering which pervades the novel, Ubesie is able to maintain a sophisticated sense of humor throughout the narrative. Indeed humor and irony are among his most embellished literary devices. They are most effectively felt in *Juo Obinna*, whereas, in the hands of a less talented writer, humor would have been an incongruity in the midst of the general cataclysm of the war.

Examples of this include the following:

1. *Anaghi ezonahu onye Igbo n'okpuru akwa. Ihe obula onye Igbo maara,*
   onye Igbo ozo maara ya, maka na ihe di n'etiti onye Igbo na ibe ya bu ahia
   mbe na nwanne ya na-azu. Mbe na mbe zukoo ahia, uru anaghi adi ya. (p.
   20)

   You can't hide an Igbo man under the bed [i.e., you can't deceive an Igbo
   man]. Every Igbo man knows what the other knows. An Igbo buying from
   another Igbo is like buying and selling between one tortoise and another.
   In such a case, there is no profit and no cheating on either side.

2. *Nwoke na ibe ya jiri ihe gbasara ego yie agba, nani ihe ga-egbochiri ha*
   ya bu onwu. O buru ma nke ahu, anaghi eji n'aka na nwoke anwuola nke
   oma ruo mgbe efere ya akwukwo ego n'ihu oghara imati aka ya. (p. 142)

   If a man [reference here is to the Igbo] makes an appointment with
   another man over a money matter, the only thing that can prevent the
   meeting is death. Even then, the only way you can tell that the man is
   dead, is if you wave money across his face, and he does not snatch it from
   you.

It is hoped that Tony Ubesie's style of writing and general narrative
techniques will serve as models for aspiring Igbo writers.

Contemporary Igbo authors have effectively and authentically articulated
the general cultural concerns of the Igbo as a people by the thematic
preoccupations in their novels. What is lacking now is a corresponding
mastery of language usage. Success in literary creativity is a manifestation
of success in the mastery of the relevant language. Literature is language in
action. A good writer of Igbo literature must of necessity be a good speaker
of Igbo language first. The medium complements the message, and vice
versa.

After years of self-denigration, literatures in indigenous Nigerian languages are in the process of rediscovery and revival. The indigenous writers
are evolving through a slow process, but the results are delightful and
encouraging. The time is, therefore, ripe for positive government intervention, as well as support from universities within and outside Nigeria.
Government intervention could be through practical commitment to the
development of Nigerian languages without the feeling that such an action
will make Nigerian ethnic groups "small nationalities" that will emphasize
group loyalties to the detriment of the central government. It is necessary
to make the study of each Nigerian language compulsory in any school
situated in the particular linguistic territory and require a pass in it for
graduation at any level of the school system. Government emphasis on
"made in Nigeria goods" and the frequent trade fairs launched to encourage
and support them need to go beyond carvings, crafts, paintings, and masks,

to include exposure to literature in Nigerian languages. The government should encourage this as an essential aspect of cultural and national development.

The universities have an equally important role to play, by expanding the focus of their programes in linguistics departments. Courses in techniques of translation will prove to be of immense value in the translation of creative works of high quality, not only from English into Nigerian languages, but from one indigenous Nigerian language into another. Literary contributions by Nigerian indigenous authors may yet prove far more significant to contemporary African literature than what has so far been experienced with writers in English.

NOTES

1. Ngugi wa Thiong'o, *Devil on the Cross* (London: Heinemann Educational Books, Ltd., 1982). Page references are to this edition and are indicated within the text.

2. Chinua Achebe, *Morning Yet on Creation Day* (New York: Anchor Press/Doubleday, 1975), p. 57.

3. *Popline*, December, 1984.

4. See Hansford Keir, Bendor-Samuel-John, and Stanford Ron, *Studies in Nigerian Languages* no. 5, 1976, Summer Institute of Linguistics, Ghana.

5. See Ibrahim Yaro Yahaya, "The Development of Hausa Literature," *The Guardian* (Lagos, Nigeria), February 9, 1985, pp. 8-9.

6. Ibrahim Yaro Yahaya, pp. 8-9.

7. For a comprehensive discussion of the literary achievements of D. O. Fagunwa see: Bernth Lindfors, *Early Nigerian Literature* (New York: Africana Publishing Company, 1982), chapter 2. Also, Ayo Bamgbose, *The Novels of D. O. Fagunwa* (Benin City, Nigeria: Ethiope, 1974).

8. Lindfors, *Early Nigerian Literature*, p. 13.

9. Lindfors, p. 14.

10. Lindfors, p. 17.

11. Abiola Irele, *The African Experience in Literature and Ideology* (Bloomington: Indiana Universisty Press, 1990).

12. Lindfors, p. 13.

13. For a detailed discussion of Pita Nwana's *Omenuko*, see my "Early Fiction in Igbo" in *Research in African Literatures* vol. 4, no. 1 (1973). Also in Bernth Linfors (ed.), *Critical Perspectives on Nigerian Literatures* (Washington, D.C.: Three Continents Press, 1976), pp. 87-100.

14. Leopold Bell-Gam, *Ije Odumodu Jere* (Lagos, Nigeria: Longman, 1963); D. F. Achara, *Ala Bingo* (Lagos, Nigeria: Longman, 1937; reprinted, Longman, 1963). For detailed discussions of these, see my "Early Fiction in Igbo."

15. D. N. Achara, *Elelia na Ihe Omere* (Nigeria: Longman, 1964, reprinted in 1981). All page references are to this edition and are indicated within the text.

16. J. U. Tagbo Nzeako, *Chi Ewere Ehihe Jie* (Onitsha, Nigeria: University Publishing Company, n. d.) All references are to this edition and pages are indicated within the text.

17. L. N. Oraka, *Ahubara Eze Ama* (Ibadan: O.U.P., 1975). All page references are to this edition and are indicated within the text.

18. Julie N. Onwuchekwa, *Chinaagorom* (Lagos, Nigeria: Lantern Books, 1978). All references are to this edition and pages are indicated within the text.

19. Tony Uchenna Ubesie, *Ukwa Ruo Oge Ya Odaa* (Ibadan, Nigeria: O.U.P., 1973). All references are to this edition and pages are indicated within the text.

20. Tony Ubesie, *Juo Obinna* (Ibadan, Nigeria: University Press Ltd., 1977, reprinted 1980). All page references are to this edition and are indicated within the text.

7

From Dialectal Dichotomy to Igbo Standard Development

Donatus I. Nwoga

What I intend to do in this chapter is to give expression to some of the ideas which I personally consider important in the now critical assignment which is to give Igbo language studies definition and direction. I want, in this presentation, to go beyond the perennial question of what dialect should constitute the core of standard Igbo to the urgent question of how to make the present standard capable of fulfilling its role in the busy world of Nigerian language policy discussions.

THE CONTEXT OF LANGUAGE POLICY

The first question in the context in which the discussion must find its base is, What responsibility do those to whom the management of the Igbo language has been entrusted have the language and the owners of the language? What is the Igbo language supposed to be used for, and what is it supposed to represent within Igboland and outside Igboland in the Nigerian context and the context of world languages?

The responsibility with which we are charged is to standardize for the Igbo people a language which unifies them and gives them an identity, a language in which they can be educated in the tradition which has now established that first language education is the best, especially in the early years of the educational process. We are charged with the responsibility to forge for our people a language which can bear the burden of giving expression to their experiences and communication to their ideas. The Igbo have always been a people who hanker after new experiences, who latch on to new developments, who travel to new places and acquire new styles. They have to have a language which is adaptable and expansive, a language which does not restrain their efforts to accommodate their experiences, a language receptive to new ideas and technology. The impatience of the

Igbo to advance cannot tolerate a language that would tie them to the apron strings of tradition or create tortuous phrases where adapted words would serve the same function of giving names to thoughts, things, and situations.

In trying to achieve such a language, we must think of the living. But, most importantly, we must think of the generations to come. This means that, in line with our traditions, those of us living today might have to make sacrifices in order that what is not possible in our own time may be possible and perhaps bear fruit in the lives of our children and grandchildren.

The second arm of the context of our discussion is that the Igbo language is not only for the Igbo people. The National Language Policy which aims at making Nigerians capable of doing their business and communicating in Nigerian languages has included Igbo among the three major languages of Nigeria. This is not a favor: it is the result of the fact that the Igbo speaking peoples have a population which is at least the third highest in Nigeria. This imposes on the Igbo language the necessity of being developed to the stage where it is capable of bearing other people's experiences, or at least being used by others to communicate their ideas and feelings. The Igbo language is therefore to be such, and to have such teaching materials and developed methods, that it can be the subject of studies by non-Igbo people in Igboland, by other Nigerians in their own homes, and by other nationals of the world as one of the developed languages of thought and literature.

THE NEED FOR A STANDARD

Can Igbo achieve its role in the present context of uncertainty generated by some of the discussions as to the viability of a standard Igbo? Some people will immediately interject that they have no objections to a standard Igbo but that they object to the choice that has been made for a variety of scholarly reasons. That quibble will not help the discussion; perhaps a little history will make my point at this juncture:

Isuama Igbo, c. 1841-72

Late in August 1841, the Rev. J. F. Schon, a Church Missionary Society representative on an expedition up the Niger, came to the court of the King of Aboh. Eager to show his interest in the people and their language, he wrote his speech in Igbo and read it to the King of Aboh. The consequence was disastrous. He found, he later reported, "that the dialect of the Ibo language, on which I had bestowed so much labour in Sierra Leone, differs widely from that spoken and understood in this part of the country. It never escaped my observation, that a great diversity of dialects existed: but I must blame myself much for not making stricter enquiries about that which would be most useful for the present occasion."[1] When Schon read his speech to the King of Aboh in Igbo, the man was so bored by pronunciation and intonation which he could not understand that he soon interrupted the speech. Schon later found Hausa more congenial to study and sustained his interest in that language to the detriment of Igbo studies.

Certain points emerge from this brief narrative. Schon, a foreigner, was interested enough to want to speak to an Igbo King in the Igbo language. But his effort was not appreciated. There was such consciousness of dialectal differences that the King of Aboh reacted with abruptness to sounds that were not familiar to him. The consciousness of dialectal differences became a prominent factor in the development of the Igbo language.

The dialect problem has bedeviled Igbo studies since then. P.E.H. Hair's 1967 exposition of "The Early Study of the Languages of the Lower Niger and Benue, 1840-1890,"[2] gives many details of how this problem obstructed the development of the early scholarship of the Igbo language:

1. The Rev. J. C. Taylor, a native of Freetown both of whose parents were born in Igboland, was one of the early missionaries to Onitsha. It would appear that his parents came from different dialect areas and gave their son no firm grounding in any dialect—specifically not in the Onitsha dialect. He had to preach to the people of Onitsha through an interpreter. And when he needed to deepen his knowledge of Igbo, he had to go to England to understudy the Rev. J.F. Schon, the same man who had experienced the linguistic fiasco at Aboh in 1841.

2. The Rev. J. F. Schon produced a grammar of Igbo in 1861. When, in 1899, a French missionary-linguist who was constructing another grammar of the language found himself in disagreement with the findings of Schon, he was willing to attribute it to the fact that they might have worked on different dialects.[3]

3. The earliest dictionary of the Igbo language had to be produced by the Yoruba scholar and missionary the Rev. Adjai Crowther and was published in 1882. In line with what could still happen today, the Rev. J. C. Taylor, of Igbo parentage, who had pioneered a lot of Igbo literature in the 1860s had been posted out of the Niger Mission under distressing circumstances. In 1883 an Igbo-English supplement to the dictionary was published under the editorship of the Rev. J. F. Schon. Again the consciousness of dialect forms and variants caused the dictionary to be an incomplete and carelessly collated publication.

4. In the 1850s, Crowther and his co-workers had selected the so-called Isuama dialect as the standard and it was in this dialect that translations of the Bible and other forms of literature were sup-

posed to be produced, and were produced. In the 1870s, when he returned to Igbo studies, he was expecting that the language would be fully developed. He had cause to hope. In the 1850s, he had also selected a dialect for the writing of Yoruba and this dialect had been gaining progressive acceptance. In 1875, he went from a conference in which the language of Yoruba translation was confirmed, to one held in Onitsha with the Igbo translators, in which the same kind of affirmation was made. But by 1876, Isuama had been discarded. By the 1880s, new translations were being made in different dialects, particularly Onitsha and Bonny.

In the end, at the turn of the century, in spite of all the work the missionaries had put into the development of the Igbo language, the printed literature in Igbo was nowhere near what was available in Hausa and Yoruba. Other languages of the lower Niger and Benue belonged to smaller populations, and that may have explained their low output of literature; but other reasons had to be found for the disappointing Igbo situation, considering the size of the Igbo population.

Reflecting on the situation, Hair attributed the poverty of the Igbo language partly to the Igbo pursuit of modernity and progress. Igbo parents made their children transit fast from literacy in Igbo to literacy in the English language, "the language of opportunity," and this was to lead to the situation whereby "the Igbo gained a position of power in the colonial and post-colonial social and administrative order in Nigeria, but the Igbo language was neglected." But the more insistent reason given by Hair was "the failure of generations of linguists to produce an accepted solution to the dialect problem."[4]

I have gone into this detail with the story of the last years of the last century in order to show the age of the various arguments that impinge on the acceptance or otherwise of an incipient standard Igbo:

1. It is not my dialect and I cannot be expected to be interested in it; I don't even understand its vocabulary and its sound patterns and its syntax;
2. It is not the best dialect and we must not be bound by it; we have to wait till comprehensive research leads to the selection of the best dialect that will form the basis of the standard;
3. It is nobody's dialect and so it has no chance for growth. This argument became the bulwark of some of the opponents of the Isuama dialect when it was found that that dialect was a composite affair formed from the adjustment of various Igbo people living together in Freetown, Sierra Leone.

Union Igbo, 1905-39

The story of the Isuama dialect was to repeat itself with the Union Igbo which was evolved for the translation of the Bible that was published in 1913. This standard, spearheaded by the Rev. T. J. Dennis of the CMS mission, held sway between 1905 nd 1939. In addition to the Bible, Union Igbo was the vehicle for some of the premier Igbo fiction of Peter Nwana[5] and D. N. Achara.[6]

G.O.M. Tasie, in his description of "*Igbo Bible Nso* and the Evolution of the 'Union-Igbo,' 1905-1913,"[7] tells the same story of missed opportunities, wrong decisions, and sectional conflicts. The missionaries, reacting to the situation whereby the Igbo, after more than fifty years of Christianity, had no complete Bible available to them, were determined to have the Bible translated. For the Yoruba, the problem had been solved by the use of the Oyo dialect. The question did arise as to whether similarly it would not be more appropriate to choose the dialect of one Igbo group for the translation. That opportunity was missed. No such easy answer was available in the Igbo case, "especially in a circumstance in which each dialect group claimed superiority over others."[8]

It appeared that the solution that had to be found was that which would appease the "rival Igbo dialects." The Rev. Thomas Dennis made a tour of the Igbo-speaking areas and "claimed that he had examined the differences and similarities of the Igbo spoken in those areas and . . . that Owerri-Igbo was as pure as he could find.[9] Yet, it was found necessary to accommodate other dialects and so Union Igbo was formed from a mixture of Onitsha, Owerri, and Bonny Igbo.

Ultimately, that compromise did not achieve the desired result and some of the usual arguments appeared. G. N. Anyaegbunam, one of those present at the conference where the decision was taken about Union Igbo, started early to say that his people in Onitsha would not accept the Union Igbo "chiefly because it would be unintelligible to them."[10] More recent criticisms of the Union Igbo are based on the fact that, as an amalgam of dialects, "it is nobody's language."[11]

Central Igbo, 1939-72, and Standard Modern Igbo, 1973 and After

Since the 1940s, there has been a greater appreciation of the need to base the development of Igbo on a meaningful selection of a core of dialects. Aida Ward's *Igbo Dialects and the Development of a Common Language*[12] placed this core in the old Owerri province with an indication that there is an affinity between this Central Igbo type and some of the northern dialects, including Nsukka, Eke, Udi. Since the early 1970s, the Society for Promoting Igbo Language and Culture (SPILC) has accepted a modified

form of this Central Igbo as the basis of the development of the Standard
Igbo. This would appear to have sorted out the problem of dialect which had
plagued Igbo studies and literature from the nineteenth century. The situation, however, is that vigorous efforts continue to be made to oppose this
standard, indicating that the Igbo have not changed in their understanding
of the possible contribution of the linguistic factor to their unity, identity,
and development.

It is clear from the first issue of *Uwa Ndi Igbo: Journal of Igbo Life and
Culture*[13] published by Okike in 1984 that we are in another phase of the
conflict. Ebo Ubahakwe, in his review of two books, one written and the
other edited by P. Akujuoobi Nwachukwu, accepts the need for a standard
Igbo to emerge from a base dialect. But his conclusion is a suggestion that
the standard, as described by Nwachukwu, has yet to be accepted. "[For] as
suggested in the title of this review, such a base dialect may well turn out
to be the Mbaise dialect but no one can say which it is yet until a systematic
and comprehensive survey of the Igbo dialect underway is completed."[14]
This is a call for holding action.

The same issue of *Uwa Ndi Igbo* goes on to some very vigorous argument
based on E. Nolue Emenanjo's review of *Aka Weta* and Chinua Achebe's
reaction to that review. Professor Emenanjo's perspective is that a standard
Igbo exists and he thinks it is a retrograde action that "those poets and prose
writers who have written beautiful verses, poems, novels, short stories,
plays, essays, and critiques in some variety of Standard English should now
be backing the horse of dialects in Igbo which too has its own standard
variety."[15] Achebe, on the other hand, resents the attempts to force writers
into any straitjackets and believes that literature has the mission "to give
full unfettered play to the creative genius of Igbo speech in all its splendid
variety, not to dam it up into the sluggish pond of a sterile pedantry."[16] In
the opposition between grammarian and creative writer, Achebe sees the
tragedy of the Igbo languages as that of having been "saddled one generation after another with egoistic schoolmen who have been concerned not to
study the language but to steer it into narrow tracks of their particular pet
allusion. That, and not dialects, has been at the heart of our long blackout."[17]

The final commentary on the Igbo language in that issue of *Uwa Ndi Igbo*
is a spirited lament by Mazi Obieze Ogbo, a sixty three-year old minstrel,
who hails from Nteje and lives in Enugu.[18] The man does commend the
Society for Promoting Igbo Language and Culture (SPILC) for having
adopted an orthography, for evolving a language of science and mathemat-
ics, for having given to grammar and syntax some order and a sense of
direction. But he laments that "the Igbo language has been mutilated
beyond recognition" because "they decided to forge a brand new Igbo
language—the Central Igbo—and ram it down the throats of all Igbo-
speaking peoples." He wants a central language to evolve from Onitsha and

Owerri dialects. He asks SPILC to "release its death grip on the Igbo language." According to him, "our Central Igbo is not the language of any existing Igbo community. It is a synthetic compromise language without roots and precedence, a still-born monster." It is at the conclusion of the essay, though, that the author's real intention is declared: "All students in schools in the old Onitsha province can be taught the Onitsha dialect and all students in schools of the old Owerri province can be taught the Owerri dialect."[19] This statement brings us full circle. We are back to the perennial tale of Igbo sectionalism, pride, and inability to yield to the common good. If we would not accept this standard, why should we stop with the Owerri dialect and the Onitsha dialect? What should we tell the people of Nsukka, of Arochukwu and Abiriba, of Agbor and Ukwuani, as to why their own children should not also be taught their own dialect?

Writing in 1929, D. Westermann identified the three main Southern Nigerian languages as Efik, Ibo, and Yoruba.[20] About Efik he saw progress: though Efik speakers were less in number than Ibibio speakers, the Ibibio speakers were "satisfied with Efik as their literary language." Yoruba was also making progress. "For a long time books have been published in one standard dialect only, which is now generally recognized. Like Efik, Yoruba possesses strong vitality and shows a tendency towards expansion." But about the Igbo, he wrote:

The second main language of Southern Nigeria is Ibo. It is spoken by at least four million people, probably by more, that is by a far larger number than any other Southern Nigerian language. It does not, however, seem to have a corresponding power of expansion, as the Ibo-speaking people, a collection of rather primitive tribes, only very loosely connected through their common language are not distinguished either by political influences or trading capacity. Also their language is not developed to any extent and has no literature which might induce others to learn it. But with all this, Ibo is of course an important language, as almost half of the Southern Nigerian population can be reached through it. Its development and educational value have been greatly impeded by the fact that the language is split up into a number of widely differing dialects.[21]

So, in spite of Igbo number, the only importance of the Igbo language was in that number, not in its development and literature. The Ibibio had solved their dialect problem and the Yoruba had solved theirs. Can the Igbo even now admit that theirs is solvable?

At the end of the story, one is faced with the questions: Will Standard Modern Igbo fail, as "Union Ibo" failed, as the mixed dialect "Isuama" failed? Will the Igbo spend more generations looking for another dialect, while other groups are busy developing their language? Shall we, again in

the language sphere as in other areas of national life, spend our emotional
energies complaining that other Nigerians, who are united and developed,
are imposing their language and culture on us while we have rather spent
our creative energies in internecine battles of prideful mutual self-rejec-
tion?

THE DEVELOPMENT OF THE STANDARD

The acceptance of a Standard Igbo is enjoined as an urgent matter by the
pressures of the times for the Igbo to have a language for literary, pedagogic,
and other communicative purposes. Without such a standard, communication between Igbo speakers and writers from different localities (hence,
dialect areas) would be almost impossible, and there is a real danger that
Igbo literature, and indeed written Igbo generally, would be fragmented
into hundreds of little autonomous units each of which would be incomprehensible to the other without passing through the translation process.

With an accepted standard, there would be a common language with
which the Igbo can participate in the national language experiment. Educational materials and texts, and the publishing of literature generally, would
gain a freedom which can only ultimately advance the creative process. And
the availability of a common Igbo will enhance the chance of Igbo as a
viable Nigerian language choice.

The difficulty which the mature adults express today about their inability
to read or understand the standard with any fluency can only be a temporary
handicap and not a restraining factor. Our difficulty today will be the
advantage of the children of tomorrow. With the problem of base dialect
solved by our generation, the next generation will have a greater challenge
to develop the language fully to accommodate all their concepts and
experiences.

But once the standard has been accepted, what we would have achieved
is an agreement on the framework, the bare bones of the language. There is
then the major and far from easy assignment of developing it, of fleshing out
the structure into a full-bodied and attractive being. One is bound to pay
here a great tribute to the Society for Promoting Igbo Language and Culture
and its Standardization Committee for all the work that has so far been done
toward the extension of the Igbo language and its capacity for handling an
increasingly large and extensive body of information and literature.

For the essential assignment of developing the Igbo language, what is
necessary is a mental outlook which has an appropriate mixture of Freedom
and Discipline, a situation in which legislative dogmatism accommodates
creative experimentation. Absolute freedom has never been to the benefit of
any human situation; beneficial freedom has to operate always within
certain boundaries. The question then is how to achieve such disciplinary

boundaries in the Igbo language situation as would allow free scope for the fullness of advantage to be derived from the rich variety within the Igbo language itself and the creative genius of imaginative individuals among the Igbo.

If language development is seen in three broad activities—the choice of standard variety (dialect), graphization (particularly of the orthography), and lexical expansion (particularly in technical vocabulary[22]), one can then summarize one's presentation as follows:

Choice of Dialect

With tedious repetitiveness, this whole chapter has emphasized the need for everybody to accept the central dialect that has emerged over the years as the basis of standard Igbo. But, again, as I have tried to emphasize, this must be seen as the framework for the development of Igbo. Regularly, there have been calls for freedom within this framework. Part of the call is for "parallel development of dialects as primary media of creation."[23] My fear about this approach, beyond its validity for giving permanent recording to those who do not want to bother with learning the standard, is that it will lead to separateness rather than enriched oneness.

I believe that the more valid approach to the enrichment of the chosen variety is that which calls for the full scope of Igbo words that have the same meaning to be retained in the language. The idea here is that instead of discarding any of the words as useless and superfluous and picking one spoken by the majority or by those in the center, the peculiar shades of meaning of the words derived from the specific environment of the Igbo people who use them should be identified, thereby giving the Igbo language a rich body of synonyms embodying those specific shades of meaning.[24]

Graphization

Again, the major disciplinary rules have been agreed here with the acceptance of the Onwu orthography. This must be recognized as a major achievement after years of religious and sectional chauvinistic attachment to particular separate orthographies. There remain, however, certain assignments for our linguists to produce an added orthography that can reproduce the peculiar sounds of some peoples of Igboland. Some scholars have identified some of these problems of the present orthography in failing to provide adequately for "the spelling of the syllabic nasal, word division, spelling of the distinctive features of aspiration, nazalization and (in some analysis) palatalization."[25] There is need to have these additional symbols, even if only so that the creative writers and scholars who have to reproduce dialect speech have the facility for writing them.

There is here an assignment for our linguists. And they can go on and discuss and speculate and suggest till some measure of agreement is reached among them which can then be injected into the general field of language studies. The confusion arises when each linguist, in writing his own books, uses his own scheme of graphization which competes with others in the school or public forum among those of us who have no equipment for making a judgment on their conflicts. Fortunately, with all its limitations, we have a fairly comprehensive Onwu Orthography, with some of the conventions worked out in the series of meetings of the SPILC and its Standardization Committee, to give us a fair fluency in the writing of standard Igbo.

Lexical Expansion

Finally, in the area of lexical expansion, again one remembers the various meetings that have been held by the Standardization Committee and the large body of technical vocabulary and metalanguage that has evolved. Again, one has to warn that there is still scope for much development here. There has been a considerable hastiness in putting into uses words and expressions which have not been tested in the field and on which there is no general agreement. Many of the new terms are too literal and some betray some amount of unfamiliarity, among the coiners, with the theoretical background of some of the terms.

I believe that the Igbo are too dynamic and too progressive to accept any lexical system that is too tortuous and involved, except insofar as they might appeal to the imagination. Of the various ways of increasing the vocabulary of the language—borrowing, coinage, absorption, composition, and so on—my conviction is that the Igbo mentality would most favor borrowing. This is not only because of the Igbo quick acceptance of what is new, but also because the Igbo are too much in a hurry to be delayed by those working on their language. Moreover, changes taking place in learning and technology are too fast to be restrained by the old methods of trying to interpret and compose new phrases and artificial terms. Admittedly, there were quick compositions like *obara mgbala elu* for hypertension and *"ncha l'anya"* for hepatitis. But these were the imaginative coinages of the people rather than the tedious compositions of scholars. Borrowings, appropriately adapted to the phonology of the Igbo language, would be a most satisfactory manner of solving the problem of lexical expansion.

THE NEED FOR AN IGBO LANGUAGE BOARD

The question may be asked whether the development of the Igbo language should be a phenomenon that evolves from the natural interaction of peoples and minds or whether there should be enforcement of some rules of exclusion and inclusion.

Those who have read the history of the English language might reflect with nostalgia on the slow process by which aspects of the language evolved into acceptance at the late stage at which standardization was achieved; might react with a sense of justification at the failure of the two attempts to establish authoritative bodies to control the English language in the seventeenth and eighteenth centuries. Our circumstances, however, are different and do not give us the time for centuries of trial and error.

Moreover, we must not be deceived as to the measure of freedom of usage in the English language. The freedom of the English language from legislation has to be taken side by side with the existence of various bodies interested in and overseeing the growth and stabilization of the English language: the British Academy, the Philological Society, the English Association, the B.B.C. Advisory Committee on Spoken English, and the Society for Pure English. Moreover, deeply researched and elaborately documented books exist which restrain the extravagances into which writers may be tempted: Henry Sweet's *A New English Grammar: Logical and Historical* (1892 and 1898); and later and even more elaborate books on English grammar. Above all, dictionaries have been given a role in the standardization of the English language; the most authoritative guide in English usage is *The New English Dictionaries on Historical Principles,* now known as *The Oxford English Dictionary.* Before its most recent edition, it was already a book in twelve volumes, covering over fifteen thousand pages, containing 414,825 words, illustrated with 1,827,306 citations.

From this it should be clear that, regardless of the appearance of freedom, the English language is not left alone. Freedom exists within a framework of discipline. Perhaps the laws are unwritten, but the conventions have the required strength. If we follow the so-called freedom of English language development blindly, we will lose our bearings and flounder. We would then be like the uncouth person who admired an air conditioner in a house in town and went home and built an empty box and put in his wall and was surprised that it did not blow cold air. We have to find our own route to the salvation of our own language.

I believe that our salvation begins in setting up a full-scale and full-time Igbo Language Board, one of whose major urgent assignments would be to hasten action on the Igbo dictionary.

Ultimately, all that has been said about the development of the Igbo language must be addressed by a body which can make the best use of all the ideas that may result from discussions. My proposal here is that, under the impetus of the SPILC and in cooperation with the universities, colleges of education, and governments within the territories in which the Igbo language is spoken, a full-scale and full-time Igbo Language Board should be set up.

The responsibilities of this Board are quickly presented in two broad activities: first, to promote the standardization and development of the Igbo language,[26] and, second, to generate the appropriate programes for increasing the viability of Igbo as a used and growing language.

I could make suggestions as to the nature, the composition, and the mode of functioning of such a Board, but I believe that what is important now is to get an agreement on its existence; the details can be worked out during the process of discussions in symposia and in other forums. The main requirement is that such a Board be manned by people with language training, with literary training, and with imagination. Their role will be to give firm guidance to the development of the Igbo language and to enrich it vigorously from its own varied resources and from the resources of the world. It will also quickly update the activities already commissioned and in progress for the production of an Igbo lexicon which will be the storehouse of all words and phrases that are in use or have been in use in any area of the Igbo speaking world.

CONCLUSION

Igbo language policy is bound to address a broad variety of issues connected, not only with the standardization and development of the language, but also with its preservation, propagation, and teaching. Let me, therefore, conclude with a few suggestions about the teaching of Igbo.

There is a need for the university and college of education departments in which Igbo language is taught to emphasize the language as against the linguistics element. Clearly, the theories of linguistics, while they help at the abstract level to elucidate what happens in language, tend not to be of much practical value in the actual usage of the language. This is why in British and American Universities, while the linguistics departments tend toward anthropology and the sciences, there are departments which study their languages and literatures. It is necessary, therefore, to see Igbo as a language in use and emphasize its language and literature rather than its linguistics. This, then, releases the strict linguists to identify and pursue their scientific studies and only transfer the results of those studies to the language and literature programe. Otherwise, we will have a body of trained linguists emerging from our universities and colleges of education without any appreciable improvement in the quality of spoken and written Igbo. This would also explain why it would be possible to continue to discuss

Igbo linguistics in English because of the shortage of a metalanguage, while insisting that Igbo language and literature should be taught in Igbo.

At the secondary level, it should be clear to our educational authorities that just as all educational systems demand a pass at the credit level in the language of the environment, our insistence on credit pass in English without demanding that Igbo students also obtain a credit level pass in Igbo constitutes an official license for the poor regard in which the Igbo language is held. "The language of opportunity" in Igboland remains the English language. Any language which one can do without becomes a hobby rather than a necessity and there is no reason why one should pay it all the attention we appear to be demanding. My suggestion is that, in all of the Igbo speaking areas, terminal examinations at the secondary educational level insist on a good pass in the Igbo language for the award of a certificate.

The Igbo language should also now be available as an optional course, at least for the first three years of the 6-3-3-4 educational system, in other parts of Nigeria. It would be taken in addition to the mother tongue of those other Nigerians as they now take French and they can then decide whether to continue study up to the school certificate level. To this end, it is important to point out the current absence from the Igbo language program of the basic language teaching material of an Igbo course with textbooks and tapes of spoken Igbo. This recommendation is crucial if this expanded program of Igbo studies is to mature.

At the elementary level, there would appear to be adequate provision for the teaching of Igbo children, but some special provision will need to be made for the teaching of non-Igbo children. Remedial classes should be provided for them till they catch up with the other children. Fortunately, children are fast in the acquisition of languages.

Other ideas that could be considered are special language courses for Youth Corpsmen who are posted to Igboland and creation of language centers inside and outside the Igbo speaking areas which should offer courses for the public, as French and German language centers offer courses, say in Lagos. We should also interact with foreign universities and institutes of African studies so as to generate in them interest in the Igbo language and have them invite lecturers from here on a reciprocal basis and sponsor research on the Igbo language.

Finally, the import of this chapter centers on the Igbo changing their orientation from internal conflict to uniting to confront external situations. Nigeria has recognized the Igbo language as one of the major languages in Nigeria, mainly because the Igbo constitute the second largest language group in Nigeria. While we waste our emotional and creative energies in internal conflict over whose dialect is to be selected, we cannot achieve the requisite level of development, sophistication, and creativity which will give Igbo language the status of competing for national use and interest.

Let us, therefore, accept the standard received by the Society for Promoting Igbo Language and Culture, develop it with the full resources of the Igbo language and creative imagination of individual Igbo artists, establish an Igbo Language Board, and produce an Igbo dictionary. The identity and dynamism of the Igbo will then be matched by the identity, wealth, and expressiveness of their language.

NOTES

1. Quoted in P.E.H. (See below).

2. P.E.H. Hair, "The Early Study of the Languages of the Lower Niger and Benue, 1840-1890," in P.E.H. Hair, ed., *The Early Study of Nigerian Languages: Essays and Bibliographies* (Cambridge: Cambridge University Press in Association with the West African Language Survey and the Institute of African Studies, Ibadan, 1967), pp. 69-104.

3. Hair notes this fact from P. A. Ganot's "Preface" to his *Grammaire Ibo,* 1899.

4. Hair, *op. cit.*

5. Pita Nwana, *Omenuko* (London: Longmans, 1963).

6. D. N. Achara, *Ala Bingo* (London: Longmans, 1963); *Elelia na Ihe Omere* (Longmans, 1964).

7. *The Journal of Niger Delta Studies* 1, 2 (1977), pp. 61-70.

8. *Ibid.,* p. 64.

9. *Ibid.*

10. *Ibid.*

11. E. C. Ilogu, 1967, and Chinua Achebe, "The Bane of Union," Paper presented at the Seminar on the Problems of the Igbo Language and Literature at the University of Nigeria, Nsukka, November, 1971.

12. (Cambridge: Heffer & Sons, Ltd., 1941).

13. No. 1 (June 1984), edited by Chukwuma Azuonye.

14. Ebo Ubahakwe, "Mbaise-nizing the Igbo Literary Standard," a review of *Readings on the Igbo Verb* and *Towards an Igbo Literary Standard,* by P. A. Nwachukwu *Uwa Ndi Igbo* I (1984), p. 88.

15. Nolue E. Emenanjo, "After the Blackout: Editorial and Linguistic Problems in *Aka Weta," Uwa Ndi Igbo* I (1984), p. 82.

16. Chinua Achebe, "Editorial and Linguistic Problems in *Aka Weta*: A Comment," *Uwa Ndi Igbo* I, (1984), p. 95.

17. *Ibid* .

18. "Saving the Igbo Language," *Uwa Ndi Igbo* I, pp. 103-4.

19. *Ibid,* p. 104.

20. "The Linguistic Situation and Vernacular Literature in British West Africa," *Africa* 11, 4 (1929), pp. 337-43.

21. *Ibid,* p. 339.

22. Pat Ndukwe, "Stnadardizing Nigerian Languages," *JOLAN* 1 (1982), pp. 141-46.

23. See, for example, Victor Manfredi, "Centre and Periphery in Ika Literacy," *JOLAN* 1 (1982), pp. 175-95.

24. These points are made variously in R. C. Duru, "Geographical Area Variation and Lexicological Enrichment of the Igbo Language," Paper presented at the Workshop "The Foundations of Igbo Civilization," Institute of African Studies, University of Nigeria, Nsukka, May 20-22, 1980; M.J.C. Echeruo, "The Future of Igbo Studies: A Very Modest Proposal," in F. C. Ogbalu and E. N. Emenanjo, eds., *Igbo Language and Culture*, vol. 2 (Ibadan: University Press, 1982), pp. 228-37; Nolue Emenanjo, "Central Igbo—an Objective Appraisal," in *Igbo Language and Culture*, vol. 1 (Ibadan: Oxford University Press, 1975), pp. 114-37; D. Ibe Nwoga, "Dialect Variation and the Development of Written Igbo," in Ogbalu and Emenanjo, eds., *Igbo Language and Culture*, vol. 2, pp. 102-14; F. C. Ogbalu, "Towards Standard Igbo: The Case of the Abagana Dialect," in *Igbo Language and Culture* vol. 2, pp. 98-101; and Bishop G.M.P. Okoye, Address to the SPILC, Enugu, January 27, 1973.

25. Emenanjo, "Central Igbo-an Objective Appraisal," pp 123-25.

26. P. A. Nwachukwu, *Towards an Igbo Literary Standard* (London: Kegan Paul International, 1983), pp. 71-73.

8

Genetic Discontinuity in Achebe's *No Longer at Ease*

Nnadozie F. Inyama

Chinua Achebe's *Things Fall Apart*[1] and *No Longer at Ease*[2] are geneti-
cally linked, not only because the latter novel followed the former in
immediate succession but also because *No Longer at Ease* continues the
saga of Unoka's family history which began in *Things Fall Apart*. One of
the most striking things about these two novels is that, in spite of their small
sizs, Achebe has been able to cram into them the histories of four generations of a family. Although all the characters are not given equal attention,
we still gain enough insight into the essential qualities of Unoka and his
grandson Nwoye, even though they may appear peripheral to the author's
concern with the fates of Okonkwo and Obi, the leading characters in
Things Fall Apart and *No Longer at Ease*.

Although other critics have made valid thematic deductions from the
works in discussion, it is my view that the two novels are as deeply
concerned with family character as with anything else. Perhaps one of the
most remarkable aspects of Igbo social behavior is the people's concern
with family histories. It is a concern which can prove decisive or disastrous
in inter-personal relationships of any depth, whether in business ventures
or marriage alliances. Whether deliberately or inadvertently, Achebe has
succeeded in highlighting this aspect of Igbo cultural behavior through the
way he focuses on the characters of Unoka, Okonkwo, Nwoye, and Obi. But
there are more than enough hints in the novels to indicate that whatever
Achebe shows us in this regard is more deliberate than inadvertent, that he
is, in fact, responding to an ancestral habit that is common to the Igbo
people.

In presenting the histories of Unoka and his descendants, Achebe focuses
on one main family trait—their wilfullness. It is a quality that manifests
itself at various points in the lives of the characters, with varying degrees
of prominence and varying degrees of positive or negative results.

One could be tempted to imagine that this quality of strongmindedness
was missing in Unoka, what with his failure in the whole scheme of manly
qualities and achievements prescribed by the patriarchal code of Umuofia.
The inclination would also be to credit him with nothing of his son's later

achievements. Yet one must not lose sight of the fact that among those who lent yams to Okonkwo to start his farming career were two friends of his improvident father; so that while Okonkwo was a hard man who, we imagine, believed that he had nothing to be grateful to his father for, the warmth which Unoka left in the hearts of his friends turned out to be a source of nourishment for his son. In this regard, C. P. Sarvan[3] has observed that much of what we read of Unoka in *Things Fall Apart* and which might be mistaken for negative authorial judgments are, in fact, Okonkwo's opinion of his father; thus we are led to see him as an unsuccessful man, "lazy and improvident," and a debtor who "owed every neighbour some money," a wanderer whose wife and child barely had enough to eat, and so on. It would also be tempting to believe that Okonkwo's strong will, which carried him to such heights of fame and prosperity, had no source in Unoka. But one has to look more closely at Unoka to see whether this is actually so.

Okonkwo came into the world and saw the lure and magic of fame and bravery, and other masculine values, such as title taking and the possession of numerous wives. Unoka had also seen these things. Both men reacted differently. One must suppose that Unoka was not really blind to these areas of manly achievements, especially the title-taking ceremonies, at which, presumably, he was regularly present, since he was a flutist in the village music group. If Unoka did not run after titles like the rest of the Umuofia men, it was not entirely due to his laziness, even though he once pretended that the gods were responsible for his farming failures. There must have been an element of deliberate indifference in Unoka's mode of life and attitude to these "achievements," an attitude that basically saw them as vain pursuits. At any rate, the title-taking ceremonies resolved ultimately into this: when a man had gathered enough, he paid a certain membership fee to previous title holders, went through some rituals of initiations, and then feasted his neighbors. We are told that Unoka feasted his neighbors whenever "any money came his way" (p. 3), so that in his own way he was doing from time to time the same things which other men spent so much time, energy, and noise to accomplish only once or twice in a lifetime.

However, the more serious point being made is that Okonkwo cannot justifiably claim to owe absolutely nothing of his capacity to sustain his choice of action or belief to his father. Unoka had chosen to stick to a way of life that suited his temperament. In a society that expected a certain uniformity of masculine actions and aspirations, it required a certain strength of will for one to refuse to be drawn into the common pursuit and remain firm in the face of common ridicule. Unoka was even capable of laughing at one of his creditors, a member of his musical group who wanted his money back for yet another title. Again, Sarvan has pointed out that "Unoka expresses the quiet but stubborn courage of non-conformity."

In a society where men of "achievement" and title were the rulers, where even children knew who was an *agbala* and who was a real man, it required a special courage, such as Unoka alone possessed, to be a dropout and not care one bit about it, and even laugh at those who went after much titles with such zest and passion. So that if we admire Okonkwo for the single-mindedness which enabled him to achieve, Unoka, in the final analysis, has to be admired for that "stubborn courage of non-conformity," the courage to be different.

In the case of Unoka or Okonkwo, the choice of a way of life or a line of action is conscious and deliberate and the consequences accepted and accommodated. When Unoka is carried off to the evil forest, for example, he does not struggle or refuse to be carried there. He quietly takes his most valued possession, his flute. One could even speculate that if Unoka had the physical strength in his final days, he would have walked to the evil forest on his own to die, without anyone's urging, quite unlike that other man who had staggered back to the village and had to be taken back and tied to a tree.

Unoka's choice of a mode of life might be considered wrong, but it is sustained till the end and its ignominious consequences accommodated. When Okonkwo could no longer take the insults from the white man and his system, he made a decision to avenge himself, even in the face of the communal disinclination to go along with him. The common trait in Unoka's lineage, varied in its manifestations, is, therefore, the ability to make individual and momentous decisions. How far does this genetic trait survive, and at what point does it break down?

One can look at Nwoye, Okonkwo's son and Unoka's grandson, in the light of the foregoing argument. Nwoye begins to judge his father's ways critically as soon as Ikemefuna is killed. Unoka had chosen a different way of life from the general communal expectations, Okonkwo had in turn judged his father (rather harshly) and taken a different way of life, and had taken a decisive action when he thought his honor needed to be restored. The values that Okonkwo admired in his community are the ones he presents to, and tries to force upon his son, Nwoye. But by his act of killing Ikemefuna, the boy-hostage who had not only established such a close bond with his family but seemed to harbor in him the seeds of all that the community admired when these qualities blossomed, Okonkwo in one swift stroke cut to death any faith which his son might have had in the justness and sincerity of the codes which were being pressed upon him. As soon as the opportunity offers itself, Nwoye swiftly abandons the old codes. His conversion by the missionaries who come to Mbanta becomes an external manifestation of the rejection of his father, a confirmation of an inner spiritual alienation.

That Nwoye could defy a father whom he was so deeply afraid of throughout his young life and that he could take an action that amounted to suicide, or at best a life in the wilderness, are testimonies to his willpower. Even though he had disappointed Okonkwo's hopes of becoming a fierce warrior and a successful man of title and wealth, he had retained Okonkwo's (and Unoka's) ability to choose a line of action and cling tenaciously to it, damning all consequences. Nwoye surely could have remained under the perpetual shadow of his fierce and imperious father, pretending to admire his ways, and thereby betraying his own nature and inclinations. But he firmly chose to escape from a system that was spiritually stifling and even physically threatening to destroy him. In order to leave no one in doubt about the firmness and irrevocability of his resolve, Nwoye abandons his family in Mbanta and returns to Umuofia to live with the Christians. Nwoye's firmness of choice is admirable. But above all, it is a choice he debated alone and within himself, just as his father and grandfather before him would have.

Nwoye reappears in *No Longer At Ease* as Isaac Okonkwo, the father of Obi Okonkwo, the novel's chief protagonist. Obi is the distinguished son of Umuofia, who has achieved the sterling feat of studying in an English university. He comes home to the adulation and expectations of his family and community. Ironically, the distinction which Okonkwo's strong and imperious ways could not achieve in Nwoye has been achieved in his grandson by Isaac Okonkwo's Christian softness.

Obi is faced with problems as soon as he arrives home, most of them financial. These range from the clan union's demand that he start repaying the loan-scholarship money they gave to him, to family demands on his lean finances. For Obi, these become very trying issues, even though one would have expected him to recognize his pioneer status and equip himself, at least psychologically, to cope with such contingencies. Even though the final external event that led to his downfall was the acceptance of a bribe, it is hardly on this that we should examine Obi's ability to retain that peculiar family trait which his forebears had demonstrated. More significantly, we are concerned with Obi's response when he is faced with the challenge of a decisive choice, when his innermost will and capacity for personal decision are put to the test.

Obi's moment of crisis (and, therefore, of choice) arises from his association with Clara. To marry or not to marry an *osu:* that's the issue. While it must be admitted that Obi had faced problems before Clara's revelation of her ancestry, it must also be admitted that these were problems of financial management which made no real demands on his moral center. Was he, after Clara's revelation, going to withdraw his promises of love and marriage because of a primitive and ill-conceived code of social stratification? Especially in the face of his education and supposed enlightenment? There is no doubt in the reader's mind at this point in the story about Obi's spiritual and emotional commitment to Clara. Clara's revelation becomes the point of decision and choice for Obi, the crossroads in their relationship and his life. When Nwoye, his father, was faced with a similar choice in *Things Fall Apart*, that is, remaining with a father to whom he no longer owed any spiritual loyalty and accepting his rigid and apparently violent codes, or following the new but yet unexplored way, which offered him a promise of his finding his true nature, Nwoye looked within himself and chose firmly and swiftly to reject father and tradition. Considering his father's reputation, even while in exile, and the comparative darkness of the age, Nwoye's action was epochal in its pioneering quality.

We could say unequivocally that Obi's education and pioneering status put him in a position to lead his people away from the more unacceptable and irrational practices of society. Isaac (Nwoye) his father had defied home and community to sit in church and mingle with the *osu*, killers of sacred pythons, and rescuers of twins. Obi was thus in a position to deal the death blow to the last of the absurd taboos—the *osu* caste system.

Apart from looking up to Obi for material benefits, the people are also looking up to Obi for a certain kind of leadership. Indeed, what Obi takes as an interference in his private affairs by the Lagos branch of the Umuofia Progressive Union is but their stating of their view of the situation, presentation of one side of the argument. In other words, they are testing Obi's willpower and the quality of his enlightenment. But one can only conclude that when he realized Clara's parentage Obi saw himself as incapable of fighting the battle that would ensue with honesty and conviction. It is true that shortly after Clara's revelation, Obi had gone the next day to buy her an engagement ring and had declared to Joseph, his Umuofia kinsman, that he was still going to marry Clara. But it seems that all these things were merely done to revive a conviction that died when Clara told him the fact. The scene needs to be quoted at some length:

"Why can't you marry me?" He succeeded in sounding unruffled. For answer she threw herself at him and began to weep violently on his shoulder. "What's the matter, Clara? Tell me." He was no longer unruffled. There was a hint of tears in his voice. "I am an osu," she wept. Silence. She stopped weeping and quietly disengaged herself from him. Still he said nothing. "So you see we cannot get married" she said, quite firmly, almost gaily—a terrible kind of gaiety. Only the tears showed she had wept. "Nonsense!" said Obi. He shouted it almost as if by shouting it now he could wipe away those seconds of silence, when everything had seemed to stop, waiting in vain for him to speak. (p. 64)

One notes, also, that when the matter is raised by the Umuofia Union, Obi leaves in a shouting and raving anger. The Igbo have little respect for an adversary who merely shouts, and Obi, if he still had a genuine determination to fight all opposition according to his own enlightened conviction, would have achieved more effect with more quiet and dignified behavior. There is none of that quiet determination which had carried his father to the new faith, or his grandfather to a strong, if somewhat misguided action on behalf of the clan. What Obi sadly loses sight of is the fact that if his Lagos kinsmen were as rigid as they appeared to be, they would have considered his association with Clara up to that point enough reason to ostracize him. If he had stuck to his decision, they would have had to choose between accepting him and his wife—and perhaps later adopting his example—or losing him completely, an "only palmfruit," in the fire. In the face of such a radical development, they would have behaved like an earlier generation of Umuofia people who chose to accommodate the white man and his "abominations" on the land rather than confront him and be liquidated, like Abame. We can only suppose that a certain central weakness in the protagonist prevented him from recognizing his tactical advantages, which would have enabled him to sit, as the Igbo say, *ka odudu bere n' akpa amu* (like a tse-tse fly on the scrotums) of his kinsmen. They could not have afforded to strike him too hard, but would have come to a sensible accommodation with him. Obi's action shows neither calm nor conviction. Privately he overdebates an issue that required only one firm act—marriage to Clara—to force all the opposition to readjust. His weakness reaches the climax of its manifestation when he goes home to Umuofia to discuss the matter with his father. Indeed, Obi's approach to the discussion deteriorates from weakness to dishonesty because he not only deliberately ignores the signs his father shows him, but maneuvers to make the older man make the decision for him.

The discussion between Obi and his father takes place in two stages. The first one is almost impersonal and abstract. They look at the issue from the religious standpoint. While Obi argues that as Christians they are above such absurd taboos and restrictions, his father counters with the argument that in spite of his exalted position, Naaman the Syrian was a leper. Obi fails to clinch the argument by reminding his father that the Syrian leper was made clean when he came into contact with a Jewish prophet, the voice of enlightenment in his age, and that he is, therefore, in an analogous position to cleanse Clara through marriage and also bring light to his people.

In the second phase of the discussion, Isaac Okonkwo cites himself as a model for his son. The final speech and scene will be quoted at length so that one can fully appreciate Isaac Okonkwo's point and the degree of Obi's deliberate misreading of the message in it:

Then his father spoke, but not about the thing that was on their minds. He began slowly and quietly, so quietly that his words were barely audible. It seemed as if he was not really speaking to Obi. His face was turned sideways so that Obi saw it in vague profile.

"I was no more than a boy when I left my father's house and went with the missionaries. He placed a curse on me. I was not there but my brothers told me it was true. When a man curses his own child it is a terrible thing. And I was his first son."

Obi had never heard about the curse. In broad daylight and in happier circumstances he would not have attached any importance to it. But that night he felt strangely moved with pity for his father.

"When they brought me word that he had hanged himself I told them that those who live by the sword must perish by the sword. Mr. Braddeley, the white man who was my teacher, said it was not the right thing to say and told me to go home for the burial. I refused to go. Mr. Braddeley thought I spoke about the white man's messenger whom my father killed. He did not know I spoke about Ikemefuna with whom I grew up in my mother's hut until the day came when my father killed him with his own hands." He paused to collect his thoughts, turned in his chair and faced the bed on which Obi lay. "I tell you all this so that you may know what it was in those days to become a Christian. I left my father's house, and he placed a curse on me. I went through fire to become a Christian. Because I suffered I understand Christianity—more than you will ever do." He stopped rather abruptly. Obi thought it was a pause, but he had finished."(p. 125)

When Obi returns to Lagos he tells Clara that they must wait a little longer. He tells her of the encounter with his parents, and his mother's threat to kill herself if he should marry Clara in her lifetime. We may assume too that he must have mentioned that his father was cursed by his grandfather for rebelling. But Isaac Okonkwo is not threatening to curse his son in the encounter. He is merely making Obi aware of the momentous nature of his decision, if he should stick with it. He presents himself as a model who defied all else to be himself. But he will not make the choice for Obi, which is what Obi is asking for. He does not really approve, but he will certainly accommodate Obi's choice if he should go ahead and marry Clara. As Eustace Palmer has observed, "Although his father expressed complete disapproval, it is obvious that he will be won over in time, since he himself was a rebel."[4] Unfortunately, Obi fails to count his teeth with his tongue, as his people would say, and arrive at the real import of his father's speech. As for his mother's threat to kill herself, even Joseph, Obi's kinsman and staunch defender of Umuofia customs, pooh-poohs it, and it is difficult to imagine her holding firm in the face of an eventual capitulation by her husband. At any rate, the woman herself had once killed a sacred he-goat that was destroying her crops and menacing her household, and cooked it for her family's dinner. The chief priest of the deity that owned the goat had threatened dire consequences and the townspeople had ostracized her for a while. She had ridden out the storm and in the end nothing happened. In other words, Obi has more than one example from his immediate family to emulate in making his decision. Obviously, Obi had not gone to Umuofia to present a decision but to seek a shoulder onto which to shift the responsibility for his unmanliness; this is why one cannot agree with Professor Palmer when he blames Clara for returning Obi's ring, and thus ending the whole farce. Clara has obviously discovered that Obi lacks the essential quality that makes men make bold and controversial decisions, that his wanting to wait further is a tactic whose aim lies in the hope that something might happen to rescue him from his will-less predicament. Indeed, one remembers that after Obi's first meeting with his father, he had looked into himself and found nothing worthy:

He was amazed at the irrelevant thoughts that passed through his mind at this greatest crisis in his life. He waited for his father to speak that he might put up another fight to justify himself. His mind was troubled not only by what had happened but also by the discovery that there was nothing in him with which to challenge it honestly. All day he had striven to rouse his anger and his conviction, but he was honest enough with himself to realize that the response he got, no matter how violent it sometimes appeared, was not genuine. It came from the periphery, and not the centre, like the jerk in the leg of a dead frog when a current is applied to it. But he could not accept the present state of his mind as final, so he searched desperately for something that would trigger off the inevitable reaction. Perhaps another argument with his father, more violent than the first; for it was true what the Ibos say, that when a coward sees a man he can beat he becomes hungry for a fight. He had discovered he could beat his father. (p. 124)

Clara offers Obi a last chance of proving his genuineness when she informs him of her pregnancy, but, predictably, he fails to respond positively, and rather takes her to an abortionist. One wonders what Isaac Okonkwo would have thought of such a line of action.

So, in the most crucial challenge in Obi's life, he fails to emulate his forebears. When the villagers of Umuofia in their admiration declare that Obi is "Ogbuefi Okonkwo come back. . . . Okonkwo *kpom-kwem*, exact, perfect" (p. 49), and that in going to England and obtaining a degree he had been to the land of spirits and wrestled victoriously against them, they are wrong on both counts. When Obi is confronted with the actual wrestling match, he is thrown with disheartening ease. A bowl of pounded yam would have thrown him, as his grandfather would say. As for his being a reincarnation of his grandfather, Okonkwo's real essence (inherited from Unoka and bequeathed to his son Isaac [Nwoye]) breaks down when it gets to Obi. Isaac Okonkwo's Christian retort that "dead men do not return" is ironically true in his son's case, for Obi does not resemble Okonkwo in the crucial qualities. If Unoka died an ignominious death, it was not because he could not make a decision on the type of life he wanted and stick to it. We sympathize with Okonkwo's tragedy because we recognize, in spite of the misguided nature of some of his actions, that he retained till the end the ability to defy both man and fate in the pursuit and sustenance of his beliefs. As Gerald Moore says, "Achebe measures the decline in the simple contrast of Obi and his grandfather; the grandson has more humanity, more gentleness, a wider awareness, but he lacks the force and integrity of his ancestor." While Okonkwo's fall was a real tragedy, Obi's fall is wretched; his tragedy eventually takes place, in his own words, "in a corner, in an untidy spot" of his life (p. 36). Long before he is convicted for bribe taking, he has lost our sympathy and admiration. When he fails to carry through his commitment to Clara, his worth evaporates. The subsequent acceptances of bribes merely emphasize the essential fall. They become a mere quickening of the downward erosion.

According to W.J.M. Mackenzie, "Freedom of choice is not a privilege but a burden; the curse of freedom is imposed on each man alike . . . each man must pick up the burden of identity, authenticity, commitment—or be accused of complicity or bad faith."[5]

Earlier generations of the Okonkwo [(Unoka)] lineage were able to pick up their "burden of identity, authenticity and commitment." In Obi this genetic factor in his lineage breaks down. Achebe concludes *No Longer at Ease* on this ironic note: "Everybody wondered why the learned judge, as we have seen, should not comprehend how an educated young man and so on and so forth. The British Council man, even the men of Unuofia, did not know. And we must presume that in spite of his certitude, Mr. Green did not know either" (p. 153). The reader, however, knows, especially if he had also known Unoka, Okonkwo, and Nwoye.

NOTES

1. London: Heinemann African Writers Series, 1964. All page references are to this edition.

2. London: Heinemann African Writers Series, 1963. All page references are to this edition.

3. C. P. Sarvan, "The Flute and the Matchet," *The International Fiction Review* 4, no. 2 (July, 1977), pp. 155-58.

4. Eustace Palmer, A*n Introduction to the African Novel* (London: Heinemann Educational Books, 1978), p. 70.

5. W.J.M. Mackenzie, *Power. Violence. Decision* (Hammondsworth: Penguin Books, 1975), pp. 186-87.

9

Of Governance, Revolutions, and Victims: Achebe and Literary Activism in *Anthills of the Savannah*

Kalu Ogbaa

Chinua Achebe is one of the few African writers who truly play the role of keepers of the conscience of their people and defenders of the values of individual freedom and human rights. His writings portray him as a conscious artist in the traditional communal sense of the term; and in telling his stories, Achebe adopts a historical approach, which is to say that for anyone to understand the events of the present, he has to know the events of the past. The knowledge of both kinds of events, of course, should enable him to predict events of the future which ultimately are influenced and mediated by those of the past and the present. And because Achebe, as a writer, has this historical sense of events, he tends to use almost the same people and names as characters, the same West African geographical areas as setting; the same gods, goddesses, oracles, and rituals and ceremonies as an expression of the people's religion and cosmology; the same folk songs and tales as well as proverbs as the stylized verbal art of the people. All these folk and traditional elements form the basis of his thematic materials. The result of all that is that Achebe's thematic concerns are predictable and his social commitment easily appreciated.

In an article simply titled "Chinua Achebe," Michael J. C. Echeruo made the following ever-enduring assertion regarding Achebe's works:

Behind his novels, short stories and poems there is this immense presence of a patrimony, a land, a people, a way of life. But while characterizing that land, detailing the history of its many crises, Achebe sees it as the one unchanging feature of the artistic and moral landscape, as the one permanent Being to which all efforts of the children of the land must be devoted. If we recognize this, we can then appreciate why Achebe is not the urban African, why his art is not the art of the metropolis. Rather Achebe is the artist in the communal sense of the term, the man of great wisdom, working within the limits and through the norms of his society as on the universality of his own personal vision.[1]

And in the concluding paragraph of the article, Echeruo predicts: "Given the pattern of Chinua Achebe's development as an artist and as conscience for his people, it would indeed be surprising—it would be doubly disappointing—if his next major work did not deal with that truly traumatic experience: The War." Reflecting on his earlier novels, Achebe once described his generation as "a very fortunate" one in the sense that the past was "still there," even if not "in the same force."[2]

Echeruo, Achebe's critic and countryman, made these assertions out of careful readings of Achebe's works and from his personal knowledge of Achebe the man. However, that "next major work," *Anthills of the Savannah,* was published in Britain in 1987 and in the United States of America in 1988,[3] more than twenty years after *A Man of the People.*[4] Although *Anthills of the Savannah* may not have dealt with "that truly traumatic experience: The War [the Nigerian Civil War]," all the same, it deals with another kind of war: bad governance of the Nigerian nation in particular, and by analogy, other African nations in general; ill-conceived revolutions; and social injustice. Whereas the Nigerian Civil War was ostensibly over in 1970, this second kind of war that *Anthills of the Savannah* deals with is still raging, though not "in the same force." Achebe has to talk about the war against the people, suggesting ways of liberating them and freeing their land. The urgency and immediacy of his literary activism enable him to maintain the "immense presence of a patrimony, a land, a people, a way of life," while he plays the role of "an artist and as conscience for his people" as he has done in his first four novels.

As a matter of fact, Achebe's failure to write about the Nigerian Civil War specifically was a personal choice, not because he was afraid to do so nor because he lacked the artistic capability. In fact, in an interview with Ann Bolsover, he says:

It seemed to me that our history was beginning and since my writing, my fiction, is really my way of recreating history in the modern world I had to come to terms with this new history. I didn't want to write about Biafra. I still don't want to write a novel of the war. I may change my mind later on but I was doing things, all of them with the war, but from the side. Not confronting it properly. And this is something I can't do anything about.[5]

That new history began with the 1966 military coup which became the start of military regimes in Nigeria. Achebe, like Ikem Osodi and Chris Oriko in *Anthills,* suffered untold hardships that shook his faith in his fatherland:

It seemed to me that Nigeria really ceased to be what it was to me six years after Independence, and the excitement, and suddenly you had this blood-letting on a horrendous scale. Before that you had the experience of running away and hiding in your country, which was my own experience. Soldiers came to the radio station in Lagos where I worked to look for me. After all that the country could not be the same. Africa couldn't be the same and I seemed to need some time, a lot of time, to rethink things.[6]

The statement not only explains the long silence between the appearance of *A Man of the People* and *Anthills*. . . . but also preempts the political nature and ambience of the latter novel. Like the fleeing Achebe (from Lagos to Igbo country), Chris Oriko, fleeing (from Bassa to Abazon Province), meets personally the people who own the land, experiences their problems firsthand, and is, thus, disillusioned with the idea that Kangan was owned by the troika, Sam, Ikem, and Chris.

At the very beginning of *Anthills*, readers are introduced to the poor governance of Kangan. Instead of using an omniscient reporter or the I-narrator to tell his tale, Achebe uses Witnesses who happen to be some of the major characters to do so. So we find on page 1 of the novel Christopher Oriko serving as First Witness. The political crime whose fallout the entire novel explores and dramatizes has already taken place. From time to time, though, allusions are made to that crime, and the suspected criminals, as it were, are called in as witnesses to say what they know about it. The effect of this technical device is that the characters, who are also members of the ruling class, are regarded by other members of His Excellency's cabinet as saboteurs; and since the narrator's point of view appears to favor the suspects, the narrator assumes the status of a character before the narratee. The overall effect of the novel's shifting narrative voice on the reader of "conventional" novels is that he becomes confused in picking the narrative thread. We will come to the examination of the narrative technique and style later on.

If one may ask, What is the political crime that has been committed against His Excellency's government and Kangan? A coup, two years ago, gives power to a Sandhurst-trained soldier, Sam, and he becomes the Head of State of Kangan. From then on, Sam is known and addressed as His Excellency or H.E. for short. He chooses a cabinet of Commissioners and senior government officials, including his boyhood friends, Chris and Ikem, to help run his government. Somewhere along the line, His Excellency wants to be President-for-Life. A national referendum is called to decide the issue; Abazon, Ikem's home province, says no to His Excellency's request, and Ikem is suspected by his colleagues in the cabinet to have had a hand in the Abazon provincial verdict. His Excellency "has already deteriorated into a paranoid despot surrounded by a sycophantic cabinet.

Trying to protect his position any way he can, he has created a 'State Research Committee' which is really a secret police."[7] Chris watches His Excellency turning into a dictator, but his own role in the government portrays him as a pacifist. On the other hand, Ikem the poet and journalist writes bold editorials which he thinks can guide the government to take the right types of action toward the downtrodden people of Kangan. Ironically, it is those crusading editorials and his meeting with the delegation from Abazon that earn him the wrath of His Excellency. Ikem is fired as editor of the *National Gazette*.

In reaction to his dismissal, Ikem delivers a speech to the students of the University of Bassa. He is misquoted in a headline, EX-EDITOR ADVO-CATES REGICIDE! Eventually, he is arrested and murdered by the grisly secret police. Chris fears for his life and goes into hiding. From that point of the novel on, His Excellency's role in the governance of Kangan is not very clear. What one reads about is the role of the State Research Council, whose activities plunge the nation into sporadic eruptions of bloody violence. With the help of the sought-after President of the Students Union, Emmanuel, the taxi drivers, and Beatrice, Chris becomes more militant. He dies as he attempts to save a student nurse, Adamma, from being raped by a drunken police sergeant in Abazon; but not before His Excellency's death has been announced. Thus the total overthrow of the triumvirate of Lord Lugard College alumni is completed. All told, His Excellency's government is a military regime. The people have no hand in its formation. The cabinet is made up of His Excellency's personal friends and their nominees whose appointment is a nepotic rather than a democratic act. So, those who are so favored as to be appointed cabinet members must of necessity work to please His Excellency with the mistaken belief that worshiping a dictator assures one of more favor and longer stay on the job. Resultantly, there is infighting in the cabinet: seeds of mistrust, suspicion, and betrayal are sown in His Excellency's mind against Chris and Ikem, who are considered as being closer, therefore more favored, than others to His Excellency. There is a crack in the relationship of the three boyhood friends. Things begin to fall apart because the apparently strong center of the cabinet cannot hold any longer. Ikem is disenchanted with the discharge of public affairs that has been shrouded in secrecy and so he questions its propriety:

At some point he had assumed, quite naively, that public affairs so-called might provide the handle he needed. But his participation in these affairs had yielded him nothing but disenchantment and a final realization of the incongruity of the very term "public" as applied to those affairs shrouded as they are in the mist of unreality and floating above and away from the lives and concerns of ninety-nine percent of the population. Public affairs! They are nothing but the closed transactions of soldiers-turned-politicians, with their cohorts in business and the bureaucracy.[8]

However fatally flawed the government activities are, the functionaries always attempt to legitimize them by claiming that action was taken in the interest and for the well-being of the people, who are usually far away from government. As a political ideologue, Ikem meditates over the hypocritical relationship of the government to the people: "'Of course,' he admitted bitterly, 'we always take the precaution of invoking the people's name in whatever we do. But do we not at the same time make sure of the people's absence, knowing that if they were to appear in person their scarecrow presence confronting our pious invocations would render our words too obscene even for sensibilities as robust as ours!'"9

Indeed, any government that fails to involve the people in the governance of the country is bound to fail; and any government that pretends total commitment to the act of true governance stands condemned even by its own members, when the truth is known. From the outset, one finds that the government of Kangan is flawed. The people know it and fake their loyalty to the government, and, even before its total downfall, Ikem knows that their government is a failure:

The prime failure of this government began to take on a clearer meaning for him. It can't be the massive corruption though its scale and pervasiveness are truly intolerable; it isn't the subservience to foreign manipulation, degrading as it is; it isn't even this second-class, hand-me-down capitalism, ludicrous and doomed; nor is it the damnable shooting of striking railway-workers and demonstrating students and the destruction and banning thereafter of independent unions and cooperatives. It is the failure of our rulers to re-establish vital inner links with the poor and dispossessed of this country, with the bruised heart that throbs painfully at the core of the nation's being.10

Here, Ikem sounds like Achebe in *The Trouble with Nigeria*.11 All the sociopolitical ills that Achebe points out in that book of essays are recreated here in *Anthills*. They include massive corruption, subservience to foreign manipulations, hand-me-down capitalism, government use of force to elicit loyalty from workers and students, and government nonchalance toward the suffering of the masses. Those ills are rife in most West African governments, especially the current military regime in Achebe's home country, Nigeria. The theme of corruption is by now a familiar one in modern African and Nigerian fiction, and it is perfect material for Achebe's polished ironies and fine anger, especially as it touches on the exploration of failed leadership and misrule.

A government such as we have described so far inhibits the people's exercise of their personal and political liberties. It must be noted, however, that although the government may use all coercive agencies such as the

State Research Council to oppress the people (with the mistaken belief that it can survive forever), there is bound to be some struggle by the oppressed for reform, change, or even outright bloody revolution against the oppressors. All the motivation that the people need in order to fight for their right may just be the right leaders and ideas. In *Anthills. . . ,* those who come close to satisfying the yearnings and aspirations of the suffering masses in that direction are Ikem, Emmanuel, Beatrice, the white-bearded leader from Abazon, and Elewa's uncle. The first three represent the modern and urban force, and the last two represent the traditional and rural force. Both forces combine to examine the conditions of the grass-roots people and attempt to protect them against the lies, corruption, and blatant abuse of power of the ruling class.

For his part, Ikem assumes, quite naively, that his editorial appointment, "public affairs so-called might provide the handle he needed" to bring about peaceful changes in some of the government policies so as to ameliorate the people's lot. As that does not produce effectual results, he decides to use people and ideas to bring about the kinds of change he has in mind. The university, being a place for developing leadership and national ideologies, among other pursuits, is where Ikem goes for a hearing. He is warmly greeted, as he is introduced. He is cautious, as he attempts to deliver his message, making sure that his audience that propounds theories and ideas that eventuate in national ideology is itself welleducated in native and workable ideologies, not in parroting and disseminating foreign ones such as "the democratic dictatorship of the proletariat" (*Anthills . . .* p. 155).

Ikem makes an immense speech that symbolizes the best in the old Africa and the new. Like his tribal elder, who speaks in metaphor and ambiguity of the injustice his people are suffering, Ikem addresses the students with subtle, but modern irony.[12] It is a fiery lecture on the failures of revolutionary idealism. Carried away by the overwhelming response of the students, Ikem makes a statement which is interpreted by the authorities as "fomenting revolt." He is so accused because, after the speech, the students are highly motivated to confront the ruling class; they take to the streets and mobilize the silent but powerful majority: the underclass.

One of those so thoroughly reeducated as a result of Ikem's propounded "new radicalism" is Emmanuel Obete, the President of the Students Union. He puts into practical use what he has learned from the speech, editorials, and practical life-style of his mentor, Ikem. His opportunity is the arrest and eventual mysterious death of Ikem. Reacting to that event, Emmanuel aids and abets the escape and activities of Chris, who is wanted by the secret police. In the process, Emmanuel learns how one dies nobly for one's beliefs and, sometimes, one's country. It is he who gives Beatrice the details of the heroic death of Chris and consoles her over it. Emmanuel's role revives the downcast spirit of Beatrice: when the cycle of tyranny ends without necessarily bringing change for the better, "death settles the score, not only for Chris and Ikem [significantly, Emmanuel and Beatrice survive, to represent youth and continuity, those hopes of the future] but also for His Excellency."[13] Indeed, Emmanuel and Beatrice remain to tell the story of the brushfire which they, the proverbial anthills of the savannah, have survived.

Beatrice's actual crusading role begins in chapter 6 of the novel, which is titled "Beatrice." In it, the narrator describes in detail her background; personality; education, relationship with the major characters, Sam, Chris, and Ikem; and general political views. Her first act of rebellion against the government takes place at the Presidential Retreat in Abichi village, where she has been invited by the President to "come and meet Miss Cranford of the American United Press. Lou is in Bassa to see if all the bad news they hear about us in America is true," and to be paraded before Lou and the new power brokers around His Excellency as "the only person in the service, male or female, with a first-class honours in English. And not from a local university but from Queen Mary College, University of London" (*Anthills*, pp. 74-75).

Beatrice notices Lou's impudent relationship with His Excellency and his cohorts and expresses disbelief:

Her manner with His Excellency was becoming outrageously familiar and domi-neering. She would occasionally leave him hanging on a word she had just spoken while she turned to fling another at Major Ossai whom she now addressed only as Johnson. And wonder of wonders she even referred to the Chief of Staff, General Lango, as Ahmed on one occasion. And for these effronteries she got nothing but grins of satisfaction from the gentlemen in question. Unbelievable! (p. 78)

In addition, Beatrice is shocked that Lou, "without any kind of preamble, began reading His Excellency and his subjects a lecture on the need for the country to maintain its present [unpopular, needless to say] levels of foreign debt servicing currently running at slightly more than fifty-one percent of total national export earnings. Why? As a *quid pro quo* for increased American aid in surplus gains for our drought provinces!" (*Ibid*). When Beatrice challenges Lou's views on foreign debt servicing by refer-ring her to Ikem's editorials in the *National Gazette*, Lou calls Ikem "a Marxist of Sorts" who admires Castro of Cuba, who, no matter what he says, never defaults in his obligations to the international banking commu-nity, while he says "Don't pay." And because His Excellency seems to be saying to Lou, "Go on; tell them. I have gone hoarse shouting the very same message to no avail" (p. 79), Beatrice is reminded of the incident of a girl who had remarked to her in England, "Your boys like us, ain't they? My girlfriend saiz it's the Desdemona complex," and decides to fight Lou the new Desdemona "this time itinerant and, worse still, not over some useless black trash in England but the sacred symbol of my nation's pride, such as it was. Corny. So be it!" (pp. 79-80).

What we see here is true nationalism. His Excellency and his high government officials are ridiculed by a foreign female journalist without their knowing that they are! So Beatrice takes His Excellency boldly by the hand and leads him to the balcony railings to the breathtaking view of the dark lake from the pinnacle of the hill, where she tells him her story of Desdemona. She asks His Excellency: "If I went to America today, to Washington DC, would I, could I, walk into a White House private dinner and take the American President hostage. And his Defence Chief and his Director of CIA?" (p. 81). As if to emphasize her patriotic zeal and achievement, Beatrice remarks: "I did it shamelessly. I cheapened myself. God, I did it to your glory like the dancer in a Hindu temple. Like Esther, oh yes like Esther for my longsuffering people" (*Ibid*).

Generally, the trip to His Excellency's retreat offers Beatrice the opportunity to see firsthand all the ills of society that are brought about by poor leadership. For instance, she recollects the arguments Chris and Ikem had over the vast sums spent on the refurbishment of the Retreat—money, incidentally, which had not been passed through the normal Ministry of Finance Procedures (p. 73). Also, she studies at close quarters the behavior of the Director of SRC, Major Johnson Ossai, whom she describes as "reticent," "controversial," and "so excessively obsequious to His Excellency during the dinner"; and that of the Chief of Army Staff, General Ahmed Lange, whom she describes as "more popularly known, more self-assured and more agreeable person altogether." What she learns about His Excellency and his men scares her, and she is apprehensive of the degenerating relationship of Sam, Chris, and Ikem, the "three green bottles standing on the wall." The final events of the novel confirm her fears and careful observations at the dinner. For, it is the Director of SRC who is so reticent and excessively obsequious to His Excellency (for purposes of deceit and betrayal) who arrests, detains, and kills people; and, it is the more popularly known, more self-assured, and more agreeable person (for purposes of the same deceit and betrayal), the Chief of Army Staff, who plans and executes a counter-coup in which His Excellency is killed. After His Excellency dies, he promotes himself President and Head of State. To make his position secure, he gets rid of Major Ossai, who was himself promoted colonel for eliminating Ikem.

Beatrice's peculiar knowledge of people also gives Ikem an insight into the world of women. Ikem acknowledges that she charged him with assigning to women the role of a fire-brigade after the house has caught fire and been virtually consumed, and that that charge has forced him to sit down and contemplate the nature of oppression. At the end of the acknowledgment, Ikem says:

The women are, of course, the biggest single group of oppressed people in the world and, if we are to believe the Book of Genesis, the very oldest. But they are not the only ones. There are others—rural peasants in every land, the urban poor in industrialized countries, Black people everywhere including their own continent, ethnic and religious minorities and castes in all countries. The most obvious practical difficulty is the magnitude and heterogeneity of the problems. There is no universal conglomerate of the oppressed. Free people may be alike everywhere in their freedom but the oppressed inhabit each their own peculiar hell. (pp. 98-99)

While Beatrice inspires Ikem, he in turn inspires her. In fact, it is out of her concern for the oppressed that she helps her boyfriend, Chris, to escape the SRC; dutifully keeps and nurses Elewa when Ikem dies and when she gives birth to Amaechina; as well as naming the child when Elewa's uncle fails to arrive in time for the naming ceremony. Generally, Beatrice's role is service to her friends, Chris and Ikem; to her fellow women, including Elewa and Agatha; to her ethnic group (the Igbo speaking people of the novel); and to her country and her leaders who are ridiculed by modern Desdemonas.

The white-bearded leader of the Abazon delegation plays a role that is important in two ways. First, when at a gathering in Harmoney Hotel Ikem is accused of failing to join in his people's monthly meetings and other social gatherings (so as to direct their ignorant fumblings with his wide knowledge), it is this leader, "tall, gaunt-looking and with a slight stoop of the shoulders," who comes to the defense of Ikem and his profession. To Ikem's accuser he says:

Going to meetings and weddings and naming ceremonies of one's people is good. But don't forget that our wise men have said that a man who answers every summons by a town-crier will not plant corn in his fields. So my advice to you is this: Go on with your meetings and marriages and naming ceremonies because it is good to do so. But leave this young man alone to do what he is doing for Abazon and for the whole of Kangan; the cock that crows in the morning belongs to one household but his voice is the property of the neighborhood. You should be proud that this bright cockerel that wakes the whole village comes from your compound. (p. 122)

What Ikem is doing is that he functions as the editor of the *National Gazette*. He has chosen journalism as a means of carrying out "all the fight he has fought for poor people in this land," and the leader "would not like to hear that he has given up that fight because he wants to attend the naming ceremony of Okeke's son and Mgbafo's daughter" (p. 123).

The defense also underscores the need for people to recognize individual talents—"To everyone his due?. . . . To every man his own! To each his chosen title!"—and natural callings, especially the art of story-telling:

To some of us the Owner of the World has apportioned the gift to tell their fellows that the time to get up has finally come. To others He gives the eagerness to rise when they hear the call; to rise with racing blood and put on their garbs of war and go to the boundary of their town to engage the invading enemy boldly in battle. And then there are those others whose part is to wait and when the struggle is ended, to take over and recount its story.

The sounding of the battle-drum is important; the fierce waging of the war itself important; and the telling of the story afterwards—each is important in its own way. I tell you there is not one of them we could do without. But if you ask me which of them takes the eagle-feather I will say boldly: the story. (p. 123)

This kind of defense and education encourages Ikem to work harder for the people as he produces more editorials in the *National Gazette*. Indirectly, he has been made to regard his editorial appointment as the most important of the cabinet appointments, since that appointment involves "telling stories."

The second significance of the leader's role is embodied in the story "The Tortoise Who Was About to Die." The story is about the struggle of the underclass against their oppression by the ruling class. It teaches people how to fight for their liberation, which could result in either sociopolitical liberty or noble deaths: *"Because even after I am dead I would want anyone passing by this spot to say, yes, a fellow and his match struggled here"* (p. 128). Abazon is oppressed by His Excellency's despotic government. Although the people suffer the worst drought in the history of Kangan and need some assistance from the government, they do not expect to receive any because they did not support His Excellency's ambition to become President-for-Life. Yet they have to send a delegation to His Excellency instead of standing still. In other words, the delegation is a form of struggle which may not result in practical solutions to their numerous problems, but it does give them some psychological satisfaction: so "that those who come after us will be able to say: *True, our fathers were defeated but they tried"* (p. 128).

A story such as the leader (symbol of age and tradition) tells to Ikem and his people in Bassa (symbol of youth and inexperience) exhorts Ikem to literary activism. And when he is dismissed as editor of the *National Gazette*, he does not take it lying down. He goes to the university to make a speech, a move which is comparable to the tortoise's going "into strange action on the road, scratching with hands and feet and throwing sand on the road furiously in all directions." Ikem's message goes in the directions of Emmanuel, Chris, Beatrice, Captain Abdul, Medina, and the taxi drivers and changes their entire lives (p. 223). They all co-operate in their individual ways and roles to fight the establishment and give hope to posterity.

In his own way, Elewa's uncle, who is another old man from the countryside, adds a new dimension to the type of education that the young men of Abazon in Bassa receive from the leader of the Abazon delegation. This second old man makes a speech in the naming ceremony of Amaechina which touches on the survival of the people. One way of surviving the modern world is for one to adjust to changes that occur from time to time in the society. When he hears that *the people* have already done his work of naming the child, he does not grow angry, especially as he can still receive the rewards of the service that "All of Us" does for him. He does not fret just because

people gather in this whiteman house and give the girl a boy's name . . . [p. 227]; for, that has been done by the people in the interest of the people. The overall import of the old man's speech as Beatrice perceives it is that "This world belongs to the people of the world not to any little caucus, no matter how talented. . . ." For she says: "It is the same message Elewa's uncle was drumming out this afternoon, wasn't it? On his own crazy drum, of course. Chris, in spite of his brilliance, was just beginning to be vaguely aware of people like that old man. Remember his prayer? He had never been inside a whiteman house like this before, may it not be his last." (p. 232)

As he says prayers before breaking the kola nut, the old man refers to the root causes of national disunity: namely, religious bigotry and intolerance, poor and selfish national planning, and ethnic bickerings. All those problems he prays against so that Kangan may once again enjoy peace, harmony, and security. As a matter of fact, before the old man joins in the naming ceremony, the effort toward national unity of all ethnic and religious groups for which the old man prays had already started. The group includes Igbo, Hausa, and Yoruba people who are also Christians, Moslems, and the "priestess of the unknown god" in ecumenical fraternization (p. 224). But what the old man's prayer does is to reinforce the importance of the ethnic and religious unity that should result in national unity, and to elicit from the up-and-coming leaders a pledge for its realization.

Achebe handles the theme of victimization from the very first page of *Anthills* through the last page. There are group victims, class victims, and individual victims. When the novel opens, readers hear His Excellency tell Chris, "You're wasting everybody's time, Mr Commissioner for Information. I will not go to Abazon. Finish! *Kabisa!* Any other business?" (p. 1). Later on, readers are made to understand that Abazon is a province whose citizens are drought victims. Everybody suffers the effect of the worst drought in Kangan, and yet the government does not come to their aid. And when, eventually, a delegation of six Abazon leaders goes to Bassa in order to say yes to His Excellency's request, the leaders are put away in jail. They are accused of collaborating with Ikem, who is charged with the crime of advocating regicide. The leaders are not released on bail pending trial nor are they given any opportunity for legal defense. There are for the leaders' isolation and deprivation abroad, and hunger and death at home for all Abazon citizens.

The leaders are thus sacrificed because of the political "indiscretion" of their people and the inordinate political ambition of His Excellency the President. The Abazon leaders' imprisonment adds more tension to the already tense society that faces starvation and extermination. Men, women, and children all suffer from the consequences of a political decision that they all may not have taken part in. It seems as if their suffering is group karma.

The leader is a storyteller. He tells tales of survival techniques, in the face of formidable adversity. His story does not give prescriptions for their suffering; instead, it gives headaches! That is why Ikem will in future determine more and more to make a speech that does not augur well for the survival of the oppressive ruling class. Ordinarily, anyone seeing what has happened to the leaders of Abazon in Bassa would think that other political enemies of the government would be cowed into fear, as is the intention of the government that is rapidly turning Bassa into a police state. Instead, the people gain strength through the suffering of the great storyteller, and there is a greater degree of suspicion and distrust of the government.

The underclass of Kangan are the class victims. The author's first graphic description of this category of victims occurs in chapter 4 of the novel in which the Second Witness—Ikem Osodi—discusses the barbarism of the public execution of armed robbers, which is becoming mass entertainment on the beach. Ikem is opposed to it and writes powerful editorials attacking all forms of capital punishment. On the other hand, his colleague Chris charges that Ikem is a romantic, "that the ordinary people of Kangan believed firmly in an eye for an eye and that from all accounts they enjoyed the spectacle that so turned my stomach" (p. 39).

While Chris misreads the apparent enjoyment of the oppressed class, Ikem expresses anger over the ease with which the ruling class has adopted attitudes of the white colonialists when he rhetorically asks:

How does the poor man retain his calm in the face of such provocation? From what bottomless wells of patience does he draw? His great humour must explain it. This sense of humour turned sometimes against himself, must be what saves him from total dejection. He had learnt to squeeze every drop of enjoyment he can out of his stony luck. And the fool who oppresses him will make a particular point of that enjoyment: *You see, they are not in the least like ourselves. They don't need and can't use the luxuries that you and I must have. They have the animal capacity to endure the pain or, shall we say, domestication.* The words the white master had said in his time about the black race as a whole. Now we say them about the poor. (p. 40)

Here Achebe, through Ikem, is commenting on the victimization complex of the poor, that is, the poor's accepting their suffering as if it were the natural order. But behind that apparent animal capacity to endure pain is the poor men's quiet but cynical rebuff of the ruling class's inhumanity to them. That is why toward the end of the novel Chris's companion can counsel a policeman on a checkpoint—an agent of oppression—who laments that he has no motorcycle:

Make you no mind. No condition is permanent. You go get. Meself as I de talk so, you think say I get machine? Even common bicycle I no get. But my mind strong that one day I go jump bicycle, jump machine and land inside motor car! And somebody go come open door for me and say *yes sir!* And I go carry my belle like woman we de begin to pregnant small and come sitdon for owner-corner, take cigarette put for mouth, no more kolanut, and say to driver *common move!* I get strong mind for dat. Make you get strong mind too, everything go all right.

And to Chris, the Commissioner for Information—another government agent—whom he teaches how to escape arrest by the police: "Ehe! Talkam like that. No shaky-shaky mouth again. But oga you see now, to be big man no hard but to be poor man no be small thing. Na proper wahala. No be so?" Chris, having undergone some transformation mentally and physically, concurs with his companion's views when he says, "Na so I see-o. I no know before today say to pass for small man you need to go special college" (p. 194)—an opportunity which his trip north to Abazon province offers to him.

The brutalization of Kangan society by its government officials turns every individual, low or high, into a victim. Sam, His Excellency the President, for example, is a victim of his own inordinate political ambition. Up until the time he becomes Head of State, he is described as a man who insists that things be done right; but he is so distant from the dispossessed of the country—"The crippled kindred in the wild savannah"—and from his cabinet members that he is unable to ensure that things are, indeed, done

right. Even in his dealings with his government officials, he is seen to be
paranoid but certainly not depraved. In fact, he exhibits qualities that prove
that he is at the helm of his government affairs from time to time; but he is
also credulous to a point of being fooled into mistrusting and hating his
close friends. His lusty credulity, therefore, makes him rely more and more
on the secret police for the day to day running of his government, and that
brings about his total undoing.

Chris is as distant from the masses as His Excellency. However, from
Beatrice's account, he is a very intelligent and debonair person. His
inability to hurt a person prevents him from seeing and challenging the
inhumane treatment of the masses by the government as quickly and as
clearly as Ikem does. Hence he calls the more militant Ikem a "romantic."
It is the same pacifistic attitude toward people, especially His Excellency,
that prevents him from resigning from His Excellency's cabinet, despite
Ikem's prodding. He does not obey His Excellency's order to fire Ikem from
his editorial appointment. It is only when Ikem has been abducted and
murdered that he gets near the people and becomes militant. Even at that,
his militancy is short-lived; but his act of defending and dying for the weak
and young is a mark of heroism that is so powerful in banding the young men
and women who are the future hope of Kangan.

Ikem, the moral embodiment of the novel and keeper of the conscience of
the society, is the one character who initiates much of the political action
of the novel which the Head of State considers subversive; therefore, Ikem
must be punished for it. In a way, Ikem suffers a kind of monomania in the
sense that he knows how dangerous the role that he is playing can be and
still he stubbornly continues with it. John Gross remarks, "A real-life Ikem
would surely have been more deeply compromised by his role as editor of
a semi-official paper; and though the fictional Ikem has his inner doubts, his
reflections tend to be impossibly abstract and wordy."[14] That may be true
but readers do not forget that "Ikem is also Achebe's alter ego," who
believes that "a genuine artist, no matter what he says he believes, must feel
in his blood the ultimate enmity between art and orthodoxy." Ikem longs for
union "with earth and earth's people." His love of truth and people tran-
scends political ideology, and he becomes a popular hero among students
after Sam dismisses him from the *Gazette*.[15]

Ikem dies because, according to Lee Leseaze, "Mr. Achebe also puts his
faith for a better future in an old tradition: storytelling." Stories are what
make us different from cattle, he tells us. What's more: "Storytellers are a
threat. They threaten all champions of control, they frighten usurpers of the
right-to-freedom of the human spirit—in state, in church or mosque, in
party congress, in the university or wherever."[16] Indeed, Ikem falls a victim
but his truth changes the world of men and ideas, and from the time he dies
Kangan is never its old self again. That is why his death is a precursor to
those of Chris and Sam.

All three men rose to power together, and all three die at the end of the revolution, thereby falling from power together. Commenting on their demise, Neal Ascherson observes that "in their very different ways, the three boys from Lord Lugard College have all expiated the sin that two of them recognized but one did not": that "failure to re-establish vital inner links with the poor and dispossessed." The three murders, useless as they are, represent the departure of a generation that compromised its own enlightenment for the sake of power—"even the power of bold opposition enjoyed by Ikem Osodi."[17] However, the other characters such as Beatrice, Elewa, Agatha, Emmanuel, and Abdul, who attempt to re-establish vital inner links with not just the poor and dispossessed but also the aged and the storytellers, are scourged but not murdered.

In addition to the three men, there are other individual victims in the novel: Beatrice, who loses her friends and intellectual companions, Chris and Ikem; Elewa, who loses her common-law husband, Ikem; Emmanuel, who loses his political mentor and revolutionary comrade, Ikem and Chris, respectively; and Amaechina, born posthumously to Ikem, are all victims of bad governance and misrule. Their unbearable pains are vividly described by the narrator and through the interior monologues of the victims themselves:

She looked at each in turn with a strained smile on her countenance. "Truth is beauty, isn't it? It must be, you know, to make someone dying in that pain, to make him . . . smile. He sees it and it is. . . . How can I say it?. . . . It is unbearably, yes *unbearably* beautiful. That's it! Like Kunene's Emperor Shaka, the spears of his assailants raining down on him. But he realized the truth at that moment, we're told, and died smiling . . . Oh my Chris!"

Two lines of tears coursed down under her eyes but she did not bother to wipe them. (*Anthills*, p. 233)

Any writer who thinks and writes the way Chinua Achebe has in *Anthills of the Savannah* is bound to offend one category of his readers or another and, therefore, must suffer one form of victimization or another, in one time or another. And since there are clear indications in the novel that Achebe's sympathy is with Ikem Osodi, critics may tend to regard Ikem as Achebe's spokesman. Therefore, whatever political and activist views Ikem expresses about Kangan (which some readers think resembles Achebe's native Nigeria) must be Achebe's personal views on that government. Hence, Achebe should, and ought to, expect on the one hand the kind of victimization that Ikem suffers in the novel, and, on the other hand, unfair critical reception by those who do not understand, or deliberately fail to

appreciate, the true role and burden of a committed third world writer like
Achebe.

That is why, in spite of the generally favorable critical comments on
Achebe's achievements in *Anthills*,[18] one can still read unfavorable comments on the novel such as the following:

Achebe's doubtlessly heart-felt message also gets in the way of *Anthills'* success
as fiction. For the most part, he speaks with the diction and verve of a first-rate
novelist; at other times, he's far too earnestly didactic, given to rhetorical comment
on the nature of tyranny, the plight of the poor and the dispossessed. . . . The trouble
with this kind of language is that it may reverse priorities, making editorializing
more important than the thrust of the narrative.[19]

Indeed, what Ken Adachi calls reversal of priorities is only a fault from
the *purist's* point of view; yet, judged from Achebe's overall aim and
technique in *Anthills*, it is rather an innovation. Achebe does not allow an
omniscient reporter to tell the tales of the novel. Instead, he wants the
participants to tell their own tales as they play the roles of witnesses. It is
a conscious choice that Achebe the artist has made, which means that to him
editorializing becomes an important weapon for bringing the testimonies of
the participants in the poor governance (which is a shared experience)
together. That is also why the narrative voice shifts from time to time,
making the authenticity of the tales depend on the candor of the characters
themselves and not on the assumed authority of the narrator.

By "editorializing" rather than "dramatizing" the events of the novel,
Achebe adds a new dimension to the art of novel writing. That is why he
declares to a *Daily Texan* reporter, "Basically, I have come to the conclusion that the novel, the form, can carry more than we have tended to give it.
Perhaps we have not been bold enough in assigning tasks to the novel.[20]
Nevertheless, the type of task he assigns to the novel makes novel writing
a highly political art, but he practices it with courage, despite the danger he
has endured in the past. He knows that "it is more dangerous to be a writer
in Africa than in America," and illustrates that assertion by recounting how
he had "predicted" the first Nigerian military coup in *A Man of the People*,
and six months later, when a counter-coup took place, some of those who
suffered from the first coup figured that if he was able to predict the
takeover, he must have been part of it. So armed soldiers went to the radio
studios where he worked looking for him, but he was at home. Staff
members telephoned him immediately. "They said that there were two
drunken armed soldiers there who wanted to know if my pen was as strong
as their guns," Achebe recalls.[21]

Achebe's victimization includes his being denied some honors that he highly deserves. For example, in January 1988, Achebe left the University of Massachusetts and returned to Nigeria, flown there by Lagos State University, which was to award him an honorary degree at an academic convocation. A day before the ceremony, the government ordered the university to cancel it. The university was never given a reason for the cancellation. "The newspapers speculated that I was too controversial and that that was the reason for the cancellation," Achebe says. "I think the newspaper speculation is accurate."[22]

While that deprivation was going on in Achebe's home country, a knowledgeable foreign critic who had just read *Anthills* was making a passionate case abroad for an international award for Achebe. In an article, "Africa and the Nobel Prize," Bernth Lindfors writes:

Chinua Achebe thus appears to be the only viable candidate from black Africa remaining [without the award], but many feel that he is easily the best and most deserving of high literary honors. Indeed, one suspects he would have won the Nobel Prize years before Soyinka did, had he continued writing at the pace at which he started. . . . However, the Nigerian Civil War threw him off his stride, turning him away from long fiction to poetry, essays, short stories, and children's books. Because he had made his initial impression with the novel some critics ignored these briefer works (even though several of them won major prizes) and persuaded themselves and others that he had stopped writing altogether. . . . Anyone doubting his present creative vitality should take a look at *Anthills of the Savannah*, a powerful new novel he published a few months ago. Nominated immediately for England's Booker Prize, it may well become the definitive treatment in fiction of military rule in Africa. Such evidence of undiminished literary prowess may also soon put Achebe, Africa's premier novelist, back into contention for the Nobel Prize. He certainly merits the most serious consideration.[23]

Lindfors writes the way he has because Achebe's writing does not threaten him; instead it serves as a study of how power corrupts itself and in doing so begins to die.

Anthills is an important novel in a lot of ways. "Considered in terms of Achebe's body of works it replays familiar scenarios. There seems, however, to have been a maturing of Achebe's perceptions about politics and the human condition."[24] Indeed, it is a maturing that derives from the author's meeting firsthand with the suffering masses during the Nigerian Civil War, and from the practical experience he gained during the brief period he served as a party official of the PRP. Both types of experience and his almost natural sympathy for the poor and the dispossessed all combine to deepen his natural creative sensibility. The result is that Achebe is

enabled to articulate a mature view of governance, revolutions, and victimization.

Hence in *Anthills*, he emphasizes that the strength of the human race is its
unpredictability: "man's stubborn antibody called surprise. Man will surprise by his capacity for nobility as well as for villainy." For that reason, all
that can be done is to understand what cannot be done, that all total solutions
fail and that therefore "we may accept a limitation on our actions but never,
under no circumstances, must we accept restrictions on our thinking" (p.
223).

Playing his usual self-imposed role of the novelist as teacher, Achebe has
used *Anthills of the Savannah* as a forum to discuss the issue of bad
governance and misrule in most West African countries and how it has
destroyed many rulers, crippled their national economy, inhibited the
citizens' political liberty, and turned both the ruler and the ruled into
victims. In the end, Achebe does not prescribe revolution as the solution to
the hydra-headed problems of the nations; for he says through Ikem:
"Experience and intelligence warn us that man's progress in freedom will
be piecemeal, slow and undramatic. Revolution may be necessary for taking
a society out of an intractable stretch of quagmire but it does not confer
freedom, and may indeed hinder it" (p. 99).

Through the discussions and conversations of the characters and the
commentaries of the narrator, Achebe has told us West Africans where the
rain started to beat us. Now we know; we ought to get to our destination
quicker.

NOTES

1. Bruce King and Kalawole Ogungbesan, *A Celebration of Black and
African Writing* (Zaria, Nigeria: Ahmadu Bello University Press, 1978), p.
151.

2. *Ibid.*, p. 162.

3. *Anthills of the Savannah* (London: Heinemann Educational Books Ltd,
1987; New York: Anchor Press/Doubleday, 1988). The edition that we
have adopted in this discussion and out of which we have quoted passages
is that of Heinemann Educational Books Ltd., the African Writers Series,
1988.

4. *A Man of the People* (London: Heinemann Educational Books Ltd.,
1966).

5. *Africa Events* vol. 3, no. 11 (November, 1987), p. 76.

6. *Ibid.*, p. 76.

7. *The Washington Times*, February 15, 1988, p. E8.

8. *Anthills of the Savannah*, p. 141.

9. *Ibid.*, p. 141.

10. *Ibid.*

11. Chinua Achebe, *The Trouble with Nigeri.* (Enugu, Nigeria: Fourth Dimension Publishing Co. Ltd., 1983).

12. *The Sunday Times* (London), September 20, 1987, p. 56.

13. *Ibid.*, p. 56.

14. *The New York Times*, February 16, 1988.

15. Charles Johnson expresses this view in *The Washington Post*, February 7, 1988, p. 10.

16. *The New York Times*, February 16, 1988.

17. *The New York Review*, March 3, 1988, p. 4.

18. Details of the favorable critical views can be seen in the blurbs of the three editions of the novel.

19. See Ken Adachi's comments in *The Sunday Star,* January 21, 1988, p. A21.

20. *The Daily Texan*, Friday, February 19, 1988, p. 11.

21. For details, see *The Hartford Courant*, Monday, May 16, 1988, pp. C1 and C8.

22. *Ibid.*, p. C8.

23. For the full argument, see *World Literature Today* (Spring 1988), pp. 222-24.

24 . See Charles Johnson's review of *Anthills* in *The Washington Post*, February 7, 1988, p. 10.

10

The Theme of Victimization in Select African Plays and Novels

Emmanuel Obiechina

Victimization is one of the main themes of African literature. African written works and oral tales and fables abound in examples of individuals, willing and unwilling, young as well as adult, male no less than female, who are occasionally sacrificed to the needs of society, to the pressures of tradition, or to the exigencies of religion. They may be sacrificed to sustain the despotism of community, the all-consuming egotism of a dictator, or the absolutism of an idea.

Modern African writers no less than traditional artists have devoted considerable attention to this question of the victimization of the individual. In their role as the keepers of the conscience of the group and defenders of the values of individual freedom and human rights, they are not indifferent to a phenomenon which is neither hypothetical nor restricted to folklore. They are not indifferent to a situation that challenges their integrity and vision as humanists and moral legislators of their people.

One point deserves to be made from the onset. The society, community, or group that sacrifices its members is already in a state which students of man and society would identify with absence of good health. A society, group, or community under pressure or in a state of tension is likely to sacrifice some of its members in its state of nervousness. It is, therefore, not difficult to see why victimization should assume such prominence in a continent that has undergone such severe and sustained stresses and convulsions. African history in the last five hundred years has been the history of a number of serious disasters, and, therefore, a history of numerous victims.

Starting with the slave trade, the African peoples have probably produced more human victims than any other race of mankind in recent times. Imperialism and white racism on the continent have also brought their own dimensions of human wastage. More recently still, the emergence of post-independence black dictatorships and bad governments has brought new styles and degrees of human destruction that provide additional material for writers whose role it is constantly to explore and evaluate the state of social and psychological health.

African writing, from the very beginning, has been the literature of victims. From the texts left behind by the eighteenth-century and nine-teenth-century Africans, texts made up mainly of autobiographies and autobiographical fragments, it is easy to observe the pervasive insecurities among individuals who were suddenly uprooted from their familiar sur-roundings and transported to the hostile, wider world of the Americas, the Caribbean, and the West Indies.[1]

It would, of course, be unrealistic to assume that traditional Africa, even if it did not undergo these upheavals, would have been completely free of victims. No human society, no matter how stable and well organized, could be without any victims whatsoever, for the simple reason that no human society has so far attained a perfect state of stable equilibrium between itself and its numerous individuals. Traditional society never was, nor has it since become, the idyllic paradise of the romantic imagination. It has always had within it certain conditions that made the sacrifice of chosen victims inevitable. African realistic artists are not deceived into striking a purely idyllic pose when they appraise the position of the marked individu-als within the traditional and modern societies on the continent.

African literary texts present the reader with two faces of victimization: collective victimization or the conversion of large segments of society into victims, and particularized victimization of single, isolated individuals. Collective victimization is sinister enough and embodies the terror that goes with any form of victimization, but, because of its public and gener-alized nature, it operates less oppressively on the psyche than the more isolated and particularized case of individual victims.

In one respect, however, collective and individual victimization cannot be neatly separated. Collective victimization tends to form a background to individual victimization and to reinforce it emotionally and psychologi-cally. Where the group has already been victimized and has a consciousness conditioned by that experience, as in the case with the blacks in apartheid South Africa or the subjects of the post-independence African dictators, victimization of separate individuals is taken for granted and regarded as an extension of group victimization. In fact, the individual tends to develop a victimization complex, which makes him almost expect to be victimized, as if it were a natural order of things.

African writers deal with victimization on the two levels of the group and the individual consciousness. The theme is explored mainly in plays and novels because these are forms which offer full scope for the exploration of human experience in its extended dimension with the possibility of attain-ing a statement or clarification of a specific human condition or predicament. Each writer determines which form might be more appropriate to his conception of this theme. There is no doubt, however, that a writer's conception of the meaning and nature of victimization goes a long way to determine for him whether the drama form or the novel form should be adopted. Where the scope of action in the treatment of the theme requires a detailed portrayal of the environment and atmosphere of victimization, the novel, which is an elaborative form, has generally proved advantageous, but in respect to symbolic or ritual approach, the drama form has generally been favored. The novel offers the widest scope possible for the examination of the conditions that give rise to the sacrifice of human victims and can track down motives and psychological factors which give significance and depth to action, while plays operate almost in the opposite directions, through a process of condensation, and use of associative and symbolically worked out movements and gestures. The three plays discussed here all deal with the victimization of individuals within traditional societies, while the two novels studied explore the predicament of the outstanding but doomed individual within the transitional society or in the vitiated world of post-independence dictatorship.

SELECT PLAYS

I have selected three plays—Wole Soyinka's *Death and the King's Horseman* and *The Strong Breed* and Tsegaye Gabre-Medhin's *Oda-Oak Oracle*—to see how their authors deal with the question of victimization. These works offer a fair sample of victimized characters and examples of situations and circumstances that make the sacrifice of human victims possible. They demonstrate that traditional societies existed in a metaphysical context which recognized the continuity between the past, the present, and the future, and, correspondingly, between the dead, the living, and those yet to be born. These societies widely accepted the need for occasional sacrifices to ease communication between the three stages of the continuum. On the other hand, it is also shown that outside the metaphysical context human beings are often prepared to lay aside all consideration of humanity and to sacrifice human victims to sustain their personal well-being.

Death and the King's Horseman, The Strong Breed, and *Oda-Oak Oracle* start from the traditionally accepted concept of sacrifice as a necessary ritual for cleansing society and oiling the wheel of transition that ensures the stability of the world. The writers examine the motives and attitudes involved and, at times, the suppressed pain, hopes, and fears which may be the features of these sacrificial rituals. They deal directly, and in varying levels of artistic subtlety, with the sort of life which specializes "in finding scapegoats for anything that steered it from its dreary course."[2]

Each of the three plays is set in a communal society. The communal society is governed by custom, which, in turn, is sustained by an ancestral code of laws and conventions. The ancestors rule the world from the land of the dead and because they also enforce the code by remote control; all manner of intermediaries and interpreters including oracles, priests, diviners, and elders exist to determine their precise intentions, especially during difficult moments when real or hypothetical threats exist against the metaphysical order. The communal world is like an orb delicately poised on a tripod. One leg of the tripod represents the dead, the second leg represents the living, and the third leg represents those yet to be born. If any of the legs suddenly gives way, the equilibrium is upset and the orb falls to pieces. It is the duty of the living to ensure that all three legs of the tripod are kept firmly fixed in their places in order to ensure the safety and stability of the world. The easiest way to upset the delicate balance is for the living to offend against the ancestral laws and conventions. That would bring instant reprisals against the living, imperil the future of those yet to be born, and create an upheaval in the land of the dead.

Each play explores, explicitly, the metaphysical determinism of the communal world. In *Death and the King's Horseman*, the world trembles at the brink of the abyss when Elesin Oba, the King's Horseman, fails to commit sacrificial suicide in accordance with the ancient custom which demands that the King's Horseman must accompany the king to the other world after the king's death. The metaphysical world-order is threatened in the *Oda-Oak Oracle* when Shanka, the strong son of the tribe who had had a bride chosen for him by the Oracle of Oda Oak, refuses "to know the warmth of his bride" because the same oracle has prophesied that the first-born son of the marriage would be sacrificed to the ancestors. The attempt to forestall the "ordained" course of events leads not to one death but to the sacrifice of four people. *The Strong Breed* presents two perspectives on the ritual significance of "the carrier" in traditional society, the recognition of the necessity for an individual to be "sacrificed" for the sake of society at large.

All three plays assume the ritual necessity of sacrifice of victims for the good of the communal society. In the details of presentation, however, the circumstances and inner rhythms of each action differ considerably from those of the others; so do the motives and attitudes that underscore each drama. These differences are seen most clearly when the plays are considered separately.

Death and the King's Horseman

Soyinka explores the theme of victimization in *Death and the King's Horseman* from various perspectives. There is the metaphysical, communal perspective which admits without question the archaic custom that demands that the Horseman of the Alaafin should accompany the Alaafin at his death to the other world. Then there is the perspective on the individual caught in the web of personal dilemma when it falls to his lot to become the sacrificial victim to serve what might appear to be other people's well-being. The outsider's perspective is present when the action is viewed from a position of ignorance attended by skepticism.

In the Author's Note to the Eyre Methuen edition of the play, Soyinka inserts this interpretative guide, meant, no doubt, to lead the producer into the heart of the play and through the dense and tangled tissue of Yoruba metaphysics which constitutes the intellectual underpinning of the action: "The confrontation in the play is largely metaphysical, contained in the human vehicle which is Elesin and the universe of the Yoruba mind—the world of the living, the dead, and the unborn, and the numinous passage which links all transition. Death and the King's Horseman can be fully realized only through an evocation of music from the abyss of transition."

The Note is beneficial. The producer who adopts a purely secular and "materialist" view of the play will experience difficulty, very much in the manner of the Polkings who, with the best of intentions and in an effort to do good, doubly confound the tragedy of those they set out to save. And not only producers but also critics who underestimate the metaphysical implications of the action will have great difficulty evaluating it. One has recently begun to hear epithets like "feudalistic" and "reactionary" being flung at Soyinka from the radical inkpots of some Nigerian critics. They are appalled that a writer of modern perceptions should use his gifts to sustain an archaic and outmoded worldview which sacrifices individuals to the "capriciousness" of a feudalpatriarchal social order.

It is not really necessary to attempt a detailed defense of Soyinka beyond saying that it is reasonable to absolve him from the more damnable imputations. Soyinka has done what any conscientious writer ought to do, which is to explore, with artistic fidelity, the historical event of 1946 (or was it 1944?) when the Elesin Oba destroyed his own life to sustain the old tradition of his people after the intervention of the British authority nearly caused a serious civic disorder. He has examined the underlying motives and underlined the intellectual and emotional impulses that conditioned the responses of those involved, with a view to wringing out of the reconstructed drama the widest range of meaning and significance. If in doing this Soyinka has chosen to lean heavily toward a metaphysical interpretation of the action, it must be that a metaphysical interpretation is the one calculated to present it more truthfully and significantly than a purely secular and physical interpretation that might in the end trivialize the experience, as well as misrepresenting the true feelings of the dramatis personae.

The traditional perspective defines the main line of the action. All the traditional characters—the Iyaloja, the Praise-Singer, Elesin Oba himself; and Olunde, Elesin's eldest son studying medicine in England—accept the custom of sacrificial suicide and the metaphysical view underlying it. They all accept the cosmic unity of all existence as a first principle, which is that a metaphysical link exists between the dead, the living, and the unborn. When Elesin fails to fulfil his "destiny," partly because of his disinclination and partly because of his arrest by the District Officer, the Iyaloja accuses him of overturning the ordered course of the communal world:

He (Elesin) knows the peril to the race when our dead father, who goes as intermediary, waits and waits and knows he is betrayed. He knows when the narrow gate was opened and he knows it will not stay for laggards who drag their feet in dung and vomit, whose lips are reeking of the left-overs of lesser men. He knows he has condemned our king to wander in the void of evil with beings who are enemies of life.[3]

The Praise-Singer is even more emphatic in condemning the Horseman: "You sat with folded arms while evil strangers tilted the world from its course and crashed it beyond the edge of emptiness . . . you left us floundering in a blind future. . . . Our world is tumbling in the void of strangers. . . ." (p. 75). Everyone, except the outsiders, recognizes the connection between the self-sacrifice of the Horseman and the mystical welfare of the community, the preservation of the cosmic stability of the communal world. Olunde more than anyone else expresses the view that physical welfare is not unrelated to metaphysical peace. This comes out in the very long debate between him and Jane Polkings, in which the insider's and outsider's perspectives are sharply contrasted:

Ever since I learnt of the King's death I've lived with my bereavement so long now that I cannot think of him [his father] alive. On that journey on the boat, I kept my mind on my duties as the one who must perform the rites over his body. I went through it all again and again in my mind as he himself has taught me. I didn't want to do anything wrong, something which might jeopardize the welfare of my people (p. 57).

It is when this "welfare of the people" is put in jeopardy by his father's failure to perform the expected sacrifice that he himself takes over and pays with his own life.

Elesin recognizes the duty which is thrust upon him by tradition. It is a duty doubly reinforced by the demands of honor. He has enjoyed peculiar privileges as the king's companion and is quick to admit that these privileges are sometimes as great as those of the king himself: "Where there was plenty I gorged myself. My master's hands and mine have always dipped together. . . . We share the choicest of the season's Harvest of yams . . ." (p. 14). And later still, as if to emphasize the point more, the Elesin underlines his obligation to fulfill a pact rooted in friendship as well as in honor:

> Life has an end. A life that will outlive
> Fame and friendship begs another name
> . . . Life is honour
> It ends when honour ends. (p. 15)

From whom much is given, much is expected. The personal indulgence allowed Elesin is in recognition of a role which his destiny has carved out for him as a sacrificial victim. His life is made as comfortable as possible, as if a deliberate effort is needed to cover up the grimness of the destiny which awaits him at the very end. He is pampered by the people and is regarded as a special favorite of the gods. He is not only the king's companion but the king's confidant and trusted adviser. His fate may be grim but everything is done to give it a human face. His last day's great splash when he dances in splendor in the marketplace shows indeed that the Elesin is a "monarch whose palace is built with tenderness and beauty" (p. 10). He is magnificently costumed by the women. He demands to enjoy the virgin bride as his last privilege. The Iyaloja, the arranger of this last tribute, testifies that Elesin is already in contact with the other world: "The voice I hear is already touched by the waiting fingers of our departed" (p. 21). His enjoyment is touched with a whiff of sadness.

The character of the man himself is attuned to receiving communal tributes steeped in the unctions of sensuality. He is described at the beginning of the play as "a man of enormous vitality, [who] speaks, dances, and sings with that infectious enjoyment of life which accompanies all his actions" (p. 9). The critical issue of the play, therefore, becomes the question of Elesin's capability to shoulder his onerous burden, to fulfill his great destiny. As a sensualist with enormous sense of life and enjoyment, how would the Elesin confront a destiny whose fulfillment requires stringent self-discipline and social self-denial?

Both Iyaloja and Praise-Singer recognize the risk involved in putting a godlike burden on a mere mortal. They are full of expectations, but the expression of these expectations is mixed with statements that suggest the possibility of disappointment and hints of doubt:

Iyaloja: The living must eat and drink. When the moment comes, don't turn the
food to rodents' droppings in their mouth. Don't let them taste the ashes of the
world when they step out at dawn to breathe the morning dew. (p. 22)

And Praise-Singer, impersonating the dead King, tests Elesin's integrity:

> If you cannot come, I said, swear
> You'll tell my favourite horse, I shall
> Ride on through the gates alone.
> If you cannot come, Elesin, tell my dog,
> I cannot stay the keeper too long at the gate.
> If you get lost my dog will track
> The hidden part to me. (p. 42)

The anxieties of the market women, the Praise-Singer, and Iyaloja are
justified in the end when Elesin becomes reluctant to fulfill his obligation
and commits what he himself calls "this blasphemy of thought," "the awful
treachery of relief." But the nature of this blasphemy ought to be recognized. Elesin's sensuality is certainly a drag on the will, but he himself tells
us that it would not have stopped his fulfillment of his obligation in the end.
The decisive intervention of the District Officer alters everything. Not only
is Elesin physically restrained from committing suicide but, and this is the
blasphemy, he begins to feel a sense of relief that this intervention may have
come as an act of the gods to free him from the obligation itself: "My will
was squelched in the spittle of an alien race, and all because I had committed
the blasphemy of thought—that there might be the hand of the gods in a
stranger's intervention" (p. 69).

As he is soon to learn, however, the gods do not act so inconsistently and
their will is not so easily set aside. The living who in most cases interpret
the will of the gods and act as their agents see to it that fitting reprisals visit
those who flagrantly attempt to set their will at nought. For, Elesin is still
driven to fulfill his sacrificial obligation by the combined pressures of his
eldest son, the formidable Iyaloja, the Praise-Singer whose song is now
steeped in acid, and, by far the most persistent force of all, the voice of the
brooding elders and people speaking through the distant drums.

The major complication of the drama is supplied by the District Officer's
intervention to stop Elesin's suicide. The intervention, even though well
meant, is based on the outsider's perspective. This perspective is first
introduced when Sergeant Amusa reports the unfolding drama in the following prosaic language: "One prominent chief, namely, the Elesin Oba, is
to commit death tonight as a result of native custom" (p. 26).

It is clear that the outsiders are not capable of understanding or sharing the metaphysical world that demands the Horseman's sacrifice at the funeral of the king. The polarization of perceptions is first handled as an intellectual argument between Olunde and Mrs. Pilkings, an argument which proves distressing and inconclusive. The limitation of Mrs. Pilkings's position is, however, shown in her conferring the status of heroic self-sacrifice on the action of the British Captain who blows himself up with his ship at the harbor in order to prevent the death of people on shors, while regarding Elesin's impending self-sacrifice for the welfare of his community as barbaric and feudalistic. The fact that the District Officer and his wife accept the Captain's self-sacrifice as something noble and good, while not conceding that even within a feudalistic context a man can sacrifice his life in the noble pursuit of the welfare of his people, takes something away from the soundness of their view. This manner of presentation indicates the author's rejection of the outsider's perspective and makes it easier to appreciate Elesin's tragedy.

Simon Pilkings's insight built entirely on the secular conception of life strengthens his determination to save the life of the Horseman. He finds his confirming authority in a proverbial statement: "The elder grimly approaches heaven and you ask him to bear your greetings yonder; do you really think he makes the journey willingly?" (p. 64).

This insight cannot be dismissed out of hand because it is based upon a fact of human nature. No one is eager to die even though all religions paint the blessings of heaven in attractive colors. From the first steps taken by Elesin Oba, there grows a certain suspicion that the posture he has struck is not altogether genuine and likely to carry him to the end of his onerous duty. There is something forced and frenzied in his sweeping movements that leaves his drummers and Praise-Singer struggling to catch up with him. He is behaving like an elder who is approaching heaven at a running pace. We suspect he will not make the distance or, if he does, that he cannot arrive there in good grace. Elesin's references to the fear of death, coupled with such emphatic affirmations as "My soul is eager. I shall not turn aside," his garrulity and rhetorical exuberance (the rhetoric is facing in contradictory directions), all create a certain uneasiness, as if the Horseman is striving to fill up the time with anything but a measured contemplation of the task which lies before him, that of dying with dignity, not living hectically. Even though he redeems himself at last, his path is rendered hazardous in the process and much lustre has gone from the act: "The passage is clogged with droppings from the king's stallion; he will arrive all stained in dung" (p. 76).

The Horseman's dilemma even when rooted in metaphysics has its stem and branches in the open-air life of secular objectivity. The reluctance to embrace death is deep in the human consciousness and manifests itself in spite of the seductions and promises of metaphysical rewards. The sacrificial victim is first and foremost a human being of flesh, blood, and bones before he transmogrifies into a metaphysical medium. His struggle to answer the needs of human nature may be blasphemous from the metaphysical viewpoint, but it cannot be altogether unworthy of the sympathy of all who are in full possession of the vulnerability of their human nature. Elesin Oba's tragedy is based on two factors: his realization of his responsibility to ensure the maintenance of the metaphysical stability of his people's world by the sacrifice of his own life and his failure to live up to this responsibility because of his too tenacious attachment to the pleasures of this life.

Oda-Oak Oracle

The efficacy of human sacrifice is also claimed for the valley people in the *Oda-Oak Oracle*. Here the sacrifice of the victims is to ensure the restoration of the cosmic order which has been disrupted in the valley. In the words of First Elder, who is spokesman of the elders, only the sacrifice of the victims will restore the shattered world:

> Their deaths will prevent
> The walls of our tribe
> From breaking down.
> The gentle quiet
> That has been crushed
> From the land of the valley
> Will soon settle among us.
> The peace of the spirits
> That have escaped our mountains shall now
> Take over.[4]

The social and cosmic order is destroyed here when Shanka, the strong son of the tribe who has had a bride chosen for him by the Oracle of the Oda Oak, "refuses to know the warmth of his bride" because the same Oracle has prophesied that the first-born son of the marriage will be sacrificed to the spirits of the dead. Shanka's attempt to forestall the "ordained" course of events leads in the end not to one death but to the sacrifice of four people. The sacrifice of the protagonists is justified as a means of restoring metaphysical order and punishing the sin of defiance.

Shanka is determined that if the dead know no mercy, he will never know his bride. His abstention is, therefore, an attempt to bring the prophecy to nought, itself a serious act of presumption—and impiety. His attitude is

culpable from the traditional point of view. No true traditional character
would publicly question the will of the dead ancestors interpreted through
the oracle and the elders. As Second Elder, who functions as Chorus, says:

> The dead only demand
> In their ancient wisdom,
> Older than the memory of men
> The living only obey
> Wondering. (p. 5)

Shanka's second sin is his conscious attempt to use his friend, Goaa, to
influence the Oracle to change its mind:

> Go back to the Oda Oak, friend,
> And face the Oracle. (p. 5)

Even after many months and the discovery that his bride has been made
pregnant by somebody else, Shanka still questions the integrity of the
elders:

> Why, Wise Elders,
> Must the dead feast
> On the sapping of life
> Of a babe,
> Who should have been materialized
> As part of my blood? (p. 33)

The reason why Shanks defies the "infallible" elders in this way is that
he has been influenced by Goaa, his friend, "the inhibited by the strangers'
ways," and can, therefore, appeal to a code of values outside those of the
communal society. Even though this specific new influence is never
mentioned explicitly, the oblique references would suggest that it is
Christianity:

> You're more than a brother to me,
> Goaa, You imparted your knowledge
> Of the wisdom of the strangers

> To me. You did. You let me share the secret
> Of your happy obsession by the Word
> Which you said is all loving. (p. 38)

Unfortunately, what would have become a concerted campaign against intolerable despotism disintegrates into absurd revolt which is systematically suppressed by the implacable elders. Goaa proves to be neither a good man nor a moral man. He publicly denounces both Shanka and Ukutee, Shanka's neglected wife, who now bears Goaa's child. He tries to buy a separate peace from the elders. Shanka, now left unsupported, is totally alienated from tradition though he is far from sure what sort of a moral code he should use to oppose the absolutism of his persecutors:

> But yes
> For the cry of the new born!
> Yes, for the daughter of peace
> Yes, for the father and mother
> Who die to give it life
> Yes, for the word
> Who becomes All! (p. 51)

He suffers persistent oppression in the hands of the elders, and even though he is physically a strong and impressive man, the elders' tactics of attrition finally wear him out and his spirit is broken. He takes refuge in self-pitying lamentations:

> Strong, I am,
> Yet I am the weakest.
> The dead are my witness
> That many a dreary night
> I lamented like a woman. (p. 5)

It is as if the ancestors and the elders are determined to ruin him at all costs, because every attempt to set himself right is interpreted as a criminal offense by the elders. The extraordinary self-control he shows by refusing to know his bride is interpreted as an affront: an attempt to ensure that the oracle of the ancestors will not be fulfilled. His sin of presumption is said to cause heartburn and teeth gnashing among the spirits and the natural upheavals in the valley. He is accused of betraying the tribe. In the trial which the elders conduct, he is condemned to fight a duel with Goaa, but his surviving that ordeal is not thought punishment enough. He is doomed to extinction.

Goaa the inhibited is accused of sowing perversity in the society as a result of his being influenced by the ways of the strangers. One does not see much of his subversion in evidence except through Shanka's claim that Goaa has indoctrinated him into the mystique of the Word.

The Oda-Man's verdict is very severe for this offense. His crimes are identified as, first, letting his head turn into a cavern "where the ghosts of strangers lingered," and, second, allowing his "inhibited soul" to instill fertility into the chosen bride of the spirits. He is condemned to vagrancy in death and life. There is a hint of suspicion that the elders are more worried about the foreign influences in the mind of Goaa than about his tampering with the bride of the spirits:

> But true, Goaa,
> Because of your inhibition
> Of the strange ones
> You defied the wisdom
> Of our by-gone fathers,
> And aroused their curse
> Upon all. (p. 26)

Ukutee is just as severely punished as the others even though she rightly pleads extenuation. She is a victim of neglect; when her lawful husband refuses to know her warmth, she succumbs to temptation. But her pleas are set aside and heavy sentence is pronounced upon her:

> And you, woman,
> Comforter
> Of every man's sweat,
> The creature in you
> Shall not come forth
> Ever. (p. 30)

And so the court of severity dispenses Draconian justice. The three victims are predictably sacrificed, as well as a fourth non-active participant in the triangular tragedy, the newly born child. But it seems the author has the last word in the matter. Toward the end of the play, when the menacing mob is about to bear down on both the Elders and the culprits, Shanka poses the following significant question:

> Who rages for sacrifice?
> Our dead?
> Or our living?

To which First Elder supplies the answer:

> We need a sacrifice
> To cool the fire
> Of the raging mob.

And Third Elder agrees:

> Let them have Shanka
> With this child of shame,
> Before they have us. (p. 53)

Shanka and the child are fed to the fury of the raging mob, but he has at least obtained some illumination which had eluded his tortured soul up till now. Sacrifice is demanded by the living for the sake of the living. The sole beneficiaries are the living, who have bought their peace at the cost of those sacrificed. And as if to emphasize the human factor in the untangling of the metaphysical web, the Oracle predicts that Ukutee's unborn child shall be a boy:

> You shall deliver
> A new son, woman,
> Strong and fierce
> Like a young leopard, yes
> He shall grow
> To become a man of the tribe. (p. 45)

When the child is born, it turns out to be a girl, who is ultimately to be fed to the fury of an angry mob. The author does not indicate whether the dead ones are playing tricks on their Oracle or the oracular vision has been dimmed by the human factor.

The Strong Breed

In *The Strong Breed*, Soyinka presents two perspectives on the ritual significance of the carrier in communal societies. The recognition of the necessity for an individual to be "sacrificed" for the sake of the society at large is common to two societies suggested in this play, but there is a basic difference in general attitudes and procedures. Whereas in the one much evil is associated with the ritual, in the other, the carrier's role is something heroic and near the sacred.

The meaning of the carrier is first suggested by the mysterious girl under Eman's window: "Do you mean my carrier? I am unwell you know. My mother says it will take away my sickness with the old year."[5] The carrier is conceived as a metaphysical medium whose role it is to purge society (at specific seasons) of its evil through a symbolic physical act. This is further confirmed by the same girl later in the play, in her words to Ifada, who has been playing with her "carrier": "But just because you are helping me, don't think it is going to cure you. I am the one who will get well at midnight, do you understand? It is my carrier and it is for me alone" (p. 120).

But attitudes to the carrier differ radically between Jaguna's village and Eman's village. In Jaguna's village, where a good part of the action is set, the carrier is seen as an outcast, and the people make use of him opportunistically. They victimize him for their own well-being and treat him abominably. In Eman's village, on the other hand, the carrier is not only a respectable member of society, but also a bearer of a special responsibility for which society is indebted to him. The lot of the carrier in Jaguna's village is outlined by Jaguna himself in this exposition at Eman's house: "A carrier should end up in the bush, not in a house. Anyone who doesn't guard his door when the carrier goes has himself to blame" (p. 128). His next in command, Oroge, goes a little further: "This is not a simple matter at all. It is not a simple task for anybody. No one in his senses would do such a job. Why do you think we give refuge to idiots like him [meaning Ifada]? We don't know where he came from" (*Ibid.*). Sunma, the alienated eldest daughter of Jaguna, gives frantic expression to the evil involved in the selfish, opportunistic attitudes of the people of her village. She repudiates them and renounces her ceremonial role as the Jaguna's eldest daughter. She warns Eman against the villagers: "You are wasting your life on people who really want you out of their way. . . . I know they are evil and I am not. From the oldest to the smallest child, they are nourished in evil and unwholesomeness" (pp. 120-121).

It is possible to see her anxiety as the selfish concern of a girl for her lover's safety, but the more dignified context in which the role of the carrier is established in Eman's native village and the subsequent development of the action vindicate her position. In Eman's village, as revealed in the flashbacks, the role of the carrier is a special one, peculiar to a special family. And here it is devoid of the ignominy and contempt which characterize it in the other village. The Old Man, Eman's father, reminds him of the sacredness of the role: "Ours is a strong breed my son. It is only a strong breed that can take this boat to the river year after year and wax stronger on it" (p. 113).

A special deterministic force seems, however, to be acting on the chosen family which makes it inevitable for its members to be found out in foreign places and given the burden of their destiny. The Old Man informs Eman of this inevitability and the futility of his attempt to leave his village in order to escape the carrier's destiny: "Your own blood will betray you, son, because you cannot hold it back" (p. 134). And his blood does betray him in Jaguna's village because, even though Eman is living here as a fugitive in search of psychological peace, he intervenes to save Ifada, the village idiot selected for the role of carrier. He takes over the burden instead and is hunted down and hanged in a tree. In the end, his father's prophecy that his blood would betray him and that he would waste his strength among those unworthy of his redemptive calling comes true. However, the bestiality and viciousness of the people at the festival render the exercise futile. Oroge and Jaguna finally admit that it has been a night of curses and that despite everything, there remains much contamination in the air. At the critical moment when the carrier should have been burdened with curses, the villagers only "looked up at the man and words died in their throats" (p. 146).

It remains a question of whether Soyinka intends in this play to examine two conflicting approaches concerning the role of the carrier, recommending the one and rejecting the other; or whether he simply wants to point out the futility of such sacrificial attitudes to life.

These plays highlight the predicament of the doomed individual in the traditional, communal society. A haunting sense of loneliness and feeling of abandonment are shared by all the protagonists. Their physical terror is only matched by the spiritual terror which seizes them from the very first movements of their victimization. The exclusion from the mystical communion of those who have decided to sacrifice them presents its own psychological problem to the victims, for in every case of victimization, there is total separation of the victim from the rest of humanity and an abandonment to a fate that must be confronted alone. The sacrificial situation represents a peculiar dialectic in which the victim ceases to be humanly autonomous. He becomes an instrument, an agent, and a means to achieving an end which is the well-being of those who sacrifice him.

There is implicit in this relationship a confrontation of interests, with the interests of the sacrificial victim subjugated to those of the beneficiaries, who gain from the sacrifice. The nature of this gain or sacrificial efficacy is explored in the three plays. On one level, it is interpreted metaphysically as the restoration of cosmic order to a previously disturbed world. On another, this gain is interpreted in terms of mass psychology, a certain craving of mobs for excitement through the humiliation of carefully chosen victims. Rulers of communities aware of this tendency in the collectivity, periodically stage such shows to draw attention away from themselves. They sacrifice scapegoats to keep the crowds happy.

J. Gronowski, author of *The Face of Violence*, states in the section of the book captioned "Death as a Spectacle": "Every spectacle has an element of this; Mr. Punch and the circus clown, and the hero of Greek tragedy and the dying gladiator alike give to those who watch their defeat a stab of shameful pleasure in the collapse of human dignity."[6] And Frantz Fanon seems to endorse the same view: "In every society, in every collectivity exist . . . a channel, an outlet through which the forces accumulated in the form of aggression can be released."[7] In other words, the sacrificial drama, elaborated often by rituals, incantations, and music, and sometimes by scenes of violence and bloody orgies, provides collective catharsis and purges communal societies of the more destructive internal upheavals. The annual expulsion of the carrier or the occasional sacrifice of a human victim insendates society from grosser forms of violence and destabilizing upheavals.

SELECT NOVELS

Gabriel Okara's *The Voice* and Ngugi wa Thiongo's *The River Between* treat the theme of victimization with great concentration. Numerous other African novels deal with the theme in a more or less diffused manner. They are not lacking in victims, because the newly established post-independence regimes are still stumbling along, lacking assurance and consistency, and are, therefore, more likely than not to hunt down individuals or groups and to offer them up as scapegoats to divert attention from their failure to meet the challenges of independence. The apartheid regime of South Africa continues to sacrifice Africans, singly and as a group, in order to ensure the continuity of the totally inhuman, exploitative, and discredited system. Works like Nurrudin Farah's *Sweet and Sour Milk*, Alex La Guma's *A Walk in the Night*, and Ayi Kwei Armah's *Why Are We So Blest?* deal with different aspects of this theme of the deliberate sacrifice of an individual or a group in order to sustain the existence of a tyrannical, unjust or perverse, and exploitative social order. Of the Contemporary African novels *The Voice* and *The River Between* are single-mindedly devoted to this theme.

Perhaps what makes these two novels so attractive is their choice of self-conscious, messianic victims. Okolo and Waiyaki are active victims. They carry a special burden, are engaged in a special mission, for the redemption of society. They are committed people who espouse a noble cause and pay with their lives to bring salvation to their people. Other victims are either too passive altogether or too lacking in vision and clarity of view of the task to be performed to be interesting even as victims. Compared with Okolo and Waiyaki, Loyaan (*Sweet and Sour Milk*) is too ensconced in his suffering, subjective soul; Willieboy (*A Walk in the Night*) is too passive in his victim's predicament; and Modin (*Why Are We So Blest?*) too vague in his vision of life. It would be difficult to see how much regenerative possibility exists in their sacrifice. Okolo and Waiyaki are sacrificed, but their campaigns have a certain earnestness that ensures that their impact would survive after the victims have been sacrificed. The handling of the theme by Ngugi and Okara is competent, revealing numerous insights and refreshing technical innovations that greatly enrich the novel form.

The Voice

The plot of *The Voice* is very slight. The hero, Okolo (which in Ijaw means "the voice"), after having studied and lived abroad, returns home to the village of Amatu. He is appalled by the moral decay which he finds everywhere and more particularly by a persuasive and all-pervading materialism which corrupts the souls of the people both within the village and in the neighboring town, Sologa of the Big One, and which destroys the people's moral vision of life. Okolo feels called upon to draw attention to his people's moral predicament by going around and asking them if they have got "It" and thereby stimulating moral revival in their lives. He assumes for himself the mantle of reformer, prophet, and messiah, but like all such moral revolutionaries, he antagonizes the corrupt establishment and is quite predictably crushed, just when his message is beginning to take root.

There is hardly any doubt as to the tradition to which Okara's tale belongs. The moral campaign which the hero mounts right from the beginning, the morally dominated atmosphere, and the inside details of the plot point irrevocably not only to an obvious analogy but to a close patterning on the Passion story of the Gospels. In his excellent study *The Novelist and the Passion Story*, F. W. Dillistone writes about such novels:

The . . . possibility open to the novelist is to write about his contemporary world openly and frankly but with the essential pattern of the Passion narrative forming the inner framework of his own story. It is, of course, impossible for him to do this unless he believes that the successive stages in the recorded life of Jesus do correspond to the general sequence of events which may be traced in the career of every heroic figure who carries out a mission of redemption for his fellow men.

Such a mission may be performed by an individual seeking consciously to follow in the steps of the Christ and to fashion his life after the pattern displayed in the Gospels. But not necessarily so. In dedicating himself to the service of his fellows he may also unconsciously find himself caught up into a sequence of temporary acceptance, growing opposition, rejection, suffering, dereliction, vindication, strangely similar to that which marked the career of Jesus of Nazareth himself.[8]

Though *The Voice* is not as closely patterned on Christ's life as, say, Kazantzaki's *Christ Recrucified*, yet there is enough of the Passion story in it to justify attention being drawn to the fact. Okolo carries on his moral campaign from a position of moral superiority—he possesses It while the people whom he sets out to convert do not possess It. He is single-mindedly devoted to his mission in spite of the obvious personal risks involved. His complete commitment to his messianic mission actually contrasts with the different kind of commitment evident in the artist who "puts his shadow into creating faces out of wood"—a kind of creative virtue which though commendable in itself is too subjectively centered to have a wide cleansing impact on the moral environment.

Okolo, like Christ, is the man who cares where everyone else is content to let things slide. In a world in which everyone else is a comedian (to use Graham Greene's famous differentiation) he is the only tragedian. He has the awareness of the extent of moral ruin which has overtaken his society, and he is prepared to risk life and security to assault the forces of darkness. One of Okolo's main targets of attack, like Christ's, is the establishment, which not only is corrupt in itself but corrupts the rest of the people. Chief Izongo and the Elders of Amatu may be paralleled to the Scribes and Pharisees; the white colonialist in charge of the Big One's security service and who imprisons Okolo in Sologa to Pontius Pilate. We even have the equivalent of Nichodemus in the Elder Tebeowei, who comes to Okolo at night, not to learn more about his message, of course, but to persuade him of the futility of his effort. Okolo's collaborators and converts, the outcast Tuere and the cripple Ukule, could be likened to Christ's humble disciples. Most of the evils denounced by Christ are also the evils deplored by Okolo in the village of Amatu and the town, Sologa of the Big One—an establishment which corrupts the ordinary people by its concupiscence and self-love as well as a general moral laxity distinguished by too much love for material security and too little concern with social morality.

All the main stages in the Passion story are present in Okolo's life—notice that the actual drama of Okolo's moral campaign is very short-lived. As with the story of Christ the most formative period of the hero's life remains inexplicably shrouded in obscurity. Like Christ also, Okolo goes through the stages identified by Dillistone—temporary acceptance (because people are beginning to listen to his moral promptings, the autocrats have to move quickly against him), suffering (Okolo has a good deal of this both in the village and in the town), dereliction (the very limit is marked by Okolo's death by drowning, tied with the unfortunate Tuere in a rudderless canoe which drifts from one bank of the river to the other like "debris carried by the current" until drawn into a whirlpool), and vindication. There is more than a little suggestion that Okolo's mission will triumph over the forces of human tyranny. Ukule the cripple assures Okolo before he is led away, "Your spoken words will not die." But even before this time, a convert to Okolo's viewpoint has said with emphasis: "Nobody withstands the power of the spoken word. Okolo has spoken. I will speak when the time is correct and others will follow and our spoken words will gather power like the power of hurricane and Izongo will sway and fall like sugar cane."[9] The story leaves no doubt that the cause for which Okolo dies will in the end triumph, just as the cause for which the Christ was crucified has since triumphed.

This patterning on the Passion story is interesting, but what is even more impressive is the means whereby Okara creates for us an overwhelming vision of evil and corruption, the vision of a wholly corrupt environment within which everyday activities are distorted into a dreamlike nightmare only comparable to life in a lunatic asylum. Here is an extract from the incident of Okolo's first arrest:

Okolo seeing the messengers, recognized them and questioned them. But the men, in spite of their grim faces, opened not their mouths. The remaining crowd hushed. The silence passed silence. The three messengers faced Okolo, opening not their mouths. A man from the back of the crowd pushed his way to the messengers. The four of them put their heads together while with their eyes they looked at Okolo. They put their heads together for a while and walked towards Okolo, as if stalking an animal. And Okolo stood looking. They moved nearer. Okolo stood. They moved nearer and suddenly, pounced on Okolo. Okolo and the men fell to the ground. Hands clawed at him, a thousand hands, the hands of the world. Okolo twisted, free. He ran. Running feet followed. He ran. A million pursuing feet thundered after him. He ran past his house without knowing and ran into another. A woman giving suck to her baby screamed. Out Okolo sprang and ran. The running feet came nearer, the caring nothing feet of the world. Okolo turned a corner and nearly ran into a boy and a girl standing with hands holding each other. They did not look at him. He turned a corner. A dog barked at him. Okolo ran. He was now at the ending of the town. Only one hut was left and beyond it the mystery of the forest. Okolo ran and as he ran past, a voice held him. "Come in" it said, "Come in quickly." (pp. 15-16)

In Okolo went, instinctively and in the gloom stood panting. And here is a description of Okolo's first night in Sologa of the Big One:

Through the black black night Okolo walked, stumbled, walked. His inside was a room with chairs, cushions, papers scattered all over the floor by thieves. Okolo walked, stumbled, walked. His eyes shut and opened, shut and opened, expecting to see a light in each opening, but none he saw in the black black night.

At last the black black night like the back of a cooking pot entered his inside and grabbing his thoughts, threw them out into the blacker than black night. And Okolo walked, stumbled, walked with an inside empty of thoughts except the black black night.

When Okolo came to know himself, he was lying on a floor on a cold floor lying. He opened his eyes to see but nothing he saw, nothing he saw. For the darkness was evil darkness and the outside night was black black night. Okolo lay still in the darkness enclosed by darkness, and his thought picked his inside. Then his picked thoughts opened his eyes but his vision only met a rock-like darkness. The picked thoughts then drew his legs but his legs did not come. They were as heavy as a canoe full of sand. His thoughts in his inside began to fly in his inside darkness like frightened birds hither, thither, homeless. Then the flying thoughts drew his hands but the hands did not belong to him, it seemed. So Okolo on the cold cold floor lay with his body as soft as an over-pounded foofoo. So Okolo lay with his eyes open wide in the rock-like darkness staring, staring.

Okolo for years and years lay on the cold cold floor at the rock-like darkness staring. Then suddenly he saw a light. He drew his hands and his hands came. He stood up with his eyes on the light and walked towards the light. As he moved towards the light, the light also moved back. He moved faster and the light also moved faster. Okolo ran and the light also ran. Okolo ran, the light ran. Okolo ran and hit a wall with his head. Okolo looked and the light was no more. He then stretched his hands forth and touched the wall. His fingers felt dents and holes. Okolo walked sideways like a crab with his fingers on the wall, feeling dents and holes, dents and holes in the rock-like darkness until his feet struck an object. As Okolo stopped and felt the object his body became cold. His heart-beat echoed in the rock-like darkness and his head expanded. Still, he felt along the object until his fingers went into two holes. As his fingers went into the holes he quickly withdrew them and ran. He ran and fell, ran and fell over other objects. He ran and knocked against the wall and fell. Still he ran, then suddenly stopped. He saw a light in front of him. He moved gently crouching forward like a hunter stalking game. Then when he nearly reached the light, he rushed forward. (pp. 84-86)

Those two passages have been selected because they illustrate the quality, range, and variety of Okara's art. In fact, what is most striking about it is the careful, deliberate manner in which Okara works the different rhetorical devices into a sustained and singularly successful medium to convey the peculiar experience which we find in *The Voice*. Okara's art would reward some study because Okara is easily the most "artificial" of all West African writers. We use the word "artificial" in connection with Okara's style in the word's old and modern connotations of having "constructive skill" or art and as the opposite to "natural."

The most outstanding feature of Okara's art is his reiterative rhetoric, his repetition of single words, phrases, sentences, images, or symbols to produce diverse emphatic effect. Notice, for example, the effort suggested in the first passage by the repetition of "Okolo stood" and "They moved nearer." It is as if Okolo is fixed on the spot under a hypnotic spell while his sinister adversaries make their sharp, furtive moves, full of menace and danger to the hero. The metaphor already suggested in "as if stalking an animal" is fully justified by what happens. In the very next lines the sinister nightmarish quality of the episode is reinforced by vividly described physical activities. The assailants "pounce" on Okolo and a struggle ensues.

"Nightmare" is the only word which adequately describes the physical sensation of "a thousand hands" and "the hands of the world" which claw at Okolo as he "twisted," "struggled," and "kicked" at his four adversaries. To Okolo, the hands of four men in that brief and silent struggle produce the sensation of "a thousand hands"—the reader feels this sensation just as he feels the sensation of being pursued by a million "thundering" feet in the dark, silent night. The reader feels these sensations because the drama is so vivid, so concrete that he has become Okolo, sees things through Okolo's hunted eyes, experiences the thrill of horror which Okolo experiences when the four silent men suddenly pounce on him and when the whole crowd begins pursuing him in the dark.

The reiteration of the action in short dramatic sentences like "Okolo ran" reinforced by clearly hyperbolic statements like "a million pursuing feet" give rise to a terrifying concrete physical sensation which is felt in the very marrow. Notice also Okara's method of giving concreteness to the action by the repetition of the proper name rather than the personal pronoun—"Okolo stood," "Okolo twisted," "Out Okolo sprang," "Okolo turned a corner," "Okolo ran."

The use of reiteration to give concreteness of physical sensation to situation is even more developed in the second passage. Here, the reiteration of "black" gives to the darkness of the night a near-tactile quality in expressions like "black black night," "black night like the black of a cooking pot," "the blacker than black night."

The sinister nature of the darkness is very much heightened by its being raised to a physical sensation. In fact, the symbol of "darkness" is so pervasive not only in this passage but also in the rest of the narrative that the atmosphere of the story could be said to be completely dominated by it. Light appears intermittently and merely helps to emphasize the darkness, not to dispel it.

The reiterative image of darkness in this passage is particularly effective, especially as it is further reinforced by Okara's invocation of the horrific in terms of the human sensations—eyes trying to pierce an impenetrable darkness, hands and feet that refuse to move in one moment and then shoot out in a single automatic movement in the next, groping of the fingers into dents and holes, crablike movement, the head knocking on the wall, the body becoming cold, the heartbeat echoing, the head expanding, the running and falling, and so on—all these physical actions and sensations which are given great vividness assume a dreamlike, nightmarish quality because they take place in the dark.

Now, this evocation of horror and nightmare would have been a point of weakness in Okara's art, mere sensation-mongering, if it had been indulged in for its own sake. But it is not. It provides superb background to the serious moral issues with which Okara is dealing in the novel. This is not a normal world but one which has been terribly distorted by evil and corruption. The very prospect of living within it assumes an aspect of physical danger and spiritual terror, especially for the only man who is courageous enough to challenge its standards of morality, its rotten values, as well as the invidious forces which dominate it.

Of course, the story is a parable with the universal theme of man's indomitable struggle against the evils of spiritual oppression and social corruption, as the blurb says, but we can only wring out the limit of its rich moral significance by apprehending it on the two levels of particularity and generality and on the literal and symbolic levels, because each level tends to reinforce the other. For this realization of his theme of "good versus evil," Okara has had to build up the physical aspect of his environment, a horrific and nightmarish environment, within which we feel, through physical sensations, the oppressive presence of evil as well as the heroic suffering and torment of soul implicit in the hero's moral campaign against it. Thus the theme has both universal significance as well as a contemporary application: the novel's setting is both the world and an African country in which the dictators have set up police states and destroyed their people's liberties. Okara's reiterative rhetoric makes the realization of the actual physical implications of the moral problem and the representation of the moral situation through physical action and physical sensations reasonably easy. But there is more to it.

Okara brings his poetic gifts to bear on his choice of images and symbols. He uses metaphors, similes, and other figures of speech to give concreteness and body to the heavily oppressive moral environment which he builds up. By such devices, even the most abstract notions are reduced to physical realities. Okara is in this sense, more than any other West African novelist, a materialist, because he attempts to reduce actions, feelings, and sensations to material or physical realities. This tendency in Okara's technique could be regarded as a process of "reification"; the process of giving the quality of "thingness" to mental and abstract constructs. Okara, for example, describes Okolo's confusion of mind in the dark room by likening it to "a room with chairs; cushions, papers, scattered all over the floor by thieves." Okolo's "thoughts in his inside began to fly in his inside darkness like frightened birds hither, thither, homeless." There is an example of the use of synecdoche to give concreteness to the squalid moral outlook which exists in the town of Sologa: "So Okolo walked in Sologa of the Big One passing frustrated eyes, ground-looking eyes, harlot's eyes, despairing eyes, nothing-caring eyes, dust-filled eyes, aping eyes" (p. 90). Only by evolving a consistent style with its own inner logic can Okara make "eyes" do duty for him in this bold unconventional manner.

The process of reification in *The Voice* is greatly enhanced by the rhythm of Okara's prose, the rhythm of words spun under the immediate pressure of what is being done, felt, or suffered. This, when accompanied by Okara's reiterative rhetoric, can enhance dramatic immediacy as well as fixing impression in a concrete and vivid way. The tremendous power of the second passage is the result of Okara's ability to capture the rhythm of action and of physical sensation through common everyday words which thus acquire sensuous and sinister overtones—words like "dents," "holes," "the thing." What give ordinary innocent words like these their quality of creeping terror are the context in which they occur and the way they are woven into the hero's movement in the dark. When the hero's fingers, for instance, enter into the "two holes" and he immediately withdraws them, we feel without really knowing why that we are in a room where there are human skeletons, and with the hero we are chilled and experience the sensation of horror and revulsion. Perhaps the term which adequately describes Okara's ability to produce physical sensations and attendant emotions by manipulating words, actions, and rhythm of language is T. S. Eliot's famous phrase "Objective Correlative."[10] The accumulation of physical sensations and emotions has the effect of fixing our moral reaction to the issues which the writer has so clearly stripped bare before the reader.

The main impulse within *The Voice* seems to derive from the oral tradition, especially the folktale. Okara's rhetoric, more especially his deliberate repetitions, his metaphoric and hyperbolic elaborations, and his colloquial rhythm, belongs essentially to the oral tradition. The ghoulish and the nightmarish which are so well developed in *The Voice* are the regular features of the folktale. Okara's interest in the Ijaw oral tradition goes much further than any other novelist's interest in the oral tradition, for Okara, of all the writers, attempts to reproduce not only literal meanings from the vernacular (such as is evident in expressions like "Okolo had no chest," "he had no shadow," "all his inside," "with all his shadow"), but also actual syntactical forms, in sentences like "Who are you people be?" "If you are coming-in people be, then come in." Even the process of reification already noted may have been derived by Okara from the vernacular since it is quite well developed in the West African languages.

It has been suggested that Okara wrote the story in "ordinary English" and then as an experiment translated it into "this medium." This may well be so, but it is equally true that Okara's experiment with language and imagery in *The Voice* was clearly foreshadowed in his poetry. We find in *The Mystic Drum*, for instance, expressions like "in my inside," "with their shadows," "the eye of the sky," and the sustained image "and smoke issued from her nose and her lips parted in her smile turned cavity belching darkness," which may have prepared the way for the dominant symbol of darkness in *The Voice*. Another poem, "Adhiambo," suggests the theme of *The Voice*. The opening lines read:

> I hear many voices
> Like it's said a madman hears;
> I hear trees talking
> Like it's said a medicine man hears
> Maybe I'm a madman,
> I'm a medicine man
> Maybe I'm mad,
> For the voices are luring me,
> Urging me from the midnight
> Noon and the silence of my desk
> To walk on wave crests across a sea!

The hero of *The Voice* is also a visionary and is said by the people to be a madman. What is being hinted at here is that *The Voice* is perhaps the sublimation in prose fiction of Okara's poetic visions of his mission through literary creativeness, to reform and purify society. The poet-reformer will bring out of his creative imagination the full image of the appalling corruption of society so that all those who see this image will be shocked into a mood of moral revival. Thus, the real key to why Okolo is a Christ-like, rather than a Promethean hero may actually lie in the fact that Okara conceived him essentially as a poet-reformer and not as a political revolutionary, as a man who appeals to the soul and the finer faculties and emotions of people rather than one who storms their emotions into revolutionary violence. Okara gives us in a very vivid way a terrifying picture of society completely corrupted by totalitarianism and extreme materialism, but Okara's moral position remains vague, veiled in elusive poetic suggestion. The "I" is the quality of moral excellence which the autocrats have emasculated in their subjects: "For him it has no name. Names bring divisions and divisions strife. So let it be without a name: let it be nameless."

The novel is sometimes criticized for taking a too rigid moral position. But this criticism is hardly fair at all. As a parabolic tale whose effect depends on a certain rigidity of moral positions, the novel may be excused for adopting a one-sided moral outlook which bears out the theme of the tale.

The River Between

In *The River Between*, the protagonist is another messianic bringer of salvation to his people. Under the pressure of European settler imperialism which alienates the land from the people, the rift between the Christian converts and the Gikuyu Council of Elders deepens into a chasm of distrust and antipathies. In the prevailing climate of zealotry, fanaticism, and fundamentalism, the people are hopelessly divided. Assuming the mantle of redeemer and teacher, Waiyaki attempts through modern education, love, and tolerance to bridge the rift and reconcile the people. However, at the critical moment, he forgets that the real cause of the pain in the hearts of the people is the loss of their independence and right over their land. His efforts to unite the people fail, and he is rejected by the Christians and the traditionalists alike. He is brought to trial and convicted by the people's assembly and handed over to the Council of Elders to face execution for breaking his oath of loyalty to the people.

Two perspectives are presented in this narrative: the traditional and the Christian. Each is essential to the action. The Kikuyu community is a traditional community but Christianity has since been introduced there and has become part of its total reality. The writer's perception of the action in this novel, therefore, necessarily takes account of this reality in the advancing of the themes and sharpening of the focus of action. The perspectives explain the dilemma of the protagonist, whose education and consciousness have been conditioned by both tradition and Christianity.

In the presentation of the traditional perspective, myths and legends are deeply drawn upon to provide a support to the framework of action. The world is viewed through the myth of its origin and the legends of its continuity; its foundation is set firmly and rooted in the land, which, to the agricultural Gikuyu, is the most important factor of life:

Murugu brought the man and woman here and . . . showed them the whole vastness, the land. He gave the country to them and their children and the children of the children, *tene na tene*, world without end. . . . From here, Murungu took them and put them under Mukuruwe wa Gathang'a. There our father and mother had nine daughters who bore more children. The children spread all over the country. Some came to the ridges to keep and guard the ancient rites.[11]

People are strengthened in their lives and actions by their myths. The Gikuyu's attachment to the land is total. Land is a force drawing them to their deepest aspirations, to their origins and roots; it is hallowed by its being harnessed to their fundamental myth. When, therefore, later in the narrative it becomes clear that Waiyaki has missed the point that his people's relationship to the land is a special one and a very emotional one, it becomes clear equally that he has missed one of the life-sustaining truths concerning the Gikuyu and is bound on a course of defeat.

Next only in importance to the myth of origin and creation is the myth of a prophecy, an ancient belief that in some unspecified future some strangers would come to Kikuyuland and would break the people and their way of life apart: "There shall come a people with clothes like butterflies . . ." But the prophecy also predicts that a savior shall arise from among the people who would rescue the people from their invaders. The existence of prophecy assumes the appearance of prophets and interpreters or seers or sages who reiterate the old idea or explain it to the masses to give it perpetuitive validity. Waiyaki's credential as leader is based on his being in the line of these seers and prophets. His father, Chege, reminds him of his special destiny which is rooted in tradition:

Now, listen my son. Listen carefully, for this is the ancient prophecy. . . . I could not do more. When the white man came and fixed himself in Siriana, I warned all the people. But they laughed at me. Maybe I was hasty. Perhaps I was not the one. Mugo often said you could not cut the butterflies with a panga. You could not spear them until you learnt and knew their ways and movement. Then you could trap, you could fight back. Before he died, he whispered to his son the prophecy, the ancient prophecy: "Salvation shall come from the hills. From the blood that flows in me, I say from the same tree, a son shall rise. And his duty shall be to lead and save the people!" (p. 24)

The coming of the missionaries and the white settlers in their wake is regarded by Chege as the fulfillment of the first part of the prophecy—the arrival in Kikuyuland of "a people with clothes like butterflies." The fulfillment of the second part Chege places on the shoulders of Waiyaki, his son, who is the last of the line of the much revered Mugo wa Kabiro. Considerable space is devoted in *The River Between* to establishing the credentials of Waiyaki as a redeemer; he comes from the right place and is the proper scion.

The induction of Waiyaki into traditional life is accomplished through the rites of passage and incorporation with the circumcision rites as climax. These rites, in addition to providing great avenues for communion through musical celebrations and dancing, offer a severe test for courage and endurance. But, even more importantly, they provide the foretaste of the sacrifice which the individual would be called upon to make at any future stage in the furtherance of the people's destiny. In a number of unobtrusive authorial remarks, we are informed that the shedding of the individual's blood during the process of circumcision is a sacrificial act, prefiguring, perhaps, the demands which the land would require of the initiates in the promotion of the collective heritage and signifying the offering of the circumcised victims to the service of the tribe and its interests and the preservation of its code. Of Waiyaki's circumcision the author comments: "Blood trickled freely on the ground, sinking into the soil. Henceforth a religious bond linked Waiyaki to the earth, as if his blood was an offering" (pp. 52-53). And much later we read the following: "To her left was open ground where the candidates for circumcision went to shed their blood. Muthoni too had come here on the morning of her sacrifice" (p. 132).

It is necessary to draw attention to this matter of circumcision, sacrifice, and the preservation of the tribe because it helps us to appreciate the importance of the circumcision rites in the polarization of the relationship of Christians who abominate these rites and exclude those who go through them from their membership and traditionalists who reject anyone who should decide not to undergo the rites. Circumcision for the traditionalists is a pact of blood in furtherance of the social, economic, and cultural life of the tribe, and since the intention of the Christians is the transcending of this life, there is no better strategy than for them to strike at its heart by destroying circumcision rites.

Ngugi presents tradition as having a validity that ensures its continuity. It has within it the vitality and power that ensure its survival and perpetuity. Thus, with the extension of the settlers' power into the hills and ridges and the people feeling "the bite of injustice" and with the campaign by Christians against tradition becoming serious, people constitute a revivalist Kiama "to preserve the purity of our tribal customs and our way of life" (p. 75). At times of serious events that require the mobilization of the emotional solidarity of the people, the people's assembly is a great force and tribunal that resolves great issues of social survival. The true strength of the traditional system is demonstrated in times of emergency when the mobilization of its psychological force has taken place. At such moments, the operators of the system who recognize the trigger points of its peculiar energy press those points and make them release their concealed vitality.

Oathing is one of the means adopted by the traditionalists to galvanize the emotional vitality of tradition, a means of unifying the response of the people and linking their contemporary conditions to the past and future destiny of the race. Circumcision rites integrate the individuals within the traditional system, but an oath binds the same individuals emotionally and psychologically to the society's aspiration in a pact of life and death. The collective oath is the people's highest covenant, their call to their members to keep faith with the things that give cohesion to their lives and provide continuity of action and aspirations to past, present, and future generations.

Waiyaki's attitude to the oath, as also his inability to realize the significance of land to the Gikuyu, shows him as very weakly informed in the ways of the tribe and poorly equipped to survive within it. When his friend and colleague Kinuthia warns him that oaths are being administered in his name, he does not see at once how that shows that his work as the teacher of his people is being assimilated into the collective consciousness of the tribe, and when he lets the people down by appearing to go over to their enemies by aspiring to marry Nyambura, Joshua's daughter who is uncircumcised, he is somewhat bewildered at the strength of the same people's rejection and anger. The people who idolize him for bringing education to their children now bellow, "The Oath! The Oath!" at him with anguish and bitterness in their voices. But Kinuthia's warning had clearly prefigured both responses:

Be careful, Waiyaki. You know the people look up to you. You are the symbol of the tribe, born again with all its purity. They adore you. They worship you. You do not know about the new oath in your name. In the name of the Teacher and the purity of the tribe. And remember Kabonyi hates, hates you. He would kill you if he could. And he is the one who is doing all this. Why? The Kiama has power. Power. And your name is in it, giving it greater power. Your name will be your ruin. (pp. 127-128)

Waiyaki is, in the end, not careful enough, for to be careful in the circumstances is to adhere to the principles of action, as well as satisfying the codes, mores, and conventions of the traditional system. It would mean sacrificing Waiyaki's personal aspirations, including his love for the Christian Nyambura. It would mean allowing the extremists in the Kiama to grind down on the Christians and probably create great devastation and unhappiness. Waiyaki's regret that he ever resigned from the Kiama, which left the field free to Kabonyi and the diehards, shows how little he understood the traditional system before the truth came to him, too late, on the eve of his tragic defeat.

It is speculated, and with substantial justification, that Waiyaki's inadequate integration within the traditional system is a result of his early upbringing in Livingstone's Siriana mission school. It is suggested that as a result of his Siriana background, he underwent incipient alienation from tradition which never leaves him to the end. It blurs his sensitivity to the demands of tradition.

Ngugi's perspective on Christianity is not as fully elaborated as the traditional perspective. This is not at all surprising. The vast majority of the Gikuyu are traditionalist, compared to the few who have only recently been converted to Christianity. The framework of the action is, therefore, largely the traditional system. Christianity plays at the fringes of the traditional system and disturbs its inner harmony and stability, but it cannot replace it altogether and so cannot claim the same attention as the former.

The Christianity presented in this novel is redemptive and is explored through Joshua and his partisans. Everyone of these adherents accepts the redemptive importance of the Christ as the main ideological prop. Everyone is also determined to achieve deliverance not only from personal sins but also from contamination through the ways of the tribe which are considered sinful. Joshua's is a religion of faith mixed with selfrighteousness; it is a fighting religion whose interest is the supplanting of the ways of the tribe. It is, therefore, an overzealous religion bound on a collision course between its members, "the people of Joshua," and its enemies, "the people of the tribe." But the redemptive strand in its ideology remains a great inspiration to the less volatile of its adherents.

Waiyaki absorbs its messianic impulse during his education in the Siriana mission. Ironically enough, his admission into that school is engineered by Chege, his traditionalist father, as part of what he envisages as the necessary preparation of Waiyaki for his messianic role: "Arise. Heed the prophecy. Go the mission place. Learn all the wisdom and all the secrets of the white man. But do not follow his vices. Be true to your people and the ancient rites" (p. 24).

Like Ezeulu's in Achebe's *Arrow of God*, this move to steal the enemy's thunder is doomed to defeat, for, it is not easy to acquire the white man's attitudes and values: "The element of love and sacrifice agreed with his own temperament. The suffering Christ in the Garden of Gethsemane and His agony on the tree had always moved him" (p. 24).

He recognizes the merits as well as the weaknesses of Christianity and is prepared to build a bridge between it and traditional religion, and between its adherents and those of the traditional religion: "Waiyaki knew that not all the ways of the white man were bad. Even his religion was not essentially bad. Some good, truth shone through it. But the religion, the truth, needed washing, clearing away all the dirt, leaving only the eternal. And that eternal that was the truth had to be reconciled to the traditions of the people" (p. 24).

This quest for reconciliation of extremes remains the most positive aspect of Waiyaki's messianic career. Where Joshua and his adherents pursue their single-minded path of puritanism and fundamentalism, Waiyaki, no less than Joshua's two daughters, Muthoni and Nyambura, pursues a course of integrating the traditional and the Christian worlds. And Ngugi seems to suggest, at this stage at any rate, that his reconciliation is necessary to avert a terrible tragedy built upon intolerance. It is significant that all three people who share the vision of reconciliation are sacrificed. It is also significant that all three find sustaining comfort in the life and sacrifice of the Christ.

The convergence of the traditional and Christian impulses in the defining of Waiyaki's mission of redemption is possible because Ngugi devotes considerable effort to describing them and how they shape the messianic temperament of the protagonist. It is clear, however, that even though greater comprehensiveness is achieved in exploring the traditional background of the action, the decisive messianic inspiration seems to have come from the brief formative Christian influence of the Siriana mission school. It is, in the final analysis, with Christ that Waiyaki identifies himself and not with Mugo wa Kabiro and the Gikuyu seers in his attempt to "lead the tribe to light" (p. 125).

Waiyaki builds his strategy for redeeming the people upon modern education and pursues it single-mindedly. Much is done to show evidence of his success in building schools and infecting his people with his enthusiasm for education. But, alas, he forgets to build into the content of this education, and to preach at the appropriate moment, the lesson of tolerance and love. From this point of view, success in the educational experiment turns into defeat when the very people who idolize the Teacher in the end reject the Redeemer. The failure of the educational vision finally compromises the task of redemption.

One aspect of *The River Between* deserves to be spotlighted. It is Ngugi's successful use of setting to underline the main lines of narrative development. The ridges and hills, the sacred trees, and the Honia River are given concrete existence in the narrative by their being related to the internal details of the story. But, even more significantly, the physical features define the rhythms of action and aid plot development. Thus, when the ridges and hills are in a relative state of stability, which corresponds to the state of relative peace among the people, the features are likened to "sleeping lions." The graphic analogy is convincing. And when the life of the region is disturbed, the sleeping lions are said to be awakened. The metaphoric extension is worthy of note, but there is also another sense in which a literal condition should be inferred. The spread of education across the hills and ridges, the conflict between the converts and the Christians, and the alienating of the Gikuyu land right up to the ridges and the hills by the settlers: these appear to disturb the atmosphere physically and to increase the tempo of crisis that plunges the people into tragedy. The landscape is peaceful and almost without people when the hills and ridges are described as "sleeping lions." But a certain restless-ness and constant human movement result when the lions are awake. The effectiveness of this novel is a result of Ngugi's successful integration of setting, character, and selected myths and legends which fuse into a well-condensed statement on the theme of victimization.

Next to the uniqueness of setting is the uniqueness of Ngugi's use of language in *The River Between*. Commentators have noted with justification the simple, colloquial rhythm of the novel's language. Others have called this use Biblical with equal justification. The fact is that the virtue of a language used simply but to a profoundly great effect cannot be lost on the reader. Here, for example, are two passages taken from the great debate at the people's assembly when the protagonist, Waiyaki, and the antagonist, Kabonyi, first bare their swords publicly and set the stage that will in the end consume the hero.

1. He [Kabonyi] reminded them of the poverty of the land. The dry months had left the people with nothing to eat. And the expected harvest would not yield much. He touched on the land taken by the white man. He talked of the new taxes being imposed on the people by the government post now in their midst. And instead of Waiyaki leading people against these more immediate ills, he was talking of more buildings. Were people going to be burdened with more buildings? With more teachers? And was the white man's education really necessary? Surely there was another way out. It was better to drive away the white man from the hills altogether. Were the people afraid? Were there no warriors left in the tribe? He, Kabonyi, would lead them. That was why he had formed the new Kiama. He would rid the country of the influence of the white man. He would restore the purity of the tribe and its wisdom. (p. 109)

2. Then he [Waiyaki] opened his mouth and began to speak. And his voice was like the voice of his father—no—it was like the voice of the great Gikiyu of old. Here again was the saviour, the one whose words touched the souls of the people. People listened and their hearts moved with the vibration of his voice. And he, like a shepherd speaking to his flock, avoided any words that might be insulting in any case, how could he repudiate Kabonyi's argument? Waiyaki told them that he was their son. They all were his parents. He did not want to lead. The elders were there to guide and lead the youth. And youth had to listen. It had to be led in the paths of wisdom. He, Waiyaki, would listen. All he wanted was to serve the ridges, to serve the hills. They could not stand aloof. They would never now remain isolated. Unless the people heeded his words and plans, the ridges would lose their former dignity and would be left a distance behind by the country beyond. (p. 110)

We observe that the two speakers are using their words simply. They are the words of everyday speech. But we are also aware that the matters at issue are deadly serious. They touch upon the things which affect the collective well-being, things like poverty, drought, imperialism and its expulsion, the problem of leadership, and the question of age and experience in the determination of a leader. The words are simple but the questions touch the very fundamentals of the community's life and survival; we can, even within this limited context, discern certain essential differences in the characters of the two speakers. One speaks almost demagogically, to score points and win arguments; the other speaks in a way that "touched the souls of people"; one speaks plainly and with candor, the other speaks rhetorically, using numerous questions that suggest their answers to the audience; one man is a politician; the other is a redeemer.

This use of language of everyday speech in very clearly and precisely structured movements around serious and fundamental issues of life and death is Ngugi's fictional asset. It is what helps most to create the sacrificial atmosphere of this novel. Everything is kept very low in profile through the low language profile. There are no big speeches, full of high-blown, emotion-saturated phrases. Adjectival and adverbial elaborations which add intensities are kept to the lowest level. The appeal is to common sense and through common sense to the common good and the common destiny of a people unified by their traditions and myths and their mystical environment. The lack of linguistic excitement is not a result of the absence of linguistic vitality but the conception of language as a means of making contact with the rational and deeper levels of people's responses. At the end of it is encounter: the justness of the position of the Teacher is established and collectively endorsed. The demagogue is temporarily defeated, though he lives to fight and win another day.

What sort of people are victimized? They are often individuals who evince certain qualities of independence and openly or implicitly threaten the custodians of tradition and the maintainers of the status quo. The elders, the priests, the oracular class, and all those who constitute the ruling class of the communal society have a stake in keeping the system pure of the virus of subversive questioning. People who manifest independence sooner or later find themselves accused of some demonstrable crime against the gods and are in the nature of things sacrificed as victims, so that the communal social order will go on undisturbed.

The victimization of Shanka, the strongest son of the tribe, and Goaa, who indoctrinates him, and Ukutee, who allows her personal passions to vindicate her individuality, has its root in their having been "inhibited" (a more modern word would be "alienated") from tradition by their contact with the new subversive idea built on the mystique of "the Word." The victimization of Okolo, the visionary quester after moral excellence, becomes inevitable when he attacks the corrupt values of post-independence African dictators. And that of Waiyaki results from his assuming a redemptive, leader role against the ambitions and intrigues of powerful elders.

The authors' handling of the theme of victimization varies considerably from play to play and from novel to novel, but they share one dominant attitude in common. That attitude is ambivalence. They see the sacrifice of victims as logical to the communal system and to certain types of human situations, but their sympathy is always with the victims, and the victims, struggle to defend the flicker which they carry within them, which is indeed, their own lives.

NOTES

1. See the Colloquium Paper presented by E. N. Obiechina before the Fellows of the Woodrow Wilson Center for International Scholars in August 1980, "Africa in the Soul of Dispersed Children: West African Literature from the Era of the Slave Trade." It dealt with the memoirs, reminiscences, and autobiographical fragments of Ayuba Suleiman of Bondu, Salih Bilali, Abu Bakr al-Siddiq, Ali Eisami, Samuel Crowther, and James Wright, all of which are in *Africa Remembered: Narratives by West Africans from the Era of the Slave Trade* (edited by Philip D. Curtin); "Autobiography of Omar Ibn Said, Slave in North Carolina, 1831"; *American Historical Review*, 30: 789-795 (1924); *Letters of the Late Ignatius Sancho, An African, London, 1783*; Ottobah Cugoano, *Thoughts and Sentiments on the Evil and Wicked Traffic of Slavery and Commerce of the Human Species*, London, 1787; Phillis Wheatley, *Poems on Various Subjects, Religious and Moral*, London and Boston, 1773; James Albert Ukawsaw Gronniosaw, *A Narrative of the Remarkable particulars in the Life of James Albert Ukawsaw—Gronniosaw: An African Prince, Written by Himself*, London, 1789; V. Smith, *A Narrative of the Life of Venture, A Native of Africa, but Resident above sixty years in the United States of America, related by Himself* (New London, 1835). See also an abridged publication of the paper in *Wilson Quarterly*, Summer 1981, titled Africa's Lost Generations.

2. Alex La Guma, *A Walk in the Night* (London: Heinemann Educational Books Ltd., 1967), p. 48. All future references are to the same edition.

3. Wole Soyinka, *Death and the King's Horseman* (London: Methuen Press, 1975), p. 71. All future references are to the same edition.

4. Tsegaye Gabre-Mehdin, *Oda-Oak Oracle* (London: Oxford University Press, 1976), p. 41. All future references are to the same edition.

5. Wole Soyinka, *The Strong Breed* in *Collected Plays 1* (London: Oxford University Press, 1973), p. 118. All future references are to the same edition.

6. J. Gronowski, *The Face of Violence*, pp. 15-16.

7. Frantz Fanon, *Black Skin, White Masks* (New York: Grove Press, 1967), p. 145.

8. F. W. Dillistone, *The Novelist and the Passion Story*, pp. 19-20.

9. Gabriel Okara, *The Voice* (London: Heinemann Educational Books Ltd., 1970), p. 110. All references are to the same edition.

10. T. S. Eliot, *Selected Prose*, pp. 107-108.

11 . Ngugi wa Thiong'o, *The River Between* (London: Heinemann Educational Books Ltd., 1972), p. 21. All references are to the same edition.

11

The Dignity of Intellectual Labor: A Fiftieth Birthday Tribute

Isidore Okpewho

It is neither by chance nor by default that, in any roll call of literary scholars on the Nigerian scene, commentators are invariably moved to begin with the names of Michael Echeruo and Emmanuel Obiechina. Quite often, in fact, the list does not go very much further. The reason is not far to seek. These are the leading two of the very few literary scholars in Nigeria who are willing to apply themselves with anything like sustained rigor to a significant concept until they have attained a defensible theoretical position. This means that, whereas most scholars are content to spin off a whole series of disconnected papers and the odd booklet that do not rise above the level of what may be called an "ethnography" of the subject, Echeruo and Obiechina give a good deal more time to exploring an idea until they can come out with a solid book on it. Echeruo, in particular, is inclined to examine various sides of an issue and come out with just as many books, and do so with such thoroughness that there is very little left to say on the issue. The difference in aims is clear. Those who write disconnected papers are quite often struggling to satisfy promotion criteria in their universities or at best stay in the public eye. The likes of Echeruo and Obiechina, on the contrary, see themselves and their efforts as primarily beholden to intellectual history and a larger life of the mind.

Echeruo has the following sole-authored books to his credit so far: *Mortality* (1968), poetry; *Joyce Cary and the Novel of Africa* (1973), scholarship; *Victorian Lagos* (1977), scholarship; *The Conditioned Imagination from Shakespeare to Conrad* (1978), scholarship; *Joyce Cary and the Dimensions of Order* (1979), scholarship; and *Distanced and Other Poems* (1975), poetry. He has also edited three other books: (with Obiechina), *Igbo Traditional Life, Culture and Literature* (1971), a collection of papers by various scholars; Joyce Cary's *Mister Johnson* (1975), introduced and annotated for Longman's Heritage of Literature Series; and Shakespeare's *Tempest* (1980), a critical edition designed and adopted for the British Open University's literature program. In addition, Echeruo has published articles in various periodicals inside and outside Africa.

In an interview with the American scholar Bernth Lindfors, published in a volume of interviews with African writers entitled *Dem Say* (1971), Echeruo would wish to be seen as a critic/teacher and a poet, in that order. The premium on criticism is certainly justified, given the burden of his published effort to date. But "critic" here goes well beyond the meaning frequently attached to it. In a recent article in the *Vanguard*, Sina Odugbemi called upon our literary critics to turn their efforts toward a larger "criticism of culture." Echeruo has, in fact, been doing that from his very first book. Most students of African literature probably know him best by his first volume of poems, *Mortality*, and, indeed, in that volume we see Echeruo take a programmatic stand on various issues of literature and culture. In the poem "Sophia" he sees no profit in an unreflective embrace of foreign values and instead advocates a cultivation of the limitless potential of wisdom (*sophia*). In "Easter Penitence" he turns his sardonic mockery on the irrational ecstasy of Christian worship and the grotesque image of divinity advertised therein. And in the final poem "Daedalus," he sees the modern African poet as duty-bound to conjure the timeless though silent profundities of the race into an inspired flight. In their book, *Toward the Decolonization of African Literature*, Chinweizu and his friends rail at Echeruo's "euromodernist obscurantism." Although the troika grossly over-simplify the oral tradition they seek so piously to defend, many of the poems in Echeruo's book are indeed unduly cerebral. But the volume is perhaps best seen in the light of Echeruo's general outlook on culture.

That outlook comes through strongly enough in his first scholarly book, *Joyce Cary and the Novel of Africa*. Echeruo had encountered Cary as an Honours English undergraduate at Ibadan. At a time when there was no such "mythical beast" (to borrow Soyinka's little quip at Cambridge) as African Literature at Ibadan, Cary and Conrad were the closest that Echeruo and his contemporaries came to seeing their culture as the subject of creative discourse. Molly Mahood, then Head of English there, was later to do a book titled *Joyce Cary's Africa* (1964) and to inspire an interest in the subject in not a few of her students. Curiously enough, when Echeruo went on to do graduate studies at Cornell, it was poetry that tended to command his enthusiasm (he had written a piece and was soon, in 1963, to win the All-African Poetry Competition) and drove him to start his doctoral research on the American poet Robert Frost. But the image of Cary continued to "insist," so to speak, fired perhaps by the reality of the racial and cultural confrontation (evident enough in *Mortality*) pervading the America of the sixties.

Even as a first book of scholarship, *Joyce Cary and the Novel of Africa* is a work of mature and balanced judgment. Its purpose is to examine Cary's African-set fiction against the record of other British writers on Africa who, using the "dark continent" as a romantic backdrop, sought to set the "light" of European civilization against the "benighted" innocence of a "savage" people whose salvation was the sacred and benevolent burden of Queen Victoria's imperial adventure. The findings of Echeruo's study are far-reaching and should perhaps have benefited those who made a habit of debating, long after Echeruo's book had been published, whether the concept "African Literature" could be stretched to embrace writers like Cary. Echeruo presents Cary as poised between the horns of a dilemma. On the one hand, he had no choice but to respect the climate of prejudice of his generation. On the other hand, during those years of retirement from colonial service when he settled down to write both fiction and essays, Cary had begun a deep study of certain ideas about life and art which "transcend race, place and time," and thus tended to guide him "away from the limited significances of the traditional foreign novel of Africa." Consequently, although Cary's African novels tried to resonate the biases and the hauteur of his age, they received rather cold treatment in the contemporary press because they did not seem to go far enough in providing the accustomed entertainment for the amphitheater of the European mind.

Two relevant insights emerge from Echeruo's book. First, his verdict on whether Cary could be seen as an "African" writer is clear: a non-African does not enter the canon of African writing simply by setting his work in Africa, when he does little more than echo "the same kind of self-satisfied comedy" and "the same imperial view of the African scene from a point outside and above it" that we see in the traditional European fiction of Africa. The second, and perhaps more deep-seated insight reveals the basic thrust of Echeruo's scholarship: the rationalization of cultural attitudes as manifested in literature and other arts. Having broached those existential ideas that are thinly veiled in Cary's African fiction, Echeruo concludes his book with these words: "It is the nature of the ideas about life and art with which he tried, belatedly, to transform his experience of Africa into works of art, that we have to look for an explanation of whatever distinction there is in his African novels." This is an attractive intellectual project, and Echeruo is hardly one to let such a challenge lie untackled.

But there was an even more pressing challenge which Echeruo's study of Cary's African fiction forced upon him. In the climate of prejudice against black people which, as I have suggested, pervaded America of the sixties, Echeruo must have felt his cultural pride considerably hurt especially by those who—to borrow a fitting vulgarity—wouldn't qualify to shovel his shit. Deep thinker that he is, the following questions must have invaded his mind: Who, really, is the black or African man? What is the nature of his culture, or at any rate, what is the intellectual environment within which this culture has been and can be construed? And what is the function of the biases guiding a people's imaginative portrait of themselves and other peoples?

The questions are, of course, at the bottom of Echeruo's assessment of Cary's African fiction within the context of victorian expectations. They are even more to the fore in his next two books, *Victorian Lagos* and *The Conditioned Imagination*. Put simply, the thrust of *Victorian Lagos* is to take our minds on a historical trip to the sources of the intellectual culture that has come to characterize the contemporary Nigerian elite. What kind of Africans were they who started this in their attempts—if we may borrow, as Echeruo did in *Mortality*, a phrase from James Joyce's *Portrait of the Artist* —"to forge in the smithy of their souls, the uncreated conscience of their race"?

The book is more an intellectual than a political history (Echeruo is careful to point out), designed "to reconstruct the patterns of life and thought in Lagos during the second half of the 19th century"; by plumbing the press of that period, he endeavors "to characterize the essential features of that civilization in its human as well as its intellectual implications." In the six chapters of the book, Echeruo shows the nineteenth century Lagos elite as they emerge through their newspaper articles and editorials: sophisticated immigrants (returned slaves and their descendants) who unfortunately, in their social, educational, cultural, and religious lives and policies, could never make up their minds whether they were Africans or Europeans but who certainly saw themselves as part of Britain's "civilizing" mission in black Africa. The conclusion to this study is a well-modulated epitaph to these disoriented men who stood at the crossroads of history and civilization:

To the extent that they had the privilege of education they seemed determined to save other Africans from the predicament of illiteracy and godlessness; to the extent, however, that they were black, they realized that they shared a common dilemma with everyone who was not just African, but black. Hence, though they had no common territorial roots in Africa, they felt a common racial obligation to it. What they lacked was not the sensibility of the condition of the African, the black man, but the sense of the ordinary, the indigenous African mind and experience . . . for all practical purposes, the major source of intellectual stimulation for this elite was Negro America; the main source of its social manners Victorian England.

It would be fair to see Echeruo's four monographs as a well-orchestrated tetralogy. The first Cary book presents African man as a dim figure circumscribed by the preconditioned perspective of the foreign observer. The Lagos book shows African man in his home setting, treading insecurely in a culture he could hardly call his own and still circumscribed by established racial and cultural prejudices. In his third book, *The Condi-*

tioned Imagination, Echeruo confronts these prejudices squarely from the point of view of the philosophy of art, to find out why certain works of Anglo-American literature have attained their classic status despite the biases they so blatantly sport. The link between this book and the first may be seen in Echeruo's recognition, in the latter, that writers like Cary and Conrad do show tremendous imaginative power; in *The Conditioned Imagination* he wonders how such an admirable poetic virtue could coexist with such a damnable vice as prejudice. In this book Echeruo examines certain "exocultural storeotypes" (caricatures conceived of one culture by another) such as Shakespeare's Jew Shylock (*The Merchant of Venice*) and "Moor" Othello (*Othello*), Conrad's "nigger" James Wait (*The Nigger of the Narcissus*), and Faulkner's "octoroon" Joe Christmas (*Light in August*) to establish that what makes these works so successful in their cultural environments is that their writers have done their utmost to resonate the accepted prejudices (the "conditioned imagination") of the society that created those caricatures, and that any honest criticism of the works must reckon with the force of those cultural prejudices—not with any specious considerations of general "human" tendencies or dispositions—as a first principle.

Abiola Irele once said, in one of his *Guardian* essays, that Echeruo was "valorizing prejudice" by arguing that it could inspire great works of literature. That, I am afraid, is a rather simple reading of the book, but it is easy to see why such a misapprehension should arise. Echeruo has put far more emphasis on these predetermined figurations than on the level of imaginative effort shown by the artist. I believe we could say that, in the final analysis, the intensity of artistic effort revealed depends to a large degree on the level of the artist's commitment to communal prejudices. Take *Light in August.* We do meet disoriented Negroes in the fiction of other Southern writers like Carson McCullers and Erskine Caldwell. But what makes Faulkner that much more "successful" (to his people) than those other artists is that he has pushed the prejudice a step (or more) further. In real life the Joe Christmases of the South are seen as a racial aberration; but Faulkner makes *his* Joe Christmas both a biological horror and a moral monstrosity. Any wonder, then, that black American critics, in particular, have equated Faulkner's genius with the level of devilry in him?

The last book in the tetralogy, *Joyce Cary and the Dimensions of Order,* sees Echeruo pressing an intellectual curiosity to its logical end, by tackling the proposition which he set himself at the close of *Joyce Cary and the Novel of Africa.* In this book, Echeruo examines those philosophical and political ideas with which Cary wrestled in the first ten years of his retirement to Oxford before starting to write fiction. These include disputations on transcendental logic largely against the backgrounds of Kant and Hume; the challenge of liberal politics in its search for "a world safe for everyone"; and the relationship between the disordered reality of human existence and the artist's effort to impose some order and beauty on it. Cary's failure to resolve these stubborn questions imposed severe limitations on his fiction and earned him considerable underestimation as an artist. But he *did* make some effort to understand man beyond time and place, and that perhaps brings us back to the logic of *The Conditioned Imagination*: if Cary was judged a middler from his attachment to universal ideals, and Faulkner was hailed a master from his commitment to local prejudices, is that not proof enough of the causal connection between artistic merit and the individual disposition?

Our discussion so far might leave the impression that Echeruo as a scholar has not concerned himself with issues in "African Literature" as conventionally understood. Indeed, I once heard someone, whose ego had been severely gored by Echeruo's assessment of him for promotion, say rather glibly, "Echeruo is not really in African literature," as though there were a unique merit in being a critic of African literature even with the brain of a chicken. Of course, if being in African criticism means tossing off fly-weight papers on the symbolism of water-goddesses and sun-birds in Okigbo's poetry, or the place of proverbs and kola nuts in Achebe's fiction, or other pet trivia of middle-minded scholarship, then Echeruo may be blissfully excused. Like Soyinka, Achebe, and Clark (the last of whom was his classmate at Ibadan), he has turned out a few programmatic (though less idiosyncratic) essays on issues in modern African literature, like the one in the *Nigeria Magazine* (No. 89, 1966) on Nigerian poetry that Chinweizu and his friends found so offensive. But Echeruo's interest in African literature and (especially) culture reflects more a commitment to traditional culture. In this regard, he has published a number of lectures and papers in areas like ritual drama and oral literature, the best known perhaps being a 1971 essay titled "The Dramatic Limits of Igbo Ritual." But perhaps his most lasting contribution in this area is his establishment of a *compulsory* course in oral literature in the English Department of Ibadan University in the mid-seventies, a step that many of our universities are yet to take.

Echeruo's commitment to traditional culture must be seen as a kind of homecoming. It may be that he is responding to the heckling of Chinweizu and his friends: *Toward the Decolonization of African Literature* may not have much scholarly merit, but it certainly has a high nuisance value. More seriously, however, Echeruo must have felt that, having disposed of the encumbrances to a proper understanding of the nature of African culture, he could now settle down and probe it right from its source. The civil war must have helped in this, because it threw Echeruo deep into the homeland to confront his roots. This homecoming has not, however, forced on him that "simplicity" that the troika recommend in *Decolonization*. His second volume of poems, *Distanced*, written mostly in the six months following the end of the civil war, is certainly more approachable and (in my judgment) more lyrical than *Mortality* and deals entirely with the trauma of the times. But there is the familiar complexity of thought and associations underlying the accessibility of diction. The man is still an intellectualist through and through!

Sometime in 1979, I encountered Echeruo along the corridors walking across to our Department of Linguistics and Nigerian Languages "to teach a course in Igbo dialectology." Only age stopped me from asking him the question that leapt to my mind, "Are you crazy?" I was sure he was on to some stupendous project or other, and I wasn't wrong. For not long after, before he departed for sabbatical leave at Houston and on to the Vice Chancellorship of Imo State University, I found him in his office working on an Igbo dictionary! I could perhaps have suspected the move from a seminar he'd earlier given us (with taped texts) on the tonal music of Igbo speech and song, but I could hardly have guessed the scope of the project. The dictionary may not materialize soon—given the rigor involved—but when it does, there will be no doubt about the quality of the effort.

In his various intellectual labors, one gets a full sense of balanced judgment and controlled zeal in Echeruo's thought. Using comparative insights from Greek and Sumerian traditions, the essay "The Dramatic Limits of Igbo Ritual" combines a commitment to traditional culture with a concern for its future growth. In his Ahiajoku Lecture titled "A Matter of Identity" (1979)—a masterly blend of linguistics, literature, history, and ethnology—he again explores the virtues of Igbo culture but takes time to warn his people against an overpromotion of personal and ethnic selfhood. This sense of balance and propriety is evident even in the style. In his inaugural lecture at Ibadan, titled "Poets, Prophets and Professors" (1976), Echeruo declares literature to be "human utterance, made important and beautiful by its argument and its structure." The emphasis is certainly no less on beauty and balance. In both his poetry and his prose, Echeruo evinces a certain measured grace and an economy of diction rooted in the unlabored choice of the *mot juste*. He is particularly judicious in his stylistic strategies. In the hard-core academic monographs, where he advances his theoretical positions and parries other scholars shot for shot, he accompanies his arguments with a copious arsenal of critical notes. But in a work like *Victorian Lagos*, which explores the journalism of the times, he abandons that strategy. Although the book is just as thoroughly re-searched as the other three (with ample references to published books as well as "journals" within the run of the text), we are invited to savor the felicitous but no less cogent discourse in the same relaxed mood that those enlightened newspapers would have coaxed from us.

The preceding survey has been based mainly on Echeruo's books, espe-cially the sole-authored ones. I have given very little time to Echeruo's articles because he has treated most of them, as any decent scholar should, as merely stages in the development of a book project. There are, of course, scholars who have felt constrained to throw together all the essays they have ever written between the covers of a book. Frankly, when I read some of these easy pieces they strike me more as aborted fetuses, with neither head nor hind, than as full-blooded products of solid intellectual labor. For Echeruo, a true scholar should prove his mettle chiefly by publishing respectable monographs of sustained argument, although he may have tested his hunches with a couple of cognate articles which will form part of his final judgment. Echeruo may eventually come out with a book of collected essays, but my guess is that, given the consistency of his trajectory on culture, there will be a more transparent logic running through such a volume than we have seen in collections published so far.

I have tried to put Echeruo's work within the context of the contemporary intellectual and academic scene in Nigeria, mainly to show that he has shunned the easy options favored by the majority of his fellows. The old saying about the dignity of labor has usually been construed in terms of physical exertion. But intellectuals are real, too, or can be. And it has been the achievement of Echeruo to translate, by dint of sustained hard work, that old saying into intellectual terms. In a profession where many hustle for elevation without having much to show for it and, having wrested it, happily abdicate every urge to do anything further: in a climate of opinion where the stridency of rhetoric strives to the plausibility of logic; in a society where ideological posturing too often masquerades as genuine social concern; in short, in an age when—to borrow a platitude from contemporary official parlance—many are doing everything but what they are paid to do, it is reassuring to know that there are a few scholars working quietly, honestly, and effectively, at some cost to their comfort and social image, to demonstrate that academic life is a worthwhile national service as well as a dignified human endeavor. Of this few, Echeruo is the undisputed guru. Which is why, in any roll call of literary scholars today in Nigeria (if not Africa), his name is usually the first.

Index

About the Contributors

CHUKWUMA AZUONYE is Associate Professor and Chairman of the Department of Black Studies at the University of Massachusetts at Boston. He served as Acting Chairman of the Department of Linguistics and Nigerian Languages at the University of Nigeria, Nsukka, and as Fulbright Senior African Program Fellow in the Department of Folklore and Folklife at the University of Pennsylvania, Philadelphia. His articles, poems, and short stories have appeared in journals and books published in Africa, the Americas, and Europe.

AFAM EBEOGU is Senior Lecturer in English and Acting Coordinator of the School of Humanities at the Imo State University at Okigwe, Nigeria. He served as a Commonwealth Fellow at the University of Sheffield, England, during the 1987-88 academic year. He has published many articles on African and English literatures in journals and books published in Africa, Canada, and Europe.

ERNEST N. EMENYONU is Professor of English and Provost of Alvan Ikoku College of Education, Owerri, Nigeria. Previously, he served as Chairman of the Department of English at the same institution, and Chairman of the Department of English, Dean of the School of Arts, and Deputy Vice Chancellor, respectively, at the University of Calabar, Nigeria. He has authored, co-authored, and edited numerous articles and books, including *The Rise of the Igbo Novel* (1978).

NNADOZIE F. INYAMA is Senior Lecturer in English at the University of Nigeria, Nsukka. He has published articles on African and English literatures.

CHINYERE NWAHUNANYA is Senior Lecturer in English at the Imo State University at Okigwe, Nigeria. His articles on African literatures and comparative drama have appeared in many journals published in Africa and India.

DONATUS I. NWOGA was Professor of English and Director of the Division of General Studies at the University of Nigeria, Nsukka. He worked hard to rebuild that institution's Department of English while serving as its first African Chairman, immediately after the Nigerian Civil War. His major scholarly interest was the development of African literature and promotion of Igbo Studies. Before his sudden demise in 1992, Nwoga had written numerous articles and books including *The Supreme God as Stranger in Igbo Religious Thought* (1984).

EMMANUEL OBIECHINA is Visiting Professor of Humanities at the University of Pittsburgh at Bradford. He previously served as Visiting Professor of English and Third World Studies at Hobart and William Smith Colleges; Director, Nigerian Universities Office, Embassy of Nigeria, Washington, D.C.; Visiting National Endowment for the Humanities Professor, Department of English, Colgate University; Deputy Vice Chancellor, Dean, Graduate School, and Chairman, English Department, respectively, at the University of Nigeria, Nsukka. He has authored, co-authored, and edited numerous books, journals, and articles on African, African American, and Third World Studies, including *Language and Theme: Essays on African Literature* (1990), *Christopher Okigbo: Poet of Destiny* (1980), *Culture, Tradition and Society in the West African Novel* (1975, 1980), and *An African Popular Literature: A Study of Onitsha Market Pamphlets* (1973).

BEN OBUMSELU was Professor of English and Dean of the College of Humanities and Social Sciences (1984-87) at the Imo State University, Okigwe, Nigeria. He has published articles in respected journals, including *Publications of the Modern Language Association of America (PMLA)* . He was one of the group of students at the University College, Ibadan, who helped to develop African literature during the colonial era.

KALU OGBAA is Associate Professor of English and Africana Literatures at Southern Connecticut State University, New Haven. He served as Visiting Associate Professor of English at Oral Roberts University and at Clark Atlanta University; as Associate Professor of English and Director of General Studies Program at the Imo State University, Okigwe, Nigeria; and as Lecturer in English at the University of Texas at Austin. He has published one book, *Gods Oracles and Divination: Folkways in Chinua Achebe's Novels* (1992), and many articles on African, African American, Afro-Caribbean, and Commonwealth literatures.

ISIDORE OKPEWHO is Professor of English, Comparative Literature, and Afro-American and African Studies, and Chairman of Afro-American and African Studies at the State University of New York at Binghamton. A Folklore Fellow, he has, for a long time, served as Professor and Chairman of English at the University of Ibadan, and has been Visiting Professor of English at Harvard University. He has published many scholarly books, including *The Epic of Africa* (1979), *Myth in Africa* (1983), *The Oral Performance in Africa* (1990), and *African Oral Literature* (1992). He has also published three novels: *The Victims* (1970), *The Last Duty* (1976), and *Tides* (1993).

EDWARD C. OKWU is Principal Lecturer in English at Alvan Ikoku College of Education, Owerri, Nigeria. He has served as guest lecturer at the Imo State

University, Okigwe, Nigeria, and has also been very active in the development of the English curriculum for high schools in Nigeria.

ISBN 0-313-29281-7

EAN

9 780313 292811

HARDCOVER BAR CODE